*Migration, Minorities and Citizenship*

General Editors: **Zig Layton-Henry**, Professor of Politics, University of Warwick; and **Danièle Joly**, Professor, Director, Centre for Research in Ethnic Relations, University of Warwick

*Titles include:*

Rutvica Andrijasevic
MIGRATION, AGENCY AND CITZENSHIP IN SEX TRAFFICKING

Muhammad Anwar, Patrick Roach and Ranjit Sondhi (*editors*)
FROM LEGISLATION TO INTEGRATION?
Race Relations in Britain

James A. Beckford, Danièle Joly and Farhad Khosrokhavar
MUSLIMS IN PRISON
Challenge and Change in Britain and France

Gideon Calder, Phillip Cole and Jonathan Seglow
CITIZENSHIP ACQUISITION AND NATIONAL BELONGING
Migration, Membership and the Liberal Democratic State

Huub Dijstelbloem and Albert Meijer (*editors*)
MIGRATION AND THE NEW TECHNOLOGICAL BORDERS OF EUROPE

Thomas Faist and Andreas Ette (*editors*)
THE EUROPEANIZATION OF NATIONAL POLICIES AND
POLITICS OF IMMIGRATION
Between Autonomy and the European Union

Thomas Faist and Peter Kivisto (*editors*)
DUAL CITIZENSHIP IN GLOBAL PERSPECTIVE
From Unitary to Multiple Citizenship

Adrian Favell
PHILOSOPHIES OF INTEGRATION
Immigration and the Idea of Citizenship in France and Britain

Martin Geiger and Antoine Pécoud (*editors*)
THE POLITICS OF INTERNATIONAL MIGRATION MANAGEMENT

Agata Górny and Paulo Ruspini (*editors*)
MIGRATION IN THE NEW EUROPE
East–West Revisited

James Hampshire
CITIZENSHIP AND BELONGING
Immigration and the Politics of Democratic Governance in Postwar Britain

John R. Hinnells (*editor*)
RELIGIOUS RECONSTRUCTION IN THE SOUTH ASIAN DIASPORAS
From One Generation to Another

Ayhan Kaya
ISLAM, MIGRATION AND INTEGRATION
The Age of Securitization

Zig Layton-Henry and Czarina Wilpert (*editors*)
CHALLENGING RACISM IN BRITAIN AND GERMANY

Marie Macey and Alan H. Carling
ETHNIC, RACIAL AND RELIGIOUS INEQUALITIES
The Perils of Subjectivity

Georg Menz and Alexander Caviedes (*editors*)
LABOUR MIGRATION IN EUROPE

Jørgen S. Nielsen
TOWARDS A EUROPEAN ISLAM

Pontus Odmalm
MIGRATION POLICIES AND POLITICAL PARTICIPATION
Inclusion or Intrusion in Western Europe?

Prodromos Panayiotopoulos
ETHNICITY, MIGRATION AND ENTERPRISE

Aspasia Papadopoulou-Kourkoula
TRANSIT MIGRATION
The Missing Link Between Emigration and Settlement

Jan Rath (*editor*)
IMMIGRANT BUSINESSES
The Economic, Political and Social Environment

Carl-Ulrik Schierup (*editor*)
SCRAMBLE FOR THE BALKANS
Nationalism, Globalism and the Political Economy of Reconstruction

Vicki Squire
THE EXCLUSIONARY POLITICS OF ASYLUM

Maarten Vink
LIMITS OF EUROPEAN CITIZENSHIP
European Integration and Domestic Immigration Policies

Östen Wahlbeck
KURDISH DIASPORAS
A Comparative Study of Kurdish Refugee Communities

Lucy Williams
GLOBAL MARRIAGE
Cross-Border Marriage Migration in Global Context

---

**Migration, Minorities and Citizenship**
**Series Standing Order ISBN 978–0–333–71047–0 (hardback) and**
**978–0–333–80338–7 (paperback)**
(*outside North America only*)

You can receive future titles in this series as they are published by placing a standing order. Please contact your bookseller or, in case of difficulty, write to us at the address below with your name and address, the title of the series and the ISBN quoted above.

Customer Services Department, Macmillan Distribution Ltd, Houndmills, Basingstoke, Hampshire RG21 6XS, England

---

# Migration and the New Technological Borders of Europe

Edited by

Huub Dijstelbloem
*Scientific Council for Government Policy, The Hague, The Netherlands*

Albert Meijer
*University of Utrecht, The Netherlands*

First published 2011 by
PALGRAVE MACMILLAN

Palgrave Macmillan in the UK is an imprint of Macmillan Publishers Limited,
registered in England, company number 785998, of Houndmills, Basingstoke,
Hampshire RG21 6XS.

Palgrave Macmillan in the US is a division of St Martin's Press LLC,
175 Fifth Avenue, New York, NY 10010.

Palgrave Macmillan is the global academic imprint of the above companies
and has companies and representatives throughout the world.

Palgrave® and Macmillan® are registered trademarks in the United States,
the United Kingdom, Europe and other countries.

ISBN 978–0–230–27846–2 hardback

This book is printed on paper suitable for recycling and made from fully
managed and sustained forest sources. Logging, pulping and manufacturing
processes are expected to conform to the environmental regulations of the
country of origin.

A catalogue record for this book is available from the British Library.

Library of Congress Cataloging-in-Publication Data
Migration and the new technological borders of Europe / [edited by]
   Huub Dijstelbloem, Albert Meijer.
     p.   cm.
   Includes index.
   Summary: "European borders that aim to control migration
   and mobility increasingly rely on technology to distinguish between
   citizens and aliens. This book explores new tensions in Europe
   between states and citizens, and between politics, technology
   and human rights."— Provided by publisher.
   ISBN 978–0–230–27846–2 (hardback)
   1. European Union countries—Emigration and immigration—Government
   policy.   2. Technology and state—European Union countries.
   3. Citizenship—European Union countries.   4. Minorities—European
   Union countries.   5. Civil rights—European Union countries.
   I. Dijstelbloem, Huub, 1969–   II. Meijer, Albert, 1967–   III. Title.
   JV7590.M52545 2011
   325.4—dc22                                                    2010050726

10   9   8   7   6   5   4   3   2   1
20   19   18   17   16   15   14   13   12   11

Printed and bound in The United States of America

# Contents

# List of Tables and Figures

## Tables

## Figures

# Acknowledgements

This book is the result of a project that was initialized by the Rathenau Institute, the Dutch office for technology assessment and science system assessment, on the use of technologies in migration policy and border control. For providing us with the time to complete this volume, our thanks goes to the Dutch Scientific Council for Government Policy (WRR) and the Utrecht University School of Governance (USG). Of the people who provided us with help and advice, a special thanks goes to Jenny Goldschmidt, Eefje van den Heuvel-Vromans, Sjors Overman, H.P. Schreinemachers, Jan Staman, Gerard de Vries, Willemine Willems, Sally Wyatt and Arre Zuurmond.

# Notes on Contributors

**Alex Balch** is a research fellow in the Department of Politics, University of Sheffield, based at ICOSS. He completed his PhD at the University of Liverpool in 2007 which was on changing immigration policies in the UK and Spain. He has also published and worked on a number of projects around the subject of migration policy, European integration and immigrant inclusion. These include a Framework Five project – 'PEMINT' (The Political Economy of Migration in an Integrating Europe), and 'The Civic Citizenship and Inclusion Index' – an annual evaluation of integration policies in the EU, with the British Council, Foreign Policy Centre and Migration Policy Group in Brussels.

**Michiel Besters** took his Research Master in Philosophy at Tilburg University. During his education he had the position of teaching assistant for a course in business ethics at the Faculty of Humanities, Tilburg University. After his graduation, Besters was a teacher in philosophy at Luzac College, a private high school. Since September 2008, Besters has worked as a researcher at the Rathenau Institute. His current research reflects two of his main interests: the cultural, political and societal aspects of healthcare, on the one hand, and surveillance technology, on the other.

**Dennis Broeders** studied international relations at the University of Nijmegen. In 1999 he joined the Scientific Council for Government Policy (WRR) as a research fellow. He worked on reports to the government on immigration and integration, on decision-making procedures in an enlarged European Union and on the working of social norms and values. Later he became a senior research fellow and project leader and was responsible for the reports *Media Policy in the Digital Age* (2005) and *Identification with the Netherlands* (2007). He is currently coordinator of the Policy, Information and Technology project group. At the Department of Sociology at the Erasmus University of Rotterdam he completed his PhD thesis on the development of internal surveillance on irregular migrants in the Netherlands and Germany and the EU dimension of these policy developments.

**Frans Brom** is head of the Department of Technology Assessment of the Rathenau Institute and Professor of Ethics of Technology Assessment at Utrecht University. He focuses on the ethical and societal impact of science and technology and the interaction between ethics and political theory. He has a special interest in the status of public morality, the role of transparency and public deliberation in techno-ethical issues and the role of trust in pluralistic democratic societies. He studied ethics and philosophy of law at the Catholic Theological University Amsterdam and the Free University Amsterdam. He received a PhD in ethics (1997) at Utrecht University with a thesis on 'Animal Biotechnology as a Moral Problem'. He is co-founder and secretary of the European Society for Agricultural and Food Ethics, EurSafe (since 1999); and European Editor of the *Journal for Agricultural and Environmental Ethics* (since 2001). He is a member of the subcommittee on ethical and social aspects of the Commission on Genetic Modification (since 2002), Board member of the Societas Ethica (since 2004) and member of the Central Ethical Compliance Group of Unilever (since 2006).

**Evelien Brouwer** is Assistant Professor of Constitutional and Administrative Law in the Law School of Utrecht University. Between 2002 and 2007 she was a researcher at the Centre for Migration Law, Radboud University of Nijmegen, where she wrote her dissertation on the right to effective remedies for third-country nationals reported in the Schengen Information System. In 2001–02, she participated in the research project 'Immigration, Asylum and Terrorism: A Changing Dynamic' of the Centre for Migration Law, University of Nijmegen. She is a participant in the 6th Framework programme CHALLENGE (The Changing Landscape of European Liberty and Security) of the European Commission and Member of the Dutch Standing Committee of experts in international immigration, asylum and criminal law ('Meijers Committee').

**Huub Dijstelbloem** is Lecturer in Philosophy of Science at the University of Amsterdam and Senior Researcher at the Scientific Council for Government Policy in the Hague (WRR). He studied Philosophy (MA) and Science, Technology and Culture (MSc) at the University of Amsterdam and in Paris at the École des Mines, supervised by Professor Bruno Latour. He wrote his PhD on the democratic deficits in the political and scientific decision-making processes at the beginning of the AIDS epidemic, environmental problems and BSE. Currently his research focuses on the political aspects of the surveillance society (especially technologies for border control) and biomedical issues (human enhancement, medical technology, commodification of body materials). In addition to that he is involved in questions concerning democracy in technological societies.

**Andrew Geddes** was appointed chair of the Department of Politics of the University of Sheffield in January 2008. He specializes in comparative analysis of politics and policy-making in Europe, with a particular interest in the politics of international migration. Current research projects include: Economic and Social Research Council-funded work on multi-level governance in south-east Europe (with Andrew Taylor, Ian Bache and Charles Lees); EU policies on migration, asylum and immigrant integration; the regional and global governance of international migration; temporary labour/agency work in the UK; the European Union and British politics.

**Albert Meijer** is Associate Professor of Public Administration and Policy Sciences at Utrecht University. He does research on public accountability and on informatization in public administration. Meijer conducted research for a parliamentary inquiry committee, carried out various research projects for the Netherlands Department of Internal Affairs and evaluated Dutch policies for biotechnology application in animals. Meijer is one of the chairs of the permanent study group on informatization of the European Group for Public Administration and a member of the editorial board of the *Electronic Journal of E-Government*. He has published extensively on the relations between technology and government in journals such as *Public Management Review, Government Information Quarterly, Information Polity, The Information Society* and *Technology in Society.*

**Irma van der Ploeg** studied at the universities of Nijmegen, Groningen and Maastricht, resulting in degrees in philosophy and science and technology studies; including a PhD in 1998 for a thesis on normative and ethical aspects of medical reproductive technologies. In 2006 she was appointed as Professor of Infonomics and New Media at Zuyd University, Maastricht/Heerlen. She has published extensively on philosophical, normative and gender aspects of medical technologies and information technologies, and is the author of *Prosthetic Bodies: The Construction of the Fetus and the Couple as Patients in Reproductive Technologies* (2001) and *The Machine-Readable Body: Essays on Biometrics and the Informatization of the Body* (2005). In 2008 she received a Starting Grant for Independent Researchers from the European Research Council, for a large, five-year research project entitled 'Social and Ethical Aspects of Digital Identities: Towards a Value Sensitive Identity Management'.

**Isolde Sprenkels** studied philosophy at Tilburg University. In March 2007 she started working as a junior researcher at the Infonomics and New Media Research Centre at Zuyd University. She conducted research on digital identities and identity management, co-developed and currently teaches a minor on 'Digital Identity and Professional Practice' and contributed to research as part of the FP7 HIDE project: Homeland Security, Biometric Identification and Personal Detection Ethics. In October 2008 she started her PhD research as part of the DigIDeas project. This project examines the social and ethical implications of digital identity management systems and is funded by the European Research Council within the FP7 Ideas programme.

# List of Abbreviations

| | |
|---|---|
| AFSJ | area of freedom, security and justice (Treaty of Amsterdam, 1997) |
| BVV | Dutch Aliens Information Interface |
| CS-VIS | Central Visa Information System |
| DSS | Dutch Decision Support System |
| EC | European Commission |
| ECHR | European Convention on Human Rights |
| ECJ | European Court of Justice |
| ECtHR | European Court of Human Rights |
| EDPS | European Data Protection Supervisor |
| EP | European Parliament |
| EPIA | European Pact on Immigration and Asylum |
| ESTA | European Electronic System of Travel Authorization |
| EU | European Union |
| EU VIS | EU Visa Information System |
| ICT | information and communication technology |
| IND | Dutch Immigration and Naturalization Service |
| INDIS | IND Information System |
| JHA | Justice and Home Affairs (Council of the EU) |
| LJN | Country Court Number (Dutch: *Landelijke Jurisprudentienummer*) |
| NGOs | non-governmental organizations |
| NI-VIS | National Interface – Visa Information System |
| N-SIS/N-SIS II | national databases |
| OMC | Open Method of Coordination |
| QMV | qualified majority voting |
| RFID | radio-frequency identification |
| SIRENE | *Supplément d'Information Requis à l'Entrée Nationale* |
| SIS | Schengen Information System |
| SIS II | Schengen Information System II |
| TCNs | Third-Country Nationals |
| VIS | Visa Information System |
| UNICEF | United Nations Children's Fund |

# 1
# The Migration Machine

*Huub Dijstelbloem, Albert Meijer and Michiel Besters*

## Europe's technological borders

Anyone travelling to Europe these days comes across not only barriers but also an increasing amount of technology. Bona fide travellers are offered high-tech initiatives (such as iris scans) in the hope that the desire for safety can still be combined with freedom of movement for all citizens. As a result, the borders of Europe are changing into an 'e-Border'. Behind the scenes, various government services are drawing up risk profiles for all kinds of aliens. If migrants risk crossing the Mediterranean to Europe illegally, there are boats, helicopters, aeroplanes and satellites on the lookout for them. In harbours and at country borders ship containers and lorry cargo space are searched using heat sensors and carbon dioxide detectors to check for the presence of human beings. Globalization is taking place but is not making travel any easier. The EU has removed its internal borders but has fortified its outer boundaries.

The abolishment of the internal borders of the EU has increased the need for controlling the borders of the Schengen area, currently covering approximately 8000 km land borders and 43,000 km sea borders. There are approximately 600 airports with extra-Schengen flights. About 250 million passengers a year pass these borders over land, about 70 million over sea and about 390 million through the air. The member states supposedly have a mutual interest in strengthening the control of the external borders. After all, 'a border is only as secure as its least well guarded area' (House of Lords 2008: 15).

In order to manage the flow of migrants and asylum seekers to Europe, governments are forced to make complicated and often controversial choices. Migrants who, according to rules that are applied, are not entitled to settle are becoming more and more inventive in circumventing the procedures. Big risks are not avoided. However, it is doubtful whether strict border control does have the intended effect (i.e. decrease of illegal immigrants). Quite often the extraterritorial surveillance leads to the so-called 'waterbed effect' or the 'squeezed balloon syndrome', the displacement of migration flows. The fact that the safe itineraries are blocked does not imply that people abandon their plans to enter Europe. Rather, these people take more dangerous routes. Since these alternative routes expose immigrants to even greater risks, the tightening of the external borders leads to an increasing number of fatalities among irregular immigrants. Between 1993 and 2006, more than 7000 deaths have been documented of people trying to reach the European border. Moreover, the number of deaths increased significantly after controls were applied to the extended borders in 1995 (Spijkerboer 2007).

Meanwhile, governments continue looking for effective measures and even exceptional solutions to translate political decisions into a policy that limits traffic across borders. Examples are bone scans for investigating the age of minor asylum seekers, speech-recognition technology for administering civic integration examinations in the country of origin, the use of biometrics and the construction of European databanks to store data on illegal migrants. The financial costs are considerable: as well as national budgets of the member states the European Commission has reserved almost €4 billion for migration affairs in its financial programme for the period 2007–13.

Migration policy does not consist solely of laws and policy measures, but increasingly of technology. Notwithstanding, the resources that have emerged are debated only incidentally. In this context, technology in the form of a new border literally functions as an 'obligatory passage point' (Latour 1987) that works as a selection mechanism for newcomers. However, whether this selection process fulfils all the conditions that are normally taken into account when inhabitants of the state are confronted with technologies that affect their position as citizen, is doubtful. The risk is that technology in migration policy and border control is deployed in a 'state of exception' where the power of the state overrules the position of the migrants (Agamben 1998; Neal 2009). Technology, however, is not just the 'means' that allows political and administrative aims to be carried out; technology creates its own possibilities and limitations which implies that any targets that are thus achieved are always 'mediated' (Latour 1999). The border, as Salter (2005) has noticed, opens a kind of 'rite de passage', however nowadays increasingly of a technological kind. Delegating policy and implementation tasks to technological resources easily results in a transformation of those tasks, thus changing the meaning of 'migrants', 'borders', 'bodies' and 'state control' and affecting the migrants' position as citizens.

*Migration and the New Technological Borders of Europe* focuses on the increasingly technological nature of borders in Europe that aim to monitor and control legal and illegal migration in particular and mobility in general. It presents a discussion of the deployment of technology in European migration policies from two perspectives: examining the nature of new forms of surveillance and evaluating these developments from a politico-administrative and legal perspective. The technological borders may increase the efficiency of immigration policies but also raise important questions concerning the correct and humane treatment of immigrants. How can we understand the creation of these technological borders? How do they process individual immigrants? How can governments find a way to implement immigrant policies in a humane manner?

The aim of this introductory chapter is to reflect on the changing meaning of both 'borders' and 'border control' and its implication for the position of migrants. Walters (2006) has noted with reference to the work of Andreas (2003) about the 'rebordering' of the state, that borders far from having disappeared in an open and transnational global space, as some theorists expected in the period between the fall of the Wall in 1989 and the 9/11 attacks in 2001, reappeared 'as spaces and instruments for the policing of a variety of actors, objects and processes whose common denominator is their "mobility" or more specifically, the forms of social and political insecurity that have come to be discursively attached to these mobilities' (Walters 2006: 188).

Technologies being used for this task have a severe effect on the position of people, discriminating them at the border as citizens or aliens, thereby making use of their body as a source of information. Borders, however, as Zureik and Salter in *Global Surveillance and Policing: Borders, Security, Identity* (2005) have observed from a surveillance point of view, are important but understudied. As Pickering and Weber in *Borders, Mobility and Technologies of Control* (2006), with reference to Donnan and Wilson (1999), have stated from an anthropological and criminological point of view, borders are sites for the expression of state power. Due to the changing position of the nation-state in a globalizing world, these sites increasingly form the expression of a mixed international regime. As a consequence, the growing intensity of European integration, not only in the economic and administrative sense, but, since the Treaty of Lisbon and the institution of the first long-term President of the European Council, also in the political sense, European countries, and especially the EU member states, find themselves back in an international political unit with border control as a common policy area.

The institution of this European political regime 'frames' the technological regime of border control in a specific way. Though technology can seldom be understood as 'neutral', in this context the specific political consequences of the technological regime deserve more study. To do so, in the next section a specification of the type of technology used in migration policy will be given. In the following sections, the context in which these technologies are deployed will be described as the interweaving of immigration, integration and security policies. The policy system is increasingly becoming a mechanism for inclusion and exclusion. The result is that migration policy is becoming a test lab of a questionable kind, both technically and politically. The consequences of this and the conditions under which legitimacy could be improved will be discussed in the final section.

## Migration technology

In the highly charged political and public debate on migration, the leading role is usually granted to the objectives: what limits should be applied to the influx of migrants and asylum seekers to the EU and its member states? This issue is one of unprecedented size: complicated, cross-border and, almost by definition, tragic. As far as the public is concerned, governments can almost never get their policy right: they either do too much, or too little. The general public seems to be much less interested in knowing how the policy aims are subsequently achieved. However, in migration policy it is not only a matter of political aims, but also the resources actually used to implement this policy. National governments and the EU use a variety of instruments to curb the influx of migrants and diverse techniques to register these migrants and ascertain their identity, age or family relationships.

As we know from other areas, such as medicine and information technologies, technological societies challenge the position of citizens and their humanitarian, political, juridical and civil rights in many respects. In a formal sense the position of citizens is challenged, for instance, where new rights need to be formulated to protect the privacy of citizens in the digital era. In a more material sense this position is challenged, for example, when people do not have the practical means to realize their rights in situations where they are confronted with the negative consequences of new technologies. In this respect, the use of technologies for border control and migration policies is of special importance because it has an immediate effect on the position of people: it supports decisions about the inclusion or exclusion of people from the state and defines them as citizens or as aliens.

The modern state controls 'the legitimate means of movement' (Torpey 2000), with the border discriminating between citizens and aliens. The result of the application of these kinds of technology is that the borders of Europe are slowly but surely changing into 'technological borders'. The use of technology for border control is at least as old as the Chinese Wall, with many recent successors such as the Great Wall of Tijuana, also known as the Great Wall of Capital, dividing Mexico from the United States to control illegal migration from the South to the North. For the use of more refined technologies in Europe, historically we can point at the invention of the passport and the introduction of identity documents that have accompanied the process of state-formation in Europe and the state's attempts to obtain control over the movements of citizens. As a result, society and the movements of its citizens have been made more 'visible' by the government (Scott 1998).

As a consequence, the mechanisms of control of the modern state are becoming more and more subtle. 'Fortress Europe' is changing into a surveillance area that makes use of quite innovative techniques. For that reason, this book does not so much consider the vessels, aeroplanes and helicopters of the EU agency Frontex, the 'brute force technology' used to survey the outer borders of the Schengen area. Rather it considers the way in which technology helps to control the outer borders of the EU and the member states, but also within country borders, with the help of very refined means that are deeply integrated into the administrative systems of the state.

The raison d'être of the modern government is mainly the management of a bureaucratic apparatus that helps to support the proper treatment of citizens. The use of information technology to achieve this task is a logical step, certainly in a modern and complex society. It is almost impossible to imagine how, for instance, the Register of Births, Deaths and Marriages could be updated or taxes collected, two classic government tasks, without using some form of technology. Undeniably, there is a certain logic in the use of technology in migration policy. Applying technological and computerized methods can help to ensure that borders are better monitored, that applications are dealt with more quickly and that procedures are used more efficiently.

However, technology is sometimes an unreliable ally, leading to undesirable side effects. If information files are unreliable, impossible to adequately check or correct, migrants may unjustly be refused entry. Biometry can violate the integrity of the body or lead to the body being regarded as an instrument. Fingerprints can be difficult to read; perhaps data has been recorded incorrectly in another country. Or someone's age is difficult to determine by means of a bone scan. Too much use of technology can put a disproportionate emphasis on the need to carry out checks.

The instruments used by the government to implement its migration policy could be called 'migration technology' – a new concept in this context. Originating in the ICT world, the concept stands for technology involved in transferring digital material from one software or hardware configuration to another, or from one generation of computing technology to the next. However, the term can also be used to refer to the many forms of technological systems used to register illegal residents, to check people crossing the border and to automate the applications for asylum and migration. Two aspects typify the use of migration technology.

In the first place, migration technology does not so much affect native citizens, but mainly foreign nationals who would like to obtain entry to the territory; in other words, migrants who apply for legal residence status with all the rights and obligations that go with it. Migration technology is thus used for people who would like to become European citizens, unlike many other forms of computerization and technology the government employs. This means the technology is employed during a decision procedure, the outcome of which is decisive: someone can be refused entry to a country or the possibility of settling here.

In the second place, not only ICT is involved in this process but also a range of other techniques. Migration technology does not only consist of the whirring computers that enhance every government building these days, but also of techniques that involve the human body, such as DNA tests (saliva, hair), age testing (X-rays) and biometric data (fingerprints and iris scans). Unlike in other government departments, the application of technology to migration policy is many-faceted, as well as focusing on countless forms of information that are not usually found in the classic weaponry of bureaucracy.

The result is that migration technology has come to occupy a special position in government policy, as it affects people who find themselves in a highly vulnerable position. Moreover, these people are confronted with forms of technology and computerization that are not just related to processing information, but which are used to identify and verify, by intervening in the human body. Control of citizens, travellers, migrants and illegal aliens is coming closer to their bodies. This kind of control of the body (Rose 2007; Foucault 1978) deserves special attention because of the increasing interweaving of immigration, integration and security policies, which puts citizens in a vulnerable position towards the state.

## The interweaving of immigration, integration and security policies

The use of 'migration technology' nowadays takes place in a highly politicized and polarized context. In all European countries migration policy has become one of the most controversial issues on the political agenda over the past 15 years. Discussions about desirable and undesirable migrants; the separation of migrants who apply for asylum for humanitarian reasons from those who, in common parlance, are somewhat disparagingly called 'economic refugees' or 'fortune-seekers'; fear of an overwhelming influx of people from the poorer South to the rich West. These are just a few of the many vexed questions that have dominated public and political debate during the past few years.

The movement of people follows on logically from globalization: the creation of a world economy with the accompanying social and technological networks such as international air traffic, but also the Internet. For a considerable part, this is sustained by the increase in the international transport of capital, goods, services and information (Sassen 1998). The border historically serves as a place for commerce itself, differentiating between social, economic and juridical regimes (Pellerin 2005). But globalization came up against a development in the opposite direction: in addition to the opening up of national borders for economic reasons, an increasing number of restrictions was imposed on the free movement of people, especially the influx of migrants from less prosperous areas to Western countries. This tension between economic globalization on the one hand and a stricter national migration policy on the other has turned migration policies into a controversial topic. From that moment onwards, most European governments began to implement a much more restrictive entry policy.

During the past few decades, many European governments' policies have consisted of measures to limit the immigration influx and, at the same time, to counter illegality. In order to achieve this, more and more measures have been developed to check people who come into a country (external control), but also those already in a country (internal control). In addition, the policy is not only becoming more restrictive, but also more selective. Not only are the numbers of migrants allowed to enter into a country being reduced, migrants are also examined more carefully according to the particular needs of those countries.

As well as becoming more restrictive and selective, migration policy has also become more and more entangled in issues relating to integration policy and – since the 9/11 attacks, the War on Terror and increasing concerns about the position of Muslims in Europe – security policy. Migration and integration policies have both been 'securitized' (Lindahl 2008). As a result, three discussions have become increasingly interrelated. The first discussion concerns migration policy and is mainly concerned with the issues mentioned above, namely, the influx of migrants and the separation of 'desirable' and 'undesirable' aliens. The second discussion is about integration policy and is dominated in the media and politics by questions and problems related to social cohesion and civic integration among newcomers (varying from the obligation to assimilate culturally to the rights to participate economically). The third discussion is about security policy, especially on border control in the countries of Europe and the outer limits of the Schengen area, and the screening and refusal of people who are suspected of being a threat to society.

Responses to 9/11 by the European Commission, suggesting a direct link between the issues of migration, asylum and security, illustrate this. In less than two weeks after 9/11 the Justice and Home Affairs (JHA) Council of the EU organized an Extraordinary Meeting which called for 'the Commission to examine urgently the relationship between safeguarding internal security and complying with international protection obligations and instruments' (Neal 2009: 338). On 15 November 2001 the European Commission announced that border control must respond to the challenges 'of an efficient fight against criminal networks, of trustworthy action against terrorist risks and of creating mutual confidence between those member States which have abandoned border controls at their internal frontiers' (Commission of the European Communities 2001).

This interweaving of immigration, integration and security policies is illustrated, for example, in the agenda produced in 2006 by the European Security Research Advisory Board which places under the heading 'border security', illegal migration in the same category as weapon and drug smuggling (European Security Research Advisory Board 2006). Even so-called knowledge migrants are checked. Because of the fear of spying or the misuse of knowledge they might acquire (it may, for example, be deployed for atomic programmes or bioterrorism) the screening of this category of migrants has become a permanent element of the policy. Also the fact that migrants have to do a civic integration examination in their own country before leaving for some of the member states is one component of the integration policy. Undeniably, the cost and effort this examination involves for the potential migrant will also affect migration policy.

The policy on security is finding its way into immigration policy. Risk analyses, based on the risk profiles of various target groups, are increasingly performed as part of migration and integration policy. Migration, integration and security all come to be regarded as part of the same problem.

## The border as a mechanism for inclusion and exclusion

The policy system that is being developed today is increasingly taking on the character of a 'machine' (Morgan 1997; Barry 2001). This machine combines social and technical reality: it is a construction that not only consists of high-tech, but also of politicians, policy-makers, civil servants, customs officers and military police. The result is a gigantic, cross-border, technology-influenced policy machine that aims to regulate the movement of aliens in Europe.

The machine metaphor offers possibilities to evaluate the role of technology, and creates space to argue both the positive and negative aspects. If the use of migration technology works as it should, one may speak of a well-oiled machine that fairly deals with the vast numbers of applications and border crossings in the EU every year. Waiting times for visas and residential permits can be reduced when policies are implemented efficiently. But there may also be less favourable scenarios. The metaphor of the machine is not only reserved for appliances (machines in the classic sense of the word), but also for people who exhibit mechanical behaviour. This can lead to an undesirable functioning of the machine in two ways.

Firstly, there is a danger that the migration policy will be unjustly regarded as a machine which can be used with ease by both politicians and civil servants. Just press a button and the policy has been amended. This, however, is a dangerous illusion. Instruments of implementation do not allow themselves to be directed mechanically, and it is also questionable whether this would be desirable. Too much emphasis on the technical deployment of tasks creates a bureaucracy which is difficult to hold responsible and accountable for its actions.

Secondly, the migration machine at its most extreme is a faceless, impersonal policy machine which, without any human intervention, performs its work with the minimum of empathy for those concerned. That, too, is undesirable. The machine then takes over the human aspect. These two scenarios represent the reverse of a well-oiled machine. Policy which is influenced by technology and computerization and which increasingly acquires the character of a machine has both advantages and disadvantages, therefore. With the help of the machine metaphor, it should be possible to detect them.

If migration policy can be compared with a machine, what sort of machine is it? The dominant theoretical viewpoint in the social and political science literature devoted to the use of technology for border controls in general and migration policy in particular, is the viewpoint of 'surveillance society' (Walters 2006; Lyon 2007). The classic example of surveillance according to Foucault (1995) is Jeremy Bentham's invention of the panopticon. Latin for 'all-seeing', this represents the idea of constant and total observation. The domed prisons were constructed according to this principle. Prison warders could check the prisoners by keeping a lookout from one specific point, without the prisoners being able to see the warder.

As a consequence, these days a wider form of surveillance is part of the repertoire used by governments to keep an eye on the population, with three important aspects.

Firstly, surveillance does not occur from a central point (a control room), but consists instead of a proliferation of procedures and practices. Such a migration machine is not, in this case, a machine that can be traced to a particular location or an all-seeing eye that keeps everybody in view from one particular point. Surveillance and control refers in this sense to the distribution of tasks and functions that focus on monitoring, registering and checking. These can be found in the clearly indicated points for border traffic (customs posts), but have also extended right into the capillaries of society; for example, the illegality checks done via personal data registration.

Secondly, surveillance is not only carried out by governments; it is also the task of other organizations (governance) such as medical institutes and welfare organizations that discipline citizens in a particular manner (take, for example, the implementation of digital files on children). Migration policy offices work together with various partners in a 'chain' and the responsibility for screening certain types of migrants (education, work, knowledge and talent) is being delegated to universities and companies. As a result, the machine is not only in public, but also in private and in professional hands.

Thirdly, border control is increasingly targeting the human body. Bones, voices, DNA and fingerprints service as the new identity documents. The fact that a person's body is increasingly being used to deploy technology and computerization is a particularly significant and worrying aspect that deserves special attention. The migration machine reaches the bodies of the people it aims to control and subjects them to a surveillance regime.

## Remote control and the readable body

These three aspects have a severe impact on the meaning and the function of 'borders' and 'border control'. Traditionally, a border is a demarcation line between two countries, thus marking and protecting the territory and sovereignty of each one. The notion of 'border' originates from the French word *bordure*, meaning 'edge'. However, the formation of the Schengen area in Europe and the strong emphasis on controls have led to a change of meaning for these demarcation lines belonging to national states.

Border checks are changing their location; they do not always take place at the border, but now form part of a much wider area of surveillance, monitoring, admission requirements and administrative processes. Actually, the border is everywhere as it is both portable (ID card) and virtual (databases) (Lyon 2005). According to Walters (2006) there is a modulation in the way that the EU renders the border controls of its members and neighbouring states into calculable, comparable data and makes them subject to continuous adjustment. As a consequence, the migration machine is more than just a wall erected to protect 'Fortress Europe' from advancing migrants. Border controls are becoming more ingenious: in the form of a 'smart border' (Lyon 2005; Côté-Boucher 2008).

In a volume with the meaningful title *In Search of Europe's Borders*, this development is described as a form of 'remote control' (Guiraudon 2003). Not only are the surveillance activities being transferred more and more from the strict border-control function at the exterior of a territorial area to the interior, for example by the coupling and interoperability of databases in the country of arrival; they are also being moved further to the exterior, for instance by taking civic integration exams in the country of origin.

Governments are also increasingly outsourcing border-control activities to non-governmental organizations. As far as the analysis of migration technology is concerned, this means that this particular technology is becoming much more than a system for guarding borders. It is also a system that distinguishes between different kinds of migrants in a subtle manner by a process of 'social sorting' (Lyon 2002). The border becomes a 'refined sieve', and migration technology is accelerating that process (Broeders 2009). This 'sieving border' is of a special kind. In the case of migration technology, the border sieves information, originating from a very special source: the migrant. And to an increasing degree, the *body* of the migrant.

The external characteristics of migrants are not only presented in terms of descriptions (height, colour of eyes) in government data files; actual imprints of the body are increasingly finding their way into bureaucracy. It becomes a 'machine-readable body' (Van der Ploeg 2002). The body is regarded as a source of information, the code of which can be read by a machine. To a certain extent, the body thus becomes a component of the machine: it is being interpreted and formatted as if it were an information storage device that simply has to be scanned in order to be registered. The body becomes 'the universal ID card of the future' (Van der Ploeg 1999: 301).

There are crude examples of this to be seen in border controls at several locations, for example the use of the LifeGuard technology in Zeebrugge harbour (Verstraete 2001). LifeGuard is a remote-sensing device that registers ultra-low frequency signals emanating from the electromagnetic field around a beating heart. Originally developed by the American army for rescue operations and for searching buildings for the presence of criminals, this technique has been deployed in Zeebrugge by a company to detect refugees and illegal migrants who had hidden themselves in the cargo space of lorries and containers on their way to the United Kingdom.

Examples of a more subtle, but not less invasive, application can be seen in the unprecedented advance in the use of biometry. Whereas illegal entrants usually find themselves being asked to give their fingerprints, travellers arriving at Schiphol Airport in Amsterdam can now have their irises scanned (using the so-called Privium programme, 'a seamless travel programme designed to offer priority, speed and comfort to the airport's most loyal users'). If the scanner does not read the correct code, the person is refused entry. Biometry thus enables the process of authentication to take place; identity claims can be checked for authenticity. Only in the case of recognition does the system open the doors for a person (Ceyhan 2005). In a society that focuses on control, the body gradually becomes a 'password' (Deleuze 1995).

## Migration policy as a test lab: questionable technical and political legitimacy

The similarity between the different forms of migration technology is that they all treat the human body as if it were an information storage device. Policy instruments used for border control and the governance of the movements of people can be increasingly compared to a machine that aims to 'read' the required information and then use it to make a judgment on which status a migrant should be given. The social, ethical, legal and administrative results of such a sorting process add another dimension to the already highly charged debate on migration policy.

Because discussions on the political aims of migration policy demand everyone's attention, the spotlight is much less often focused on what happens during implementation, let alone the specific role of the type of technology used. More and more forms of technology are being applied in a policy setting in which the political wish is for limitations to be placed on the movements of aliens and, more specifically, for selections to be made. This makes the question *how* these restrictions and selections should be carried out, which resources should be used to do so and how they should function, even more urgent. The risk is that migration policy starts to function as a kind of test lab for all kinds of new technologies, with the migrant as a test subject.

This risk results from the increasing emphasis on control by the interweaving of immigration, integration and security policies. Because of a lack of attention amongst the public and in the media for the ins and outs of the technical aspects of migration policy and its consequences, and the weak position of migrants to give voice to the consequences, this test lab is not only of a doubtful technical legitimacy but also of a questionable political legitimacy.

With regard to the technical legitimacy, some examples may illustrate the precarious character of the 'migration machine'. Experts cannot agree about the reliability of bone scans in, for instance, the Netherlands where X-ray technology is used on minor asylum seekers. Speech-recognition technology, deployed abroad in civic integration examinations, has far-reaching consequences for the person using it. It is questionable whether this technology is sufficiently developed for use in this context. Speech-recognition technology has not previously been used where the outcome is so crucial as, for example, in the case of the civic integration examination in one's country of origin. Little experience has so far been acquired in this field. It is doubtful whether we know enough about the teething problems that are undoubtedly present at some examination locations. Biometrics, another example, is also not completely error-free. Not every fingerprint is read correctly and not every fingerprint can be read correctly. Fingerprints are also subject to change, as for instance people suffering from cancer may experience. In other words, every form of identification is fundamentally unstable.

In the present Schengen Information System (SIS), personal data is not always removed within the statutory period or according to the conditions of use, which can lead to a wrongful refusal of entry. Small errors in a system can have enormous consequences. Crucial decisions depend on it. For example: may someone enter a particular country or not? Furthermore, these are decisions that can have repercussions for a long time, and not just in one country. It is also true to say that migrants have less chance of obtaining rectification, compared to native citizens of a country. In short, migrants have a weak position in the everyday practice of migration policies with little means to check or to correct data that are gathered from them.

With regard to political legitimacy, it is unclear how effective the various technological systems are. There are no clear statistics and evaluations, and a new version of the SIS is being produced, even though the present system has not yet been sufficiently well evaluated. Next to that, there is the danger that the objectives will change, just as they did with the civic integration examination. Although this examination is formally part of integration policy, it has been subject to change (in a political sense) and is now part of migration policy. Here it functions as a means of making migration more difficult and more selective by raising the required language levels.

Another problem is the danger of stigmatization; exclusion of people due to race, skin colour, ethnic or social background or religion. Of course, this is against the law, but databases and biometry make it increasingly easy to use such characteristics to distinguish between people. This may lead to categorical surveillance and thus to discrimination of migrants who have very little chance of rectifying this or of appealing (Van der Ploeg 2002).

An overarching problem that keeps cropping up is the impenetrability of these technological systems. Two examples: the 'decision trees' migration offices use when deciding on a request for asylum, and the Information Systems they use in verifying asylum seekers' accounts of their escape. Automated decision-making is not allowed, and such systems should not be permitted to take over the role of the civil servants. However, in practice it becomes difficult to avoid taking the smooth path laid out by information technology.

Finally, monitoring and public checking methods have their shortcomings. Supervisory bodies such as the European Data Protection Supervisor (EDPS) have not been granted authority to provide legal advice. Their recommendations are, therefore, often ignored. In addition, staffing and competence do not always go together. This results in insufficient supervision.

## Turning the test lab into a public laboratory

The use of technologies brings new risks, new inequalities and unforeseen consequences. The integrity of migrants and their bodies, their privacy and the protection of their personal sphere are put to the test. It becomes harder to control, to check and to correct the collection of data. There is less room for exceptions and for making special decisions in individual cases, because the information process involved and, therefore, also the decision-making process become increasingly standardized.

The crucial question is whether those who, according to the current policy rules, have no right to an entry ticket are treated as aliens or as citizens. In theory a migrant who is turned away for the wrong reasons or because of a technological failure may obtain a lawyer and finally go to the European Court. However, his position is weaker than the citizen who always has his democratic rights: to go to the media, put an issue on the agenda, organize resistance and to vote at election time.

In order to appreciate more clearly the difference between the position of citizens and that of aliens, it is worthwhile to compare the use of technology in migration policies with another traditional area of the state; namely, the tax office: each year it faces the challenge of dealing accurately with every tax declaration. Whether this (one of the oldest and most important tasks carried out by the state) is done adequately depends almost entirely on the information technology used. The watchful eye of the general public guarantees, however, that there is continuous pressure to do so accurately.

This form of counter-surveillance is absent in migration policy. Those affected are not citizens of the desired country but come from elsewhere. The usual mechanisms for democratic control are missing. Moreover, in a technological society it cannot be assumed that all public and technological issues will find their way into the democratic arena by way of representation, let alone to a public of non-state residents. Neither can we assume that such a diverse and fragmented group of people as migrants can participate in the design of the border and its procedures. Therefore, possible mistakes need to be brought to the authority's attention in alternative ways so as to enable real control.

To be democratically controllable, new existing technological practices with a political goal should be open for debate. The effects of technology and the changing meaning of 'borders' and 'border control' should be rendered more visible in order to strengthen public involvement. To technically and politically legitimize the role of technology in migration policy, mechanisms need to be developed to make such technologies part of a more public endeavour. The test lab should be turned into a public laboratory.

Turning the deployment of technology into a public laboratory means that techniques have to be developed to evaluate technology, by learning from mistakes and by making it a more public tool by strengthening its visibility and 'publicity'. In such a scenario, an important role must be given to migrants themselves. In theory, they may be outsiders of the democratic community; in practice, they are the most directly affected by the workings of the migration machine. As such, they form a fragmentized and excluded public. Currently, migrants are treated as the object of the migration machine. When they are treated as subjects, greater justice is done to their status as citizens.

## Outline of the book

In the following chapters of this book, the questions raised in this introduction will be analysed from various disciplinary and thematic perspectives.

In Chapter 2 Alex Balch and Andrew Geddes examine the development of migration policy in Europe and provide a context for the following chapters that discuss the European 'migration machine'. In order to do so, they make use of a politico-legal perspective, and conceptualize the recent development of the EU migration regime (since Amsterdam) as constituent of an evolving and complex system. Through a survey of European integration in this area they map this system, consider its future development and, via discussion of Europeanization, identify linkages with policy at the nation-state level.

The next two chapters examine the nature of the main technological developments, large-scale information systems and biometrics. In Chapter 3 Dennis Broeders uses the concept of the 'surveillance society' to analyse the role of large-scale database systems in migration policies. The development of modern technological tools to implement immigration policy can be characterized as the construction of a European Border Surveillance System. From a sociological and political science point of view, Broeders examines how the increased potential for digital surveillance is influencing the state's choices in migration management. He studies the way in which the state deals with mobility and migration and the influence that surveillance and technology have had on the possibilities for migration policy at both the national and the EU level. The analysis focuses on the actual development and operation of one component of the new border surveillance: the commissioning and operation of the three major migration databases developed by the EU in recent years, namely the SIS, Eurodac and VIS. How do these systems attempt to prevent irregular migrants from entering Europe? How are they used as an instrument of expulsion policies? Modern border surveillance increases the focus of what governments see, but also makes the selective nature of this vision all the more evident.

In Chapter 4 Irma van der Ploeg and Isolde Sprenkels focus on a second set of technologies in the 'migration machine': biometrics. The authors use sociological and philosophical perspectives to show that biometrics renders the human body of immigrants as 'machine-readable'. They describe present-day developments and practices concerning the digitalization of identification in the context of migration and migration policy, together with the associated transformations that have taken place in how migrant surveillance is performed. The analysis focuses on the increasing extent to which a migrant's body is being used for carrying out identification and surveillance and especially the fact that the deployment of biometrics is proliferating in the context of this policy. Several elements are explained of the context in which the present deployment of identification technology for migration purposes should be placed. To do so, they describe the identification methods used in the present implementation of migration policy. This emphasizes, in addition to the considerable complexity of this policy area, the increasing importance of biometrics. Van der Ploeg and Sprenkels demonstrate the difficulties surrounding every application of biometrics, thus indicating where, within this context, the socio-political and normative-ethical problems surrounding the application of biometrics can be expected now and in the near future. Now the computerization of the body has extended to the body of migrants, a group that is often vulnerable anyway, proper thought should be given to how the new possibilities and methods of carrying out controls are created.

The next chapters shift the focus to a more evaluative appreciation of the 'migration machine'. In Chapter 5 a political science perspective is applied by Albert Meijer to highlight the shortcomings in political and administrative responsibilities for Europe's new technological borders. He shows how the use of information technology in immigration policy goes hand-in-glove with a growing complexity and substantial shifting in the practical working of responsibilities. Governments and parliaments have the difficult task of searching for new structures of responsibilities in migration policy that fit modern information technologies. A responsible approach to information technology is crucial in order to minimize risks. Meijer presents a critical discussion of political and administrative responsibilities for the 'migration machine'. The use of information technology in migration policies is discussed at different levels: the individual government agency, the chain of government agencies within a country and finally the level of European cooperation. At all of these levels this chapter discusses the past, present and future in order to establish how these responsibilities have been formed, take their present forms and are being formed. Responsibilities are being discussed on the basis of a normative framework which highlights the roles of civil servants, administrators and politicians. The empirical research focuses on the Netherlands but the chapter presents arguments that apply to other European countries as well since, to a large extent, these countries use the same technologies.

In Chapter 6 Evelien Brouwer takes the analysis to a legal evaluation of the 'migration machine'. Brouwer applies a legal science perspective on the lack of attention for legal frameworks in the development and deployment of technologies for border control. She aims to reach a better understanding of the standards that are frequently neglected against the backdrop of current developments. She therefore examines the legal boundaries in the use of databases and biometrics in border surveillance and migration policy. She aims in particular to reach a better understanding of the standards that are frequently neglected against the backdrop of current developments. The thrust of the argument is based on the assertion that policy-makers and politicians who do not take account of the legal boundaries – the right to privacy, the principle of non-discrimination, the purpose limitation principle and the prohibition on automated decision-making – at an early stage will inevitably find themselves confronted by them when implementing these measures. The decision to focus specifically on these rights and principles is related to four significant trends in information policy. Firstly, the increased use of central databases and the application of RFID chips and biometrics have enabled the ever closer and more systematic tracking of individuals' movements. A second trend is the desire on the part of policy-makers to use information systems for multiple purposes as far as possible. A third trend is the automation of the decisions made in migration law: government agencies increasingly act on the basis of information from a range of databases, irrespective of the origin of these data. A fourth and final trend is the increasing use of profiling. Profiling is a classic instrument which compares a range of information sources to identify the characteristics of a specific target group.

The final Chapter 7 by Huub Dijstelbloem, Albert Meijer and Frans Brom draws lessons from the analyses and presents suggestions to strengthen the position of citizens and migrants towards the migration machine. The analysis focuses mainly on the risks and the unintentional and undesirable side effects of using migration technology and discusses opportunities to mitigate those risks. To what extent can the 'growth' of the machine be regulated? In a way the machine has already developed its own dynamic, with technical system questions dominating the decision-making around policies and their implementation. However, it is not necessary merely to accept this scenario. Whenever technology is involved, it is always possible to make choices and suggest alternative designs. The authors reclaim the role of citizens as *subjects* who are actively involved in controlling and shaping Europe's technological borders. The chapter therefore concludes that different strategies of counter-surveillance are needed to strengthen the position of migrants and citizens to reclaim control over the 'migration machine'.

## Bibliography

Agamben, G. (1998) *Homo Sacer: Sovereign Power and Bare Life* (Stanford University Press).

Andreas, P. (2003) 'Redrawing the Line: Borders and Security in the Twenty-First Century', *International Security*, 28(2): 78–111.

Barry, A. (2001) *Political Machines: Governing a Technological Society* (London: Athlone Press).

Broeders, D. (2007) 'The New Digital Borders of Europe: EU Databases and the Surveillance of Irregular Migrants', *International Sociology*, 22(1): 71–92.

Broeders, D. (2009) *Breaking Down Anonymity: Digital Surveillance on Irregular Migrants in Germany and the Netherlands* (Amsterdam University Press).

Brouwer, E. (2008) *Digital Borders and Real Rights: Effective Remedies for Third-Country Nationals in the Schengen Information System* (Leiden and Boston: Martinus Nijhoff Publishers).

Ceyhan, A. (2005) 'Technologization of Security: Management of Uncertainty and Risk in the Age of Biometrics', *Surveillance & Society*, 5(2): 102–23.

Commission of the European Communities (2001) 'Communication from the Commission to the Council and the European Parliament on a Common Policy on Illegal Migration', *COM* (2001) 672 final, 15 November.

Côté-Boucher, K. (2008) 'The Diffuse Border: Intelligence-Sharing, Control and Confinement along Canada's Smart Border', *Surveillance & Society*, 5(2): 142–65.

Deleuze, G. (1995) 'Postscript on Control Societies', in G. Deleuze (ed.) *Negotiations 1972–1990* (New York: Columbia University Press).

Donnan, H. and T.M. Wilson (1999) *Borders: Frontiers of Identity, Nation and State* (Oxford: Berg).

European Security Research Advisory Board (2006) *Meeting the Challenge: The European Security Research Agenda* (Luxembourg).

Foucault, M. (1978) *The History of Sexuality*, vol. 1: *The Will to Knowledge* (London: Penguin).

Foucault, M. (1995) *Discipline and Punish: The Birth of the Prison* (New York: Vintage Books).

Guiraudon, V. (2003) 'Before the EU Border: Remote Control of the "Huddled Masses"', in K. Groenendijk, E. Guild and P. Minderhoud (eds) *In Search of Europe's Borders* (The Hague: Kluwer).

Haggerty, K.D. and R.V. Ericsson (2000) 'The Surveillant Assemblage', *The British Journal of Sociology*, 51(4): 605–22.

House of Lords (2008) *FRONTEX: The EU External Borders Agency. Report with Evidence*, HL Paper 60 (London).

Latour, B. (1987) *Science in Action* (Cambridge, MA: Harvard University Press).

Latour, B. (1999) *Pandora's Hope: Essays on the Reality of Science Studies* (Cambridge, MA: Harvard University Press).

Lindahl, H. (2008) 'Border Crossings by Immigrants: Legality, Illegality, and Alegality', *Res Publica*, 14: 117–35.

Lyon, D. (ed.) (2002) *Surveillance as Social Sorting: Privacy, Risk, and Digital Discrimination* (London: Routledge).

Lyon, D. (2005) 'The Border is Everywhere: ID Cards, Surveillance and the Other', in E. Zureik and M. Salter (eds) *Global Surveillance and Policing: Borders, Security, Identity* (Cullompton: Willan Publishing).

Lyon, D. (2007) *Surveillance Studies: An Overview* (Cambridge: Polity Press).

Morgan, G. (1997) *Images of Organization* (London: Sage).

Neal, A.N. (2009) 'Securitization and Risk at the EU Border: The Origins of FRONTEX', *Journal of Common Market Studies*, 47(2): 333–56.

Pellerin, H. (2005) 'Borders, Migration and Economic Integration: Towards a New Political Economy of Borders', in E. Zureik and M.B. Salter (eds) *Global Surveillance and Policing: Borders, Security, Identity* (Cullompton: Willan Publishing).

Pickering, S. and L. Weber (eds) (2006) *Borders, Mobility and Technologies of Control* (Dordrecht: Springer).

Ploeg, I. van der (1999) '"Eurodac" and the Illegal Body: The Politics of Biometric Identity', *Ethics and Information Technology*, 1(4): 37–44.

Ploeg, I. van der (2002) 'Biometrics and the Body as Information: Normative Issues in the Socio-Technical Coding of the Body', in D. Lyon (ed.) *Surveillance as Social Sorting: Privacy, Risk, and Automated Discrimination* (New York: Routledge).

Rose, N. (2007) *The Politics of Life Itself: Biomedicine, Power, and Subjectivity in the Twenty-First Century* (Princeton University Press).

Sabel, Ch. and J. Zeitlin (2008) 'Learning from Difference: The New Architecture of Experimentalist Governance in the EU', *European Law Journal*, 14(3): 271–327.

Salter, M. (2005) 'At the Threshold of Security: A Theory of International Borders', in E. Zureik and M.B. Salter (eds) *Global Surveillance and Policing: Borders, Security, Identity* (Cullompton: Willan Publishing).

Salter, M. (2006) 'The Global Visa Regime and the Political Technologies of the International Self', *Alternatives: Global, Local, Political*, 31(2): 167–89.

Sassen, S. (1998) *Globalization and its Discontents: Essays on the New Mobility of People and Money* (New York: New Press).

Scott, J. (1998) *Seeing Like a State: How Certain Schemes to Improve the Human Condition Have Failed* (New Haven: Yale University Press).

Spijkerboer, Th. (2007) 'The Human Costs of Border Control', *European Journal of Migration and Law*, 9: 127–39.

Torpey, J. (2000) *The Invention of the Passport: Surveillance, Citizenship and the State* (Cambridge University Press).

Verstraete, G. (2001) 'Technological Frontiers and the Politics of Mobility in the European Union', *New Formations: A Journal of Culture/Theory/Politics* (Spring): 26–43.

Walters, W. (2006) 'Border/Control', *European Journal of Social Theory*, 9(2): 187–203.

Zureik, E. and M.B. Salter (eds) (2005) *Global Surveillance and Policing: Borders, Security, Identity* (Cullompton: Willan Publishing).

# 2
# The Development of the EU Migration and Asylum Regime

*Alex Balch and Andrew Geddes*

## Introduction

This chapter examines the development of policy in Europe in order to provide a context for other chapters that discuss the European 'migration machine'. The chapter provides a politico-legal perspective, and conceptualizes the development of the EU approach to migration and asylum since the late 1990s, demonstrating how it can be seen as constituent of an evolving and complex system. Our purpose here is to consider analytically the meaning and significance of the emerging EU framework on migration and asylum. We ask what kind of system the EU is able to develop and in what ways this is limited and constrained given the questions over EU competency and legitimacy in these areas. In order to do this we critically evaluate developments in the EU on the migration and asylum system, charting its course from Tampere, Finland (in 1999) through to Stockholm (in 2009). In each of the various phases of its development, we ask about the main ideas and arguments that have underpinned this process. How, for example, has the EU balanced security concerns over the openness of borders with demographic and economic arguments for more migrants? We then consider how these compare with the actual outputs and outcomes of the legislative process. The final section draws together our main findings, discusses the rationale for integration in this area and identifies the key characteristics of the developing EU framework on migration and asylum.

## The institutional setting

It is important to understand the emergent and evolving institutional architecture which provides the context for EU action over migration and asylum. Through the course of this chapter we will see that this has become one of the busiest and most expansive areas of EU action with major developments on migration and asylum policy. However, this is an area where the power of the member states has traditionally been jealously guarded. That means that migration and asylum has typically been an area dominated by the executive branch of national governments cautious of integration or harmonization. Despite this, it now makes sense to talk about 'common' migration and asylum policies in the EU, while noting that these cover some but not all aspects of migration. In order to make sense of these developments we need to understand the forms and types of politics at EU level – in other words the distribution of legislative, executive and judicial authority and how this has changed over time. This section will explore how the institutional framework around migration and asylum in the EU has developed since the early 1990s and into the contemporary 'post-Lisbon' situation at the end of the first decade of the twenty-first century.

Following the formation of the European Union in 1993 (through the Treaty of Maastricht) a three-pillar structure was created. The first pillar was the 'community' method of policy-making – with the involvement of the European Commission (EC), European Parliament (EP) and the Court of Justice (ECJ) – and involved issues around the single market. The second pillar was the Common Foreign and Security Policy (CFSP), and the third was Justice and Home Affairs (JHA). In contrast to the first pillar, JHA was explicitly 'intergovernmental', which means it had a separate mechanism for decision-making with reduced input from the EC, EP and ECJ – or the 'supranational' institutional structures of the EU.

Since the pillar structure was introduced there has been a gradual 'communitarization' of certain aspects of Justice and Home Affairs, including policies on migration, with greater influence of the supranational institutions; however, the historical character of action in the context of the EU over migration and asylum has been predominantly intergovernmental. The placement of asylum and immigration in the third pillar with police, judicial and criminal cooperation effectively meant that policies were clearly in the domain of the Interior Ministries of the member states. This is important because it could be argued that the issue of immigration could be located under Employment Ministries; the traditional policy concerns of Interior Ministries meant that matters around migration and asylum in the EU have acquired a predominantly security focus.

After Maastricht, subsequent treaties changed the institutional balance and gradually ceded a growing role to the EC and EP (as 'co-decision-maker') and the ECJ in the areas of asylum and migration.

The Treaty of Amsterdam (1997) was a key moment in this evolution. By shifting parts of the JHA portfolio (including migration and asylum) from the third to the first pillar, the Treaty aimed to inject a greater degree of democratic legitimacy to cooperation in these areas. It also attempted to enhance the emphasis on European citizenship and the rights of individuals, and introduced the objective of constructing an 'area of freedom, security and justice' (AFSJ). This conceptualized cooperation in JHA as a necessary countermeasure to the removal of internal barriers (to movement of persons, goods, capital etc.). The other parts of JHA – Police and Judicial Cooperation in Criminal Matters (PJCC) – remained in the third pillar. The result was a significant increase in EU activity in the area of migration and asylum, while cooperation over police and judicial matters stagnated.

The Lisbon Treaty (2007) can be seen as the culmination of the institutional changes begun at Amsterdam (1997) and its impact is highly significant for the areas of migration and asylum (CEU 2009). The Treaty finally removed the 'pillar structure' of EU legislation, bringing all 'third pillar' issues into the 'first pillar'. As a result of this, measures in these areas became subject to the judicial review of the ECJ. The voting rules in the Council were also changed for a number of areas – legal immigration joined asylum policy, illegal immigration as being decided by qualified majority voting (QMV) and co-decision with the European Parliament (CEU 2009).

What does this mean for how decisions are made over migration and asylum in the EU? The short answer is that this depends on which specific aspect of migration and asylum, and the period during which the decision was taken. The rules have historically been different for each policy sub-field: illegal immigration has been subject to QMV and co-decision for longer than any aspect of legal migration, for example. The effects of the changes brought in by Lisbon should mean some simplification as there are now a greater number of policy sub-fields in migration and asylum subject to the same rules, but it is too early to say how this will operate in practice.

The slow evolution of the structure described briefly here illustrates the difficulty of concluding that decision-making over migration and asylum can be captured by a simple intergovernmental versus supranational dichotomy. Instead, the picture is one of a gradual erosion of an original intergovernmental logic, with migration and asylum loosely incorporated into the EU at Maastricht (1992) and then from Amsterdam (1997) onwards, brought gradually closer to the supranational core of the EU decision-making. An obvious point to make is that by maintaining for as long as possible close control over policy-making in these areas the member states have been able to maintain a close grip on the policy-making process, and keep to a minimum the influence of other actors and agencies at national and EU level. The outcome in terms of the policy framework that has been built up since the 1990s, and the resultant agenda for JHA going forward post-Lisbon, therefore reflects these interests.

There have been many attempts to characterize the overall nature of the EU polity, but the evidence suggests that it encompasses multiple forms of governance that are dynamic over time and vary by policy area (Wallace 2005). Before the Lisbon Treaty came into force Wallace described migration and asylum as an instance of 'intensive transgovernmentalism', which means a key role for state actors, but with a strong sectoral (Interior Ministry) focus and intensive interaction with a range of other actors from other member states and the EU.

The changes ushered in by Lisbon mean that we are entering into an interesting phase of policy-making at EU level for migration and asylum. However, and considering the majority of legislation that was passed pre-Lisbon, we can characterize EU-level developments on immigration and asylum as having broadly transgovernmental logics with somewhat opaque decision-making procedures. There are some examples of transnational NGOs having limited influence on policy development, for example over anti-discrimination legislation (Evans Case and Givens 2010), but in general the areas of immigration and asylum are closely related to the power of the member states. This has led to forms of transgovernmental cooperation spanning diverse institutional settings, and the agenda-setting role of the Council in the EU context as paramount (Monar 2009). In the Council, it has been the Strategic Committee on Immigration, Frontiers and Asylum (SCIFA) which has had overall responsibility for cooperation over a common European asylum and migration policy.

One of the themes regarding the development of JHA after Amsterdam has been continuing concerns among civil rights activists about the content of policies over migration and asylum, and the nature of agencies and initiatives that have actually been set up to facilitate in the overarching aim an 'area of freedom, security and justice' (AFSJ). It is to this content that we now turn.

## What kind of EU framework on migration and asylum?

The nature of the achievements at the European level since the late 1990s has allowed some to continue to claim that the EU is creating a 'fortress' or 'gated community' (van Houtum and Pijpers 2007), or complain of a liberal deficit (Carrera and Wiesbrock 2009). Others are more hopeful, seeing 'soft' forms of integration as a way of moving away from the securitization of immigration (Velluti 2007). One thing is fairly clear – immigration and asylum are policy areas where the older, and relatively larger, member states (such as Germany, France and the UK) have traditionally been among the main receiving states in the EU, and have been particularly keen to maintain national controls. These states, along with others such as the Netherlands and Austria, have been consistently successful in shifting the agenda towards more restrictive aims (Groenendijk 2004).

It is certainly the case that the EU has found it easier to achieve cooperation on efforts to reduce irregular migration than on a framework of legal migration. Indeed, the creation of the series of EU agencies and information systems designed to deal with cross-border crime and irregular migration has led to questions about exactly what kind of system of control is being constructed over immigration and asylum. The agencies in question here include Europol (an organization which facilitates cross-border cooperation and coordination between EU national law-enforcement agencies), Eurojust (involved in judicial cooperation), Frontex (facilitates operational cooperation at the external borders of the EU) and Eurosur (the European border-surveillance system). The three main information systems the EU has constructed are the SIS (the Schengen Information System), Eurodac (fingerprints of asylum seekers) and VIS (the Visa Information System). The next section examines this apparatus of border governance, beginning by looking at the collection of data before considering the role of EU-level agencies in migration and asylum policies.

The Schengen Information System (SIS) has been operational since March 1995, and as its name suggests was set up as a 'countermeasure' to the creation of the Schengen area (which now includes Iceland and Norway) – which aimed to gradually remove border checks between member states. It allows the member states to share data relating to immigration, policing and criminal law. Eurodac was set up to collect the fingerprints of all asylum seekers over the age of 14 and was operational by 2003. The database was seen as a measure to facilitate the implementation of the Dublin Convention (1990) which aimed to stop 'asylum shopping' (or the possibility that an individual could be rejected in one country and then reapply in another). Eurodac started with 12 countries (including the UK and Ireland) and has since expanded to include non-EU member states such as Switzerland. In this sense the system is similar to Schengen in that it is integral and embedded within – but also apart from – the EU institutional infrastructure.

The VIS (Visa Information System) is a 'system of systems' consisting of the CS-VIS (the Central Visa Information System) and structural linkage with each member state (National Interface – Visa Information System, or NI-VIS) for communication of data. Work began on the new version of the SIS – SIS II – as early as 2001. The new system was proposed in order to accommodate the EU's new member states. Due to advances in technology, the creation of a new system was seen as an opportunity to have more features added – particularly the incorporation of biometric data (i.e. data on physical characteristics such as fingerprints, DNA profiles or retina scans). SIS II also incorporates additional access to information on the database regarding Third-Country Nationals (TCNs) for the purposes of immigration control (CEC 2005). The SIS II project, managed by the Commission, has been delayed by a series of arguments – over the tendering process, and where it should be located – along with all the technical difficulties. As the Commission conceded: 'the complexity of the project itself also had a negative impact on the planning'.

Aspects of these systems that concern civil liberties campaigners include the interlinkages and sharing of data between databases (that were set up for different reasons), and the increasing number of authorities that can gain access to the data. For example, for reasons of border security, national authorities and Europol can have access to VIS data entered into the VIS; likewise asylum authorities also have access to search the VIS with fingerprint data. These concerns were hardly allayed by plans announced in 2009 by the Commission to launch a 'Management Authority' to oversee the running of all three systems, claiming that: 'The best way to improve productivity and reduce operational costs is to exploit synergies. This could be achieved if all three systems, and possibly other systems, were housed in one location and running on the same platform' (CEC 2009).

While the creation of EU-wide databases raises issues around transparency and data security, it is the EU agencies charged with border control that have been seized upon by critics as signs that the EU is militarizing its borders (Lutterbeck 2006). Frontex is an agency charged with managing cooperation between member states over border security and taking part in joint operations. The body worked on a series of operations with the border agencies of a number of countries, for example, as part of efforts to tackle irregular migration into Europe via the Canary Islands. The role of Frontex has certainly been enlarged since its creation – so much so that the organization has apparently struggled to deal with the extra resources it has been given (Monar 2009).

Eurosur is a long-term, strategic plan to support member states' authority at the southern border of the EU. It is about assisting member states in terms of knowledge of security risks and in increasing reaction capabilities through 'greater unity of effort'. Much as with the VIS, Eurosur is described by the Commission as a 'system of systems' – that is, instead of an entirely new web of border technologies at the EU level, it concentrates on creating similar national-level structures (national coordination centres) in each member state that can then communicate with each other and the EU.

There certainly appears to be a political appetite for technological solutions to the perceived problems of irregular migration at the EU level – as explained by the Future Group, which will also be dealt with in the next section (Future Group 2008). This predisposition to technological solutions to security issues is perhaps best illustrated by the Eurosur system which 'inevitably fuelled critical reactions from NGOs and some political groupings about the EU's "fortress Europe" rationale, now enhanced by an almost futuristic emphasis on advanced technology use' (Monar 2009). However, while these instruments have developed in a dynamic way (another proposal to strengthen Frontex was announced by the Commission in February 2010) they tend to remain at the level of coordinating agencies rather than constituting either a nascent or independent EU border force.

Alongside these 'control' measures and instruments, the EU has developed a parallel agenda regarding the 'fair treatment' of migrants. In this area the most important pieces of EU legislation are those on antidiscrimination (agreed in 2000 and in 2003), the rights of long-term residents (2003) and the right to family reunion (2003). Both the directive on family reunion and the directive on the rights of long-term residents contain provisions related to the integration of migrants. On the admission of TCNs, the Treaty of Lisbon expressed the intention to create a common policy but importantly made clear that this 'shall not affect the right of Member States to determine volumes of admission of third-country nationals coming from third countries to their territory in order to seek work, whether employed or self-employed' (Article 79.5).

From a slow start by comparison with other policy areas (e.g. economic integration), the EU policy framework over migration and asylum now represents something much more substantial than that which existed by the end of the 1990s. Furthermore, the development of regulatory activity seems to be gathering pace and it has become one of the most productive areas in the EU in terms of legal instruments, adopted texts (144 in 2008 alone) and initiatives. At the core of this work is the ability for the EU to enunciate, and achieve agreement on, common issues over migration and asylum between its member states. Once it has created this common ground and outlined a policy programme, there is then a basis for building a more concrete institutional and organizational framework for the purposes of implementation. This is well illustrated with the case of Eurodac, which was a database system that was created to implement the Dublin Convention. The key to understanding the trajectory (past, present and future) of the emerging EU framework in this area, therefore, is to examine how policy programmes have been negotiated and how the common ground has shifted and developed since the EU acquired policy-making powers post-Amsterdam. It is to these developments that we now turn.

## From Amsterdam to Stockholm

As part of the wider JHA remit, the construction of a common immigration and asylum policy since Amsterdam has generally proceeded in the format of five-year programmes, starting with Tampere (1999–2004), moving through the Hague (2005–09), the European Pact on Immigration and Asylum (EPIA) and finally to the Stockholm programme (2010–14).

Despite being notable as the first time a 'common' policy was outlined for these areas at the level of the Council, the Tampere (1999) programme set the precedent for subsequent agreements with the degree of complexity which it necessarily introduced to maintain unity among its member states. There were opt-outs for some countries, a five-year transition period where unanimity would remain, and the likelihood in the case of legal migration that this would be maintained beyond the five-year period. The presidency conclusions provided four elements to the definition of a common policy on asylum and immigration: (1) partnership with countries of origin; (2) a common European asylum system; (3) fair treatment of third-country nationals; and (4) management of migration flows. There was a definite emphasis on fighting illegal migration, and using bordering countries and applicant countries as a means of remote-controlling immigration.

Overall, security, restriction and control would be the best description of the results of Tampere (Bendel 2005: 23). This contrasts markedly with the rationale for community action being developed in parallel by the Commission. Here, attempts to develop a common approach to managing migration were based less on common threats than on a rejection of 'the "zero" immigration policies of the past 30 years' (CEC 2000: 3); linking the issues of immigration, integration and employment (CEC 2003) (or the Tampere programme with the Lisbon Strategy); and 'mainstreaming' immigration policies within other areas of social and economic policy.

In its assessment of the achievements of Tampere, the Commission conceded there had been difficulties and highlighted the legal and institutional constraints of the Treaties, the right of initiative shared with member states (meaning that national priorities dominated) and restrictions on the Parliament's role (less transparency).

In terms of legislative progress, there were directives on legal migration: the right to family reunification; EU long-term residence status for third-country nationals; conditions of entry for third-country nationals who are students; and for the admission of researchers. However, independent evaluations of how European legislation actually operates in the member states in the area of immigration have found that countries are often slow at transposing this legislation and there are wide variations in the ways in which countries implement their commitments (Geddes and Niessen 2005).

### New forms of legal and policy integration

One of the lessons from the limited eventual outputs of the Tampere programme was that 'harder' forms of integration (legislation) were more difficult to obtain, leading to a turn to 'softer' forms such as the Open Method of Coordination (OMC). The application of the OMC to Community Immigration Policy was outlined in a communication released in parallel with the 2001 proposal for a council directive (CEC 2001). The rationale given was: (1) to gain consensus in a 'sensitive' area; (2) to move gradually to identify common aims and objectives (the OMC in immigration has an initial period of six years); and (3) the need to improve the exchange of information on migration (something reiterated at the European Council in Laeken in December 2001).

The results of the OMC in immigration have been mixed. The member states have been less than enthusiastic about the harmonization of a policy process that is usually fiercely guarded by national governments (Caviedes 2004). Also, one could argue that the mechanism itself does not adequately fit the policy area. The OMC might be more suitable when there is a growing consensus at EU level on general principles, but fairly wide divergence in national practices – that is, labour market policies. There are some doubts as to whether the OMC can really foster learning among states and be 'steered' in some way from above (Radaelli 2004). In the case of immigration it seems that rather than establishing common objectives, the OMC operates as a mechanism for member states to find out what their neighbours are up to.

When it comes to the integration of migrants there are a whole host of 'softer' measures adopted by the EU in this area. Apart from the OMC, there has been the creation of a network of National Contact Points on Integration; the development of Common Basic Principles on integration; the European Integration Forum – a 'platform for dialogue'; annual reports on migration and integration trends; a handbook on integration for policy-makers and practitioners (now into its third edition); and the creation of a European Immigration Fund; there is of course a European website on integration: http://ec.europa.eu/ewsi/en/. There have also been attempts by NGOs at the EU level to influence the agenda – for example the European Programme for Integration and Migration (EPIM).

### The Hague programme (Tampere II)

The Hague programme, designed to build on the achievements of the five-year Tampere programme, was framed much more explicitly in terms of the terrorist threat. The opening paragraphs of the presidency conclusions referred to the terrorist attacks of 11 September 2001 (New York) and 11 March 2004 (Madrid). There was also for immigration and asylum a marked 'externalization' of policy.

The four-way division of the Tampere programme became five: (1) a common European asylum system; (2) legal migration and the fight against illegal employment; (3) integration of third-country nationals; (4) the external dimension of asylum and migration policy; and (5) the management of migration flows. Legal migration was now mentioned explicitly in the context of the fight against illegal working, and the 'management of migration flows' becomes a part of the 'external' dimension, with a host of proposals on border checks, biometrics and visa policies.

### The European Pact on Immigration and Asylum (EPIA)

The predictably slow implementation of the Hague objectives increased somewhat in 2007 and 2008, although this was often a case of quantity over quality (Monar 2008). The European Pact on Immigration and

Asylum (CEU 2008), developed during the French presidency of 2008, builds upon Tampere and the Hague but is very much a continuation – legal migration largely left to the member states, more aggressive measures for illegal migration, returns and asylum. The UK Parliament's response was that 'it appears to us that the draft Pact contains little that is new'. The proposed directives on conditions for different types of workers remain from the Hague programme and will likely be absorbed by the new schedule.

The EPIA has further clarified the main aims of the EU migration system: to attract more skilled immigration and deter the lower-skilled. This is clear in the text of the EPIA as put forward by Sarkozy during the French presidency, and can be seen by the creation of the 'Blue Card' and the Directive on Sanctions against Employers of Irregular Migrants, both adopted in 2009 (Peers 2009). The more controversial elements such as the integration 'contracts' (including obligations for TCNs to speak the host language and the prohibition of mass regularizations) found opposition (e.g. from Spain) and this aspect of the French plan was watered down (Monar 2009).

### Returns Directive

The Returns Directive, considered as one of the central planks of the EPIA, was adopted in August 2008 and defines procedures for the return of illegally resident third-country nationals. The directive was badly received in some quarters – reviving charges of neo-colonialism, and described as the 'Directive of Shame' (Morales 2008). President of Venezuela Hugo Chavez threatened to stop oil supplies to Europe, and Spain was forced to react to avert a diplomatic crisis. A key principle of the Returns Directive was to establish maximum rather than minimum rules – allowing EU member states to retain more liberal rules or adopt new ones of a more permissive nature. Under this (Article 15) the maximum detention was set at 18 months (6 months, plus a possible 12-month extension). NGOs such as Amnesty International have been especially critical, and the European Parliament was divided on the issue (although voted in favour).

### The Future Group

In 2007 an informal High Level Advisory Group on the Future of European Home Affairs Policy was set up by the German Minister of the Interior, Dr Wolfgang Schäuble, and the Commissioner for Justice, Freedom and Security, Franco Frattini. The committee, known as the 'Future

Group', continued the traditional style of cooperation in JHA. The UK House of Lords made the criticism that: 'Given the importance of the work of this group, and its influence on the preparation of the (Stockholm) programme, it is unfortunate that its work was conducted without any sort of public consultation or involvement' (House of Lords 2008–09).

The Group published a report in June 2008 which renewed the call for a 'comprehensive' common immigration policy, with more emphasis on 'mobility partnerships' or 'mobility and security pacts' with the EU's near neighbourhood. Some have branded these 'immobility' partnerships, as member states have made it clear these agreements are not intended to mean an increase in migration from these countries. The Future Group also underlined the link between abolishing internal borders and greater cooperation between law-enforcement teams on external borders. In general the Group was notable for its embrace of technology – the report advocated a speeding up and convergence in databases and for research and development activity on European-level security equipment to be made a priority (Future Group 2008).

## The Stockholm programme (2010–14)

The Stockholm programme takes a more pragmatic approach to increased integration in the area of immigration and asylum. It draws from the work of the Future Group and makes a general push for a rationalization of policy (into an immigration code). In concrete terms this seems to focus on family reunification where there will be a Green Paper and a proposal for a modification of Directive 2003/86/EC (on the right to family reunification) by 2012. On integration of immigrants there is only a continuation of the previous programme, with a vague request for the Commission to develop a 'co-ordination mechanism'. Legislation on admissions (e.g. intra-company transferees and seasonal workers) has been quietly dropped. Instead the 'information-exchange' paradigm which was developed through the common integration policy is applied. Here the focus is on improved data on skills needs of member states, and matching these with third countries. Perhaps the more ambitious element is the commitment to grant third-country nationals 'rights and obligations comparable to those of EU citizens' by 2014.

At least theoretically, the Lisbon Treaty and the Stockholm programme provide an enhanced involvement for the EU's citizens in the policy process with changes to the decision-making process and the abolition of the pillar structure. Not only has the position of the European

Parliament been strengthened, but there are also other measures that at least in theory open up more possibilities to strengthen involvement. However, as we are at the very beginning of this new programme (at the time of writing), it is too early to say whether these measures will inject much-needed legitimacy, accountability and transparency in an area that has traditionally scored low in these areas. Overall, the mixed results of developments from Amsterdam to Stockholm show fairly clearly that on the issue of immigration it has been easier to find collective agreement on restrictive measures (for example regarding asylum or irregular migration) than it has to harmonize legislation in areas such as labour migration or the integration of third-country nationals (TCNs). It is also notable that there are more resources on this 'repressive side' of migration policy (Monar 2008: 113), for example for Frontex (Neal 2009), or for the Returns Directive (the associated Community Return Fund is €676 million for the period 2008–13).

## Conclusions

What kind of system has the EU developed in the area of migration and asylum? An initial conclusion to draw is that the term 'regime' is probably more accurate than 'policy'. This is because most definitions of regimes are broad enough to encapsulate the complex and nebulous legal formulas applied in the EU's regulation of immigration and asylum. One of the most widely cited definitions of a regime is: a set of 'principles, norms, rules, and decision-making procedures around which actor expectations converge in a given issue-area' (Krasner 1982). As we have seen in this chapter, there is a greater level of convergence over the 'repressive' side of migration and asylum policies in the EU, which tells us something about the kind of 'regime' which is being constructed. When used to refer to the practice of governance, the word 'regime' is also provocative because it has historically been used to refer to authoritarian rather than democratic systems. The point here is not to come to a final conclusion about the precise categorization of the system of governance the EU has developed over migration and asylum. As we have hopefully demonstrated, this is a dynamic, evolving and complex area. Although there is not the space here to enter too deeply into political theory, it is important to highlight that questions remain regarding legitimacy and competency of the EU to act in this area.

As areas closely linked to notions of security, sovereignty and the integrity of national borders there has historically been strong resistance on the part of member states in terms of ceding any real control to the supranational level. Despite the growing relevance of developments beyond the nation-state, the national domestic arena remains the primary location where policy is decided for the established 'immigration' states (Freeman 1998: 87). Research also suggests that in these countries immigration policies are determined in a relatively top-down way by elites that have the capacity to act against the will of a restrictionist public (Statham and Geddes 2006: 266–7). For newer member states in the South and East, it is possible that legislation on immigration will be linked to accession to the EU. Spain's first (1985) law on immigration, for example, was 'almost entirely the result of external pressure associated with Spain's entry into the European Community' (Cornelius 1994).

However, as we have seen, EU competence over aspects of immigration and asylum has developed substantially since they were recognized by the Treaties of Maastricht (1992) and Amsterdam (1997). Given this, an obvious question becomes why states would willingly subject these areas to EU integration. The liberal intergovernmentalist response is that European integration, including the enlargement of the EU, has been shown to be a useful means of extending and strengthening state power in the face of global challenges (Moravcsik and Vachudova 2003). In the case of immigration and asylum, Guiraudon (2000) also argues that European cooperation becomes attractive to state actors that are prevented from enacting restrictive policy by the liberal features of their national liberal democratic institutions (such as courts and bureaucracies). From this perspective, integration is a strategy to circumvent such constraints (Guiraudon 2000).

Despite these arguments, the prospect of neofunctionalist competence-creep might seem to make integration over immigration and asylum a high-risk strategy by the member states. By assigning policy-making capacity to Brussels, the areas of immigration and asylum automatically acquire elements of multi-level governance, and thus a theoretical dispersal of power away from the nation-state. However, as is illustrated in this chapter, it is sometimes the very complexity of integration which has allowed member states (particularly the more powerful ones) to maintain tight control over the system. Any appearance of a straightforward step-by-step evolution of a coherent and unitary EU migration regime since Amsterdam would be illusory: integration in this area has been characterized by a fractured, fragmented and asymmetric process resulting in multiple overlapping competences and styles of integration.

How has integration resulted in such a complex system? To begin with, integration has been asymmetric from the outset because of the negotiation of opt-outs by the UK, Ireland and Denmark. Then there are the deep and pre-existing differences in terms of the principles and practices of migration governance across the EU. Added to this the impact of the EU is also variable – with newer member states for example more susceptible to influence due to the raising of barriers to entry via conditionality, and differences in the development of countries' political development. This combination of factors has led to a number of institutional and organizational measures and safeguards being put in place over integration.

The adoption of new binding forms of legislation has been slow because of the high barriers in terms of institutional decision-making. Voting has generally been by unanimity, at least at the start of the integration process. There was, for example, a transitionary period of five years after Amsterdam in terms of voting procedures – only after this period (May 2004) were aspects of immigration and asylum subject to QMV (qualified majority voting) and co-decision with the European Parliament. As explained earlier, this has led to a range of alternative or 'softer' forms of integration, such as the Open Method of Coordination. It has also meant that significant parts of the migration regime, such as Schengen, were initially constructed outside the formal structures of the EU (although the EU operates the Schengen Information System). Indeed, the Schengen system now includes three non-EU members (Iceland, Norway and Switzerland) but excludes a much larger number of EU member states.

The idea of the EU representing a single or unitary migration 'regime' is further challenged by the complications of enlargement. In 2004 and 2007 the EU accepted 12 new member states, and as part of this process was pushed by existing members to adopt a series of transitionary arrangements which were driven by concerns over migration. This has internal consequences in terms of creating a two-tier EU, but also means that other states are likely to differentiate between 'new' and 'old' Europe. The USA, for example, delayed extending its visa-waiver programme to all 27 states, often conducting bilateral negotiations.

What are the outcomes/effects of this complex system? For some the result is a hierarchy, or 'civic stratification', of rights similar to that seen in certain member states (Morris 2004), where low-skilled workers enjoy less freedoms and rights than their better-skilled counterparts. Others point to the ways in which less liberal visions of integration developed in certain countries (Netherlands, Germany) have spread across the EU (Groenendijk 2004; Carrera 2008).

The evidence gathered here regarding the EU migration regime overwhelmingly illustrates that it is perceived as a source of power and control for the member states. As such, it conforms to other analyses of EU integration as a 'solution' for collective action problems (Moravcsik 1991). However, the scope and coherence of integration on immigration and asylum since Amsterdam have been limited. The outputs and outcomes of this process can be characterized as partial, and differential. The latest Action Plan for the Stockholm programme shows that in the ten-year period after Tampere there has been a shift away from the notion of policy harmonization and a corresponding shift towards more practical or pragmatic attempts to find alternative methods to achieve common goals. This reduced ambition is perhaps clearest over admissions policy, where instruments of legal labour migration have been overlooked in favour of improved exchange of information on skills demand/supply with third countries.

However, notwithstanding these challenges and the imperfect or even semi-constructed nature of the EU migration regime, the division between EU and non-EU is growing, rather than narrowing. While the 'fortress' metaphor might be inaccurate or oversimplified (Geddes 2003: 175), integration in these areas presents the EU as an increasingly closed (geo)political entity. The most powerful effects of integration over immigration and asylum in the EU are likely to be felt outside the borders of the EU, or by the millions of third-country nationals within.

## Bibliography

Bendel, P. (2005) 'Immigration Policy in the European Union: Still Bringing up the Walls for Fortress Europe?', *Migration Letters*, 2: 20–31.

Carrera, S. (2008) *Benchmarking Integration in the EU: Analyzing the Debate on Integration Indicators and Moving it Forward* (Gütersloh, Germany: Bertelsmann Foundation). www.bertelsmann-stiftung.de.

Carrera, S. and A. Wiesbrock (2009) *Civic Integration of Third-Country Nationals: Nationalism versus Europeanisation in the Common EU Immigration Policy*, CEPS Report, October (Brussels: Centre for European Policy Studies).

Caviedes, A. (2004) 'The Open Method of Co-ordination in Immigration Policy: A Tool for Prying open Fortress Europe?', *Journal of European Public Policy*, 11(2): 289–310.

CEC (2000) Communication on a Community Immigration Policy. COM (2000) 757 final (Brussels: Commission of the European Communities).

CEC (2001) Communication on an Open Method of Coordination for the Community Immigration Policy. COM (2001) 387 final (Brussels: Commission of the European Communities).

CEC (2003) Communication on Immigration, Integration and Employment. COM (2003) 336 final (Brussels: Commission of the European Communities).

CEC (2005) On the Establishment, Operation and Use of the Second Generation Schengen Information System (SIS II) COM (2005) 236 final (Brussels: Commission of the European Communities).

CEC (2009) Legislative Package Establishing an Agency for the Operational Management of Large-Scale IT Systems in the Area of Freedom, Security and Justice. COM (2009) 292 final (Brussels: Commission of the European Communities).

CEU (2008) *European Pact on Immigration and Asylum*. 13440/08 (Brussels: Council of the European Union (Presidency)).

CEU (2009) *The Lisbon Treaty's Impact on the Justice and Home Affairs (JHA) Council: More Co-Decision and New Working Structures* (Brussels: Council of the European Union).

Cornelius, W. (1994) 'Spain: The Uneasy Transition from Labour Exporter to Labour Importer', in W.E. Cornelius, Philip L. Martin and James Frank Hollifield (eds) *Controlling Immigration: A Global Perspective* (Stanford University Press).

Evans Case, R. and T.E. Givens (2010) 'Re-Engineering Legal Opportunity Structures in the European Union? The Starting Line Group and the Politics of the Racial Equality Directive', *Journal of Common Market Studies*, 48(2): 221–41.

Freeman, G. (1998) 'The Decline of Sovereignty? Politics and Immigration Restriction in Liberal States', in C. Joppke (ed.) *Challenge to the Nation State* (Oxford University Press).

Future Group, The (2008) *Freedom, Security, Privacy: European Home Affairs in an Open World*. Policy (Brussels).

Geddes, A. (2003) *The Politics of Migration and Immigration in Europe* (London: Sage).

Geddes, A. and J. Niessen (2005) 'Europe and Immigrant Inclusion: From Rhetoric to Action'. http://fpc.org.uk/articles/324.

Groenendijk, K. (2004) 'Legal Concepts of Integration in EU Migration Law', *European Journal of Migration and Law*, 6: 111–26.

Guiraudon, V. (2000) 'European Integration and Migration Policy: Vertical Policy-Making as Venue Shopping', *Journal of Common Market Studies*, 38: 249–69.

House of Lords (2008–09) European Committee, Session 2008–09, Twenty-Fifth Report: 'The Stockholm Programme: Home Affairs.' www.publications. parliament.uk/pa/ld200809/ldselect/ldeucom/175/17503.htm.

Krasner, S. (1982) 'Structural Causes and Regime Consequences: Regimes as Intervening Variables', *International Organization*, 36(2): 185–205.

Lutterbeck, D. (2006) 'Policing Migration in the Mediterranean', *Mediterranean Politics*, 11: 59–82.

Monar, J. (2008) 'Justice and Home Affairs', *Journal of Common Market Studies*, 46 (Annual Review): 109–26.

Monar, J. (2009) 'Justice and Home Affairs', *Journal of Common Market Studies*, 47: 151–70.

Morales, E. (2008) Letter of the Bolivian President, in regards to the 'Returns Directive'. President of the Republic of Bolivia.

Moravcsik, A. (1991) 'Negotiating the Single European Act: National Interests and Conventional Statecraft in the European Community', *International Organization*, 45(1): 19–56.

Moravcsik, A. and M. Vachudova (2003) 'National Interests, State Power, and EU Enlargement', *East European Politics and Societies*, 17: 42–57.

Morris, L. (2004) *The Control of Rights: The Rights of Workers and Asylum Seekers Under Managed Migration* (London: Joint Council for the Welfare of Immigrants).

Neal, A. (2009) 'Securitization and Risk at the EU Border: The Origins of FRONTEX', *Journal of Common Market Studies*, 47: 333–56.

Peers, S. (2009) 'Legislative Update: EC Immigration and Asylum Law Attracting and Deterring Labour Migration: The Blue Card and Employer Sanctions Directives', *European Journal of Migration and Law*, 11: 387–426.

Radaelli, C. (2004) 'Who Learns What? Policy Learning in the Context of the Open Method of Co-ordination.' Paper presented at the ESRC (Economic and Social Research Council) Seminar Series: 'Implementing the Lisbon Strategy: Policy Learning Inside and Outside the Open Method', European Research Institute, University of Birmingham, 26 November.

Statham, P. and A. Geddes (2006) 'Elites and the "Organised Public": Who Drives British Immigration Politics and in Which Direction?', *West European Politics*, 29(2): 248–69.

van Houtum, H. and R. Pijpers (2007) 'The European Union as a Gated Community: The Two-Faced Border and Immigration Regime of the EU', *Antipode*, 39: 291–309.

Velluti, S. (2007) 'What European Union Strategy for Integrating Migrants? The Role of OMC Soft Mechanisms in the Development of an EU Immigration Policy', *European Journal of Migration and Law*, 9: 53–82.

Wallace, H. (2005) *Policy-Making in the EU* (Oxford University Press).

# 3
# A European 'Border' Surveillance System under Construction

*Dennis Broeders*

## Introduction[1]

'The border is everywhere,' wrote David Lyon, one of the leading scholars in surveillance studies in 2005. The increasing proliferation and diversification of the concept of the border is closely related to surveillance as a phenomenon and more particularly its recent technological transformation. In its broadest sense Lyon defines surveillance as 'the focused, systematic and routine attention to personal details for purposes of influence, management, protection or direction' (Lyon 2007: 14). Though surveillance is a much broader theme than just surveillance by governments, the references in this chapter to borders and migration largely relate to state surveillance. Historically, this primarily concerned border surveillance which was much 'professionalized' with the introduction of the passport (Torpey 2000). As state bureaucracies grew in size and organizational complexity, national states played a growing role in the regulation of international mobility. This chapter will present the concept of surveillance as essential to understanding the development and the implementation of Europe's technological borders. Surveillance will be positioned within the framework of worldwide increases in cross-border movements and the increasing pressure on states to adequately control and manage these movements.

In the digital era, surveillance only truly transformed through an exponential increase in the possibilities for storing and accessing the personal data of passengers systematically and on a routine basis. This transformation of surveillance has led to the notion of the border being everywhere. Technology plays an ever-increasing role in determining the nature and 'place' of the border. This applies in the first instance to the border in its geographical sense, increasingly monitored by motion sensors, infra-red equipment and surveillance cameras. More recently, massive migration databases have been deployed at both national and European level, capable of logging, storing and monitoring the personal details and movements of passengers, creating a digital border that is becoming distinct from the physical, geographical border (cf. Broeders 2007).

While it may be tempting to see a one-to-one relationship between technology and surveillance, technology is not its first or even foremost characteristic. ICT is an important catalyst for surveillance that can massively increase its scale and reach, but ultimately surveillance is the work of people. 'Surveillance may be direct, face-to-face, or it may be technologically mediated. In today's world, the latter is growing fast' (Lyon 2007: 1). Technology enables new and previously unimaginable forms of surveillance but in many cases still needs human intervention in order to be effective, as an example from migration literature shows. In certain places on the US border, fully functional infra-red scanning technology is in place but the absence of border guards to deter or arrest illegal immigrants makes these expensive scanners amount to little more than counters that record how many people cross the border illegally (Koslowski 2002). At the other extreme, there are also data systems capable of making decisions based on software profiles without the need for any human intervention. Logarithms take the place of the decision-maker. As a result, the relationship between surveillance and the human-surveillance officer is a complex one.

This chapter focuses on the emergence of the surveillance state and more particularly on the way in which European states attempt to control 'friendly', but, above all, unwanted or 'unfriendly' flows of immigrants. It is structured as follows: section 2 examines how the increased potential for digital surveillance is influencing the bureaucratic state. In other words: how is the 'surveillance state' developing in the light of the increasing options technology offers? Section 3 looks at the way in which the state deals with mobility and migration and the influence that surveillance and technology have had on migration policy. Section 4 examines the link between the member states and the European Union in terms of deploying digital surveillance technology in migration policy. Section 5 looks at the actual development and operation of the new border surveillance, focusing especially on one component, the commissioning and operation of the three major migration databases developed by the EU in recent years (SIS, Eurodac and VIS). Finally, section 6 further investigates the case of the EU databases and looks closely at how these systems attempt to prevent illegal immigrants from entering Europe and how they are used as an instrument of expulsion policy. Section 7 draws some conclusions and raises some points for discussion.

## The 'brave new world' of the surveillance state?

'Surveillance' encompasses more than the actions of the state and precedes the computer age. Even so, the state is one of the oldest and largest collectors of information about citizens and non-citizens. In itself, this is not a new development: after all, knowledge has always been power. It is safe to say that the state is one of the foremost drivers and funders of technological developments and applications for use in its own policies. The development of the modern state is closely interwoven with the development of the bureaucratic state which has become increasingly capable of tracking, cataloguing and controlling its population. Scott described the emergence of the modern national state as a process in which these states made their populations 'legible' by collecting and recording information about citizens in a variety of roles and functions (Scott 1998). Caplan and Torpey emphasized the role of 'documenting individual identity' (Caplan and Torpey 2001: 1) in the development of the modern state. The population is sorted into categories that document individuals in their role as taxpayers, employees, soldiers, travellers, criminals, etc. According to Giddens, the rise of surveillance in the modern state is in fact one of the building blocks of modernity (Giddens 1985). Documentation and registration enabled the state to gain greater control over its territory and population. Bureaucracy and registration have often been closely associated with the darker side of state control. Both fiction – Orwell's all-seeing Big Brother – and history – the highly organized bureaucratic power of the German Third Reich – have provided vivid images of the power of surveillance when it is not morally or legally restrained.

In spite of this, the numerous authors have highlighted the fact that bureaucratic registration and documentation can serve not only as instruments of control but also as a means of redistribution (see e.g. Lyon 1994; Marx 2001). Surveillance lies somewhere on the continuum between 'control' and 'care' (Lyon 2007: 3). The welfare state, which would be unable to function without bureaucracy, is the most obvious example. As the welfare state gradually developed in post-war Europe, bureaucracy was deployed not only to ensure that citizens had fulfilled their duties and responsibilities towards the state, but also increasingly to record their rights and entitlements vis-à-vis the state. Bureaucracy is an important agent of redistribution, and surveillance can serve as a tool to ensure that citizens are treated equally in terms of social security, healthcare and government services. However, the risks inherent in this kind of 'well-intentioned' application of surveillance is that it may lead to excessive concentration and centralization of information about individuals in the hands of government, the risk of data errors and other faults in the system with potentially far-reaching consequences and new opportunities for identity fraud (Prins 2006; Kohnstamm and Dubbeld 2007).

In most cases, surveillance is used to categorize people and to select groups for preferential or other treatment, depending on the imperatives of underlying policy. As a rule, the aim of surveillance is social sorting, the classification of populations as a precursor to differential treatment (Lyon 2004: 142). The population is divided into different segments with different rights and responsibilities. Gary Marx calls this 'boundary maintenance' techniques. 'Surveillance serves to sustain borders through defining the grounds for exclusion and inclusion – whether to physical places, opportunities or moral categories' (Marx 2005: 13). The best known and studied applications of new surveillance technologies are firstly those relating to security, policing and the penal system, such as camera surveillance and prisoner tracking systems. And secondly those relating to counterterrorism with its many applications in data collection and analysis, and migration policy in which technological applications have been introduced in order to distinguish between and identify those to be given access to the territory, visa or asylum procedure and those to deny it to.

Numerous recent academic studies have expressed concern about the development of state surveillance, especially about the steps taken in the wake of the attacks of 11 September 2001 (Lyon 2003; Zureik and Salter 2005; Monahan 2006; Haggerty and Ericson 2006). As part of their efforts to increase international security and to fight terrorism, Western states, with the USA 'leading the way', have accelerated the development and deployment of various new forms of surveillance. In many cases, this was not a matter of introducing new applications and technologies but a political choice to side-step conventional political and legal restraints in order to push forward legal instruments and technological applications that had been subject to lengthy political debates. This applies primarily to the large-scale deployment of new surveillance technology in the fight against terrorism and ranges from the enormous increase in the use of surveillance cameras to the wide-scale storage of data and analysis systems culminating in the now defunct American 'Total Information Awareness' programme.[2] A second example involves the introduction of new surveillance technology in migration policies. This has come about partly as a result of the convergence of migration and security and counterterrorism and partly on its own merits in order to facilitate border access by 'wanted' migrants and to hinder or prevent such access by 'unwanted' immigrants. The new instruments used to enable selection before, on and after the territorial border include databases of migration data and personal data, high-tech passports and visas and the inclusion of biometric data in documents and computer records. As these systems store vast amounts of personal data, including biometric identifiers, Intelligence agencies and other organizations responsible for national security and counterterrorism have taken a notable interest in and have requested access to the information stored in immigration databases (Broeders 2007; Balzacq 2008).

## Surveillance and mobility

In a world of increasing globalization and mass movements of goods, capital and people, modern surveillance technology is an important tool in the hands of governments who wish to keep control of their borders. The desire to demarcate and secure borders is by no means new, but there has been a significant increase in the available options to patrol borders against unwanted entry. Torpey has asserted that modern states have become increasingly successful in monopolizing the 'legitimate means of movement' (Torpey 1998, 2000). In the same way as Weber describes the process in which states appropriated and monopolized the legitimate use of violence, Torpey has highlighted the way in which states have taken the right to cross borders out of the private domain by codifying that right and making it dependent on documents and records which only governments can provide. The introduction of the passport in particular marked the end of an era for those groups who had previously enjoyed free movement between states. The issue of enforcement was of great importance. Identifying and documenting new subdivisions in society through the introduction of passports meant very little, if the state could not enforce its policies and regulate the movement of its subjects. 'The successful monopolization of the legitimate means of movement had to await the creation of elaborate bureaucracies and technologies that only gradually came into existence, a trend that intensified dramatically toward the end of the nineteenth century' (Torpey 2000: 35).

Modern European bureaucracies are better equipped than ever, in terms of both their administration and the available technology, to appropriate the 'legitimate means of movement' and monitor their borders by means of modern surveillance technology. But the nature of the border itself has also been transformed. Boyne asserted that 'The prime function of surveillance in the contemporary era is border control. We do not care who is out there or what they are doing. We want to see only those who are entitled to enter' (Boyne 2000: 287). Yet, this short quote outlines the problematic coherence between irregular migration, surveillance and exclusion in a nutshell. In the case of irregular migrants – which, since the 1990s, have superseded asylum seekers as the most important category of 'unwanted migrants' – it is of material interest to know whether immigrants are who they say they are and whether they actually originate from the country they claim to come from. Surveillance is increasingly adopted for identification purposes because the countries of origin refuse to accept the return of illegal migrants if it cannot be proved that they are actually subjects returning to their country of origin. In the everyday practice of expulsion policy, immigrants whose identity cannot be ascertained are therefore *de facto* undeportable. Van der Leun asserts that 'unidentifiable immigrants are constitutionally rather invulnerable to expulsion' (2003: 118). As a result, illegal immigrants have developed a range of strategies to ensure that their identity and origin remain concealed (see Broeders and Engbersen 2007: 1597 ff.). The fact that a simple lie about your name and origin and the destruction of all documentation that might identify you can offer such an effective shield against expulsion has not gone unnoticed by illegal migrants. There is therefore little doubt that identification and surveillance will become increasingly important in the migration technology used and developed in the years to come. The state is starting to take a keen interest in '*who* is out there'.

The increase in mass mobility has placed increasing pressure on the need to ensure that the border can function as an effective and selective filter. Andreas stated that the border is seen as a means of distinguishing between 'desirable' and 'undesirable' border crossings (Andreas 2003). At the same time the massive increase in such border crossings has reduced the available time to do so. Legal goods and freight, business people and tourists must be able to pass the border with minimum hindrance while smugglers, terrorists and undesirable immigrants must be filtered out. The long queues at border crossings that are necessary to ensure effective and tight border controls do not match the needs of an open economy. Guiraudon and Joppke call this the paradoxical union of 'open' economies and 'closed' national states in the age of global-ization (Guiraudon and Joppke 2001). In terms of the mobile global population, the border surveillance is therefore expected to make a rapid and accurate distinction between desirable and undesirable migrants, a distinction perhaps best characterized by Zygmunt Bauman. He drew a distinction between 'tourists', the primarily Western elite enjoying unhindered international mobility, and the 'vagabonds', the underclass of international mobility for whom travel to most Western countries is made as difficult as possible (Bauman 1998). The tourist and the vagabond are the extremes in the spectrum. The well-dressed business-man who rushes across the airport to meet his connection between two world cities is as much an archetype as the desperate illegal immigrant who crosses the Straits of Gibraltar in a ramshackle boat in search of the promised land. Both exist, but neither constitute the majority of those involved in international mobility.

Surveillance is applied to all groups. For the elite, much of the world may be travelled without visas, and in order to ease and accelerate border crossing at an airport such as Schiphol in the Netherlands, state-of-the-art biometric technology is in place, such as the Privium programme, in which an iris scan replaces passport control for regis-tered members (Van der Ploeg 2005: 128, see also Chapter 4 by Van der Ploeg in this book). On the other hand, the vagabonds, who cannot travel to the West without a visa, are hindered by the fact that carri-ers are subjected to heavy sanctions if they transport people without the right paperwork. The state-of-the-art technology they encounter is designed primarily to prevent their crossing of the border or to register and identify them so as to enable their expulsion at a later stage of their migration. Most people can expect a level of surveillance that is largely dependent on a range of (risk) factors determined by the immigration authorities, and the country of origin serves as one of the primary risk indicators in this.

In other words, the border is becoming a much more precise instru-ment and, as highlighted above, is increasingly to be found everywhere. It is at the consulate, at the desk of the airline, on the Frontex boats that patrol the international waters of the Mediterranean and at the systems borders of the modern welfare state where access to work, housing and education are granted or denied. But most of all, the border houses in the large data systems that store personal and travel details and whose profiles demarcate the lines between the 'ins' and the 'outs', the wanted and the unwanted, the legal and the irregular. And if the border is everywhere, than logic dictates that it can also be crossed everywhere.

In order to track and trace populations before, on and after the border, it becomes necessary for the state to record and store their personal data and the data related to their travels. The border surveillance of the future will be powered by information, personal characteristics and profiles, and its product will be identification. Because migration is in essence an international phenomenon that manifests itself locally, the technological, and political, requirements to do so are vast. The surveillance of migrants requires an information and detection system that enables international cooperation, interoperability and accessibility from an enormous number of points of entry. The technology capable of achieving this scale is relatively young. Torpey has asserted that the capability of a state to effectively penetrate society depends on its ability first to embrace that society (Torpey 1998). To put it another way, it is necessary for a large amount of information to be collected about a wide range of mobile populations in order to effectively intervene at a later stage in the activities of a small group, such as terrorists and irregular migrants. The effective regulation of international mobility sets high demands for this collection of information since 'individuals who remain beyond the embrace of the state necessarily represent a limit on its penetration' (Torpey 1998: 244). As such, border surveillance can be seen as a sorting machine designed to earmark, standardize and sometimes even privilege part of the migrant population whilst at the same time earmarking, denying access and attempting to exclude and expel another part.

## European border surveillance digitalized

The fact that the border may be considered to be everywhere is largely related to the fact that traditional European state borders have undergone significant changes, in part as a result of Europeanization and Schengen. Although hermetically sealed borders must be considered a myth and a political nostalgia for a non-existent past rather than a historical fact (Anderson and Bigo 2002; Andreas 2000), the paradox of the open economies and the closed national states does present new questions to governments. Torpey has asserted that states are both territorial and membership associations (Torpey 2000: 33) and as such the state may be considered to be both the clubhouse and the club. Rights and facilities are reserved for club members. These are primarily state citizens. Legal immigrants also have rights and responsibilities within the state which vary from a very strong legal position for citizens of EU member states to a relatively weak legal position for asylum seekers during the asylum process. Gaining access to the club in the form of citizenship or legal status is at the very least just as difficult if not more difficult than gaining access to the clubhouse. Despite the numerous border-surveillance measures deployed, the Schengen border remains a barrier that can be crossed by serious numbers of migrants. This is why modern border surveillance works on different levels. Surveillance not only takes place *at* the border, but also *before* and *after* the border. This means that surveillance shifts also to the country of origin and to the inner workings of the state institutions, such as the labour market, the welfare state and the housing market. In order to effectively monitor all these levels, identity and identification have increasingly become central concepts in the development of surveillance technology.

At a European level, there has certainly been no lessening of the preoccupation with identification in an era of terrorism and illegal migration and the associated fears. Guild points to the fact that the EU no longer trusts anything as proof of identity other than the visas it issues itself: 'Documents issued by non-member States are no longer definitive for determining identity.... The Union takes over the task of identifying all persons who seek to come to the Union and determines where they belong' (Guild 2003: 344). After the monopolization of the 'legitimate means of movement' it would seem that the monopolization of the 'legitimate means of identification' has now become the state's new project (Lyon 2007: 122). Identity, nationality and more particularly their documented and digital manifestations are an important instrument for facilitating certain movements and preventing others.

The modern border is made up of a variety of new technologies and applications. Its main constituents are technology on the one hand and the human body on the other. Firstly it involves the hardware of new technologies (such as the storage and calculation capacity of databases) and the software that enables new forms of detection, recognition, information exchange and tracking. Secondly it relates to the integration of biometric features stored in data profiles and/or the use of medical and biological information to determine age and family relationships. All of this is based on the notion that the human body is incapable of lying. Creating a new digital border at the level of the individual EU member state would be pointless as the object of surveillance can move relatively easily between member states, especially when the free movement of people within the Schengen zone applies. Europeanization has meant that the surveillance of migrants cannot be achieved solely with information and technology from one member state. Only a truly European system of border surveillance has the required scale because separating the 'ins' from the 'outs' in international migration is essentially related to the external borders of the EU. These external borders of the EU are also 'everywhere', but this fact becomes less problematic if all legal and, where possible, illegal border crossings are recorded and stored. In addition to the national immigration databases, it is these European systems that enable the surveillance of immigrants in a Europe 'without' borders. These are the new digital borders of Europe (Broeders 2007) which combine new hardware and software on the one hand and the storage of biometric and other identity data on the other.

## The digital border: a network of EU databases under development

Since the mid-1990s, the member states of Schengen and the EU have been building towards a comprehensive network of immigration databases. Some of these are already in use and others are being developed or redeveloped. This network comprises the Schengen Information System (SIS) and its successor currently under construction (SIS II), the already operational Eurodac system and the Visa Information System (VIS), also currently under construction. This move may be regarded as the digitalization of the European borders (see Broeders 2007). The territorial borders, and physical border controls, are being supplemented by the surveillance of a legal border marking the distinction between the legal and the illegal and realized by means of digital data systems. Combined, these three systems cover all forms of migration to the EU that are considered undesirable and/or might result in illegal residence in one of the member states. The development of these databases follows a logic based on migration types and their perceived risks in terms of irregularity. Obviously, illegal immigration, in the sense of a successful illegal border crossing, defies registration in databases, but illegal immigrants caught at or behind the border can be and are recorded in the Schengen Information System and can be monitored in the Eurodac system. Migrants who apply for asylum in one of the EU member states are registered in the Eurodac system. In the future, the Visa Information System will be used to record the details of migrants who wish to travel to the European Union on a visa. As a result, the EU will soon have a digital border focusing on all categories of migrants viewed as problematic, a portion of whom could disappear and become illegal aliens.

## SIS and SIS II

The Schengen Convention of 1990, essentially a long list of measures to compensate for the free movement of persons agreed in the Schengen Treaty of 1985, also included the planned introduction of the Schengen Information System (SIS). The convention laid the groundwork for a wide range of instruments intended to record and track large groups of people moving to, from and within the Schengen zone (Mathiesen 2001). The SIS is the central database of the Schengen states and aims to enforce 'public order and security, including state security, and to apply the provisions of this convention relating to the movement of persons, in the territories of the contracting parties, using information transmitted by the system' (Article 93 of the Schengen Convention, cited in Mathiesen 2001: 7). The system stores information on objects and people. In both the category of people and that of objects, most of the information stored relates to immigration. Although the main purpose of the SIS is related to public order and security, its predominant preoccupation seems to be with immigration, illegal or otherwise (Guild 2001). Of the five categories of people that can be entered into the system, the majority are registered under Article 96 (persons to be refused entry into the Schengen area because they are undesirable aliens).[3] The most important category of objects in the SIS is 'lost and stolen identity documents'. The information about people that is permitted to be entered into the system is rather sober and limited to first name and surname, known aliases, first initial of the second or middle name, date and place of birth, distinguishing physical features, gender, nationality, whether the person may be considered to be armed and/or dangerous, the reasons for the SIS report and the measures that need to be taken. The latter is related to the fact that the SIS is what is termed a 'hit/no hit' system: an individual is entered into the system and if he or she is recognized (i.e. produces a hit), the system responds with an instruction, such as 'apprehend this person' (De Hert 2004: 40). According to the German Ministry of Foreign Affairs, there were more than 30,000 terminals with access to the SIS in the Schengen area in 2005.

The SIS is a relatively modest system, offering only limited options for the user, which is why the member states have linked up a second system (SIRENE – an acronym derived from *Supplément d'Information Requis à l'Entrée Nationale*) to this database. In everyday practice, the SIS serves as an index for SIRENE, which does offer the possibility of exchanging additional information such as fingerprints and photographs. In most member states the national SIS and the SIRENE bureaus are entrusted to the same organization. Although SIRENE is often referred to as the 'operational core of Schengen', the Schengen Convention itself does not include a single reference to its existence (Justice 2000: 19).

The SIS has proved to be a popular policy instrument. The rapid growth of the Schengen group, even outside the EU through association agreements with Norway, Iceland and Switzerland and the prospect of further enlargement of the EU, led to the decision to develop a second generation of the system as early as December 1996, to accommodate the growing number of participants and enable new functions to be added to the system. This new system, SIS II, was scheduled to be already up and running, but the date has been repeatedly postponed as a result of various delays. The prospect of a new generation of the system enticed the member states to propose a series of new 'wish lists' during the development phase. The Schengen Joint Supervisory Authority aptly summarized the nature of these wish lists in two trends: one trend which involved the inclusion of additional information categories in the system, in particular biometric information, and the second granting new organizations (such as Europol and Eurojust) access to the information stored in the system (Joint Supervisory Authority of Schengen 2004: 14). There were also proposals to link the various EU immigration and other data systems to each other, and certain documents also included a call to integrate the SIS into a new single large-scale 'European Information System' (Brouwer 2004: 5).

The European Commission adopted a relatively pragmatic approach to the uncertainty about the outcome of the political negotiations on the functions of the new system. In 2003 the Commission wrote that, pending the decision of the European Council, SIS II 'must be designed and prepared for biometric identification to be implemented easily at a later stage, once the legal basis, allowing for the activation of such potential functionalities, has been defined' (CEC 2003: 16). In other words, politics should simply follow in the footsteps of technology, a concern that was again expressed recently by the European Data Protection Supervisor: 'One can safely assume that technical means will be used, once they are made available; in other words, it is sometimes the means that justify the end...legal changes quite often confirm practices which are already in place' (cited in Balzacq 2008: 78). The definitive decision on the development and functions of SIS II, that took effect in January 2007, provides clarity on the new functions and other additions. The most important addition involved the inclusion of biometric data in the database. For the time being, this is limited to the inclusion of fingerprints and photographs, but according to a research report of the British House of Lords, the system would also be capable of including iris scans and DNA, if the legal framework is created to enable this in the future (House of Lords 2007: 20, n. 43). The inclusion of biometric data marks a significant change to the character of the SIS. Sweeping searches, in which fingerprints are compared with all the other fingerprints stored on a database, have now become possible. As a result, this makes the system much more like an investigative system than its predecessor, which in turn makes it more attractive for various intelligence and crime fighting authorities but also places high demands on the quality of the biometric data stored. The European Supervisor has already warned against overestimating the reliability of biometrics.[4] Furthermore, the number of organizations given access to the second generation of the SIS has also increased; Europol and Eurojust have been granted direct access to parts of the database.[5]

### Eurodac

The Eurodac system is the database intended to aid in the implementation of the Dublin Convention. This convention, now an EU regulation, is intended to establish which member state is responsible for an asylum application and to prevent so-called asylum shopping (making an asylum application in several EU member states). Eurodac (*Euro*pean *Dac*tylographic System) was established in order to determine whether an asylum seeker has already submitted an asylum application elsewhere. It is an EU-wide data system designed to record all asylum applications in the European Union and enable comparison based on fingerprints. The development of the system has a history of political controversy that started in 1999 with the decision to develop it, led to its establishment in 2003 and continues into the current era of 'security and terrorism' (see Aus 2006). Between 1991 and 2003 the scope of Eurodac increased significantly. The database was intended originally to include only the fingerprints of asylum seekers, but in 1998 Germany exercised considerable pressure to also secure the inclusion of illegal migrants in Eurodac. In the 'parallel world' of the development of the SIS, there were also proposals to include the fingerprints of illegal migrants (see Brouwer 2002: 235), but since this was not possible in the first generation of the system, the member states were forced to look for solutions elsewhere. Mathiesen wrote that the 'history of the issue of fingerprinting illegal immigrants shows how Schengen and Eurodac concerns are intertwined' (Mathiesen 2001: 18).

Eurodac went online in January 2003 with an empty database which filled up rapidly with a total of three categories of people and fingerprints. Category 1 contains the fingerprints of all individuals over the age of 14 who apply for asylum in one of the EU member states. These are the fingerprints required to meet the objectives of the Dublin system. Category 2 contains the fingerprints of irregular migrants arrested whilst attempting to cross the border illegally, and category 3 contains the fingerprints of irregular migrants arrested in one of the member states. The fingerprints in category 3 are compared to the fingerprints stored in the first two categories, but are not themselves stored. In addition, the use of this category is optional; member states are free to decide whether or not they use it. This last category in particular illustrates the growing interest on the part of a number of member states to apply modern surveillance technology to the issue of illegal residency (see Table 3.1). Like the SIS, Eurodac is a 'hit/no hit' system that includes only limited information.

Eurodac's empty database filled up quickly. Most of the data entered are asylum applications in a member state of the European Union and the majority of the hits are detections of double or even multiple asylum applications (in 2006 there was even one person who had accumulated a total of 13 applications), which was the reason the system was established in the first place. According to the Commission in its evaluation of Eurodac's first three years, the system appears to operate effectively as a tool for identifying 'asylum shopping' (CEC 2007). However, this provides little information on whether countries actually pass on Dublin asylum seekers to each other in practice. According to the Commission, the entry of category 2 data is much too low and it has called upon the member states to carry out their legal obligations. However, several authors (Brouwer 2002; Aus 2003, 2006) have pointed out that fingerprinting and submitting information on those crossing the border illegally is hardly a logical option from the perspective of the border states. Indeed, the only possible outcome is that this migrant can be sent back to the border state if later identified in another member state. As the Table suggests, the use of category 3 has met with rather more enthusiasm. The rapid increase in the number of hits involving category 3 data – from 1,181 in 2003 to 15,612 in 2006 – indicates that Eurodac has become an important tool in the domestic part of the European 'battle against illegal immigration'. Illegal immigrants with a history of asylum seeking (from 2003 onwards) can be linked to an asylum dossier in the state in which they made their asylum application by means of cross-checking their fingerprints in the Eurodac system. For

*Table 3.1* Data entered and hits in the Eurodac system, 2003–06

| Category | 2003 | | 2004 | | 2005 | | 2006 | |
|---|---|---|---|---|---|---|---|---|
| | Data entered | 'Hits' | Data entered | 'Hits' | Data entered | 'Hits' | Data entered | 'Hits' |
| Asylum applications (cat. 1) | 246,902 | 14,960[a] | 232,205 | 28,964[a] | 187,223 | 31,778[a] | 165,958 | 27,014[a] |
| Persons crossing border illegally (cat. 2) | 7,857 | 673[b] | 16,183 | 2,846[b] | 25,163 | 4,001[b] | 41,312 | 6,658[b] |
| Illegal residents arrested (cat. 3) | 16,814 | 1,181[c] | 39,550 | 7,674[c] | 46,229 | 11,311[c] | 63,341 | 15,612[c] |

a: Fingerprint of an asylum seeker submitted by a member state matched with the stored fingerprint from an existing asylum application (cat. 1 cross-checked against cat. 1). Only foreign hits, i.e. matches with an asylum application in a different country, are included.
b: Fingerprint of an asylum seeker submitted by a member state matched with the stored fingerprint of an alien who crossed an external border illegally (cat. 1 cross-checked against cat. 2).
c: Fingerprint of an illegal alien resident submitted by a member state matched with the stored fingerprint of an existing asylum application (cat. 3 cross-checked against cat. 1).
*Sources:* CEC 2004, 2005, 2006, 2007.

the authorities that apprehended the irregular migrant, the dossier represents a source of information about his identity and country of origin. This information, which many irregular migrants are extremely eager to conceal, is necessary in order to enable expulsion to the country of origin. In other words, Eurodac enables illegal migrants to be 're-identified' (Broeders 2007). In the same way as the SIS and SIRENE can be used to exchange information that makes expulsion possible, Eurodac can play a significant role in a country's expulsion policy. In practice, only a limited number of countries are responsible for the increasing use of the category 3 data. Countries such as the Netherlands, Germany and Great Britain, where illegal residence is considered to be a major political problem, are the most frequent users of this part of the system. The popularity of this category has not gone unnoticed by the European Commission. As a result, the Commission proposed in its evaluation that in the future these data should also be stored in the system, rather than merely cross-checking them against category 1 data. This evaluation also included a proposal to examine the options for increasing the scope of Eurodac in the light of 'law enforcement purposes and as a means to contribute to the fight against illegal immigration' (CEC 2007: 11). Put another way, the system is still being stretched in order to fulfil an increasing number of different types of function than those for which it was originally established. The development of Eurodac is a prime example of how data collected for one specific purpose is also made available for other purposes if this is deemed to be opportune (i.e. 'function creep').

## VIS

The Visa Information System was the logical next step in the development of the network of EU migration databases. After all, undesirable migrants do not only enter illegally or via the asylum process. A large portion of those who later become irregular migrants enter the European Union perfectly legally on a tourist visa and only cross into irregularity when their visa expires. These migrants are known as overstayers in Eurojargon. In the conclusions of the Presidency of the European Council of Seville in 2002, there was a call, under the heading 'measures to combat illegal immigration', for the 'introduction, as soon as possible, of a joint identification system for visa data' (CEU 2002: 8). This system, known as the VIS, is currently under development. The VIS is intended to serve a number of purposes, including improving the way in which the joint visa policy is implemented and enabling cooperation between consulates by means of data exchange on visa applications and decisions, combating 'visa shopping' and visa fraud. The system is also expected to play a role in determining which member state is responsible for an asylum application (a Dublin task) and, completely in line with current preoccupations, to help prevent threats to internal security within member states. In terms of undesirable migration, the system has the following identification task: 'to assist in the identification of any person who may not, or may no longer fulfil the conditions for entry, stay or residence of the territory of the member states' (CEU 2007). In other words, the system also has a specific role to play in 're-identifying' illegal migrants. In the same way as Eurodac can generate a link with an asylum dossier, VIS can alert the national immigration authorities to the existence of the visa application dossier of an irregular migrant who overstayed his or her visa.

Like Eurodac, the Visa Information System will also start with an empty database. The data that will fill this system are much less limited in nature than the data stored in Eurodac and the SIS. Firstly, it includes all the basic information about the applicant (a digital version of the application form), and details of the dates on which visas were applied for, granted, refused, cancelled, withdrawn or extended. This basic information also includes data about the person or the company supporting the application and who are often held responsible for the subsistence costs of the applicant during his or her stay. In this system, therefore, the family and companies vouching for the applicant are clearly part of the picture and are also recorded and stored. This can increase the risk for them, or their perception thereof, and make it less attractive to bring family members to Europe who later become irregular. Indeed, research among irregular migrants in the Netherlands has shown that over 40 per cent entered the country on a tourist visa and had come to the Netherlands after a formal invitation from their family (Staring 2001: 99). The second category of information stored by the VIS is biometric data: ten fingerprints and a photograph of each applicant will be stored in the system. According to the Commission this will make the VIS the world's largest ten fingerprint system.

The VIS is therefore ambitious in its aims. The feasibility study conducted by the Commission envisaged a system able to link together at least 27 member states, 12,000 VIS users and 3500 consulates. This was based on an estimate that the EU member states would process around 20 million visa applications per year (CEC 2003: 26). In the press release issued by the Commission when the European Parliament and the Council reached political agreement about the system in 2007 it was announced that the VIS can store the data of up to 70 million people. In the development of the VIS, interoperability and synergy were key concepts, especially with SIS II, which shares the same technical DNA. The database, the technical layout and even the physical location for the central database (the SIS bunker in Strasbourg) are identical. The systems are sharing the development costs of a 'joint technical platform' to enable the databases to link up effectively and readying the systems for possible future interoperability and data exchange. For the time being, there has been no political agreement about this and the two systems remain 'separate containers', but the desire to link or even merge the different EU immigration data systems is clearly manifest. In the development of the VIS, this desire was frequently expressed, with the other databases to be linked invariably being Eurodac and SIS II. The demand for wider access to the VIS, particularly for the security authorities, is also very much in evidence and led to the European Supervisor issuing a further warning that the VIS has been developed 'in view of the application of European visa policy and not as a law enforcement tool' (European Data Protection Supervisor 2006: 2).

### The EU's Border Package and beyond

In 2008 Franco Frattini, then the EU's Justice and Home Affairs Commissioner, launched his 'Border Package' which envisioned taking border surveillance to the next level. An important part of this border package is focused on the large-scale collection of travellers' data for the use of migration control which builds on the systems described above but aims at an even more encompassing digital border management for the future. Technology, digitalization and the use of biometrics are and remain the defining characteristics of the new digital borders of the European Union. The 'first generation' of EU migration databases – of the SIS, VIS and Eurodac – is now set to be complemented by a 'second generation' of databases. The shift to a new generation is marked by the fact that the first generation was aimed at migrants from countries of origin considered a risk (i.e. under visa obligation) or migration procedures that are considered a risk (asylum procedure) for irregular stay, while the second generation spreads the net much wider and aims at the worldwide population of travellers, including EU citizens (Hampshire and Broeders 2010). The proposals for these new data systems are aimed at travellers who are usually considered to be 'unproblematic' from a migration policy perspective, such as travellers who have no need for a visa and EU citizens. The Commission's 'Border Package' therefore includes the introduction of an EU-wide 'entry-exit system' (CEC 2008). The proposed 'entry-exit system' would require setting up a new EU-wide database that would register all travellers as they enter or exit at an external border of the EU. In order to be fully effective this new system would have to be interoperable with the older databases, especially the ones using biometric identifiers like VIS and Eurodac (Guild *et al.* 2008). This new system would be modelled on the American US VISIT system which has been operational since 2004, though the underlying rationale of the systems is different. The US VISIT system is part and parcel of the American anti-terrorism legislation while the EU's entry-exit system is primarily aimed at detecting and identifying visa overstayers (see Koslowski 2008; Hobbing and Koslowski 2009). Overstayers are still high on the EU's political agenda for border management. EU citizens also come into play as the member states started to roll out the European biometric passport from late 2009 onwards. In 2019 all EU citizens should be in possession of a machine-readable passport with biometric identifiers that can be 'swiped' on entering and leaving the EU territory. To this end the Commission's Border Package envisages an 'Automated Border Control System' that will automatically verify the authenticity of the EU passport and, by default, of the EU citizenship of its bearer. Although these data will not be stored, the Commission states that the system will nonetheless 'read and extract the information from the travel document, capturing biometrics and performing the verification to enable entry or exit, as well as random checks of the SIS and national databases' (European Commission, quoted in Guild *et al.* 2008: 3). In short, the new EU proposals are testimony to the enthusiastic political embrace of new technologies and, more importantly, continue on the path of making (biometric) identification the cornerstone of EU policies on mobile populations.

## Irregular 'migrants': systems for exclusion and identification

The primary aim of the European network of data systems is to ensure that migration processes run smoothly and quickly: asylum applications should be processed in the appropriate country and visa applications processed quickly and cross-checked to identify any illegitimate and fraudulent applications. This is the primary function of these systems for the immigration officials that access them at consulates, at airports, at ports and in the offices of the immigration services. However, these data systems are also increasingly being used to exclude and where possible to expel the group of migrants who have succeeded in travelling to Europe and are living illegally in one of the member states. EU databases and national registration and documentation systems lie at the heart of the exclusion policy for irregular migrants in Europe. This exclusion can take two different, essentially contradictory, forms. The first is based on the logic of 'exclusion *from* registration and documentation' and the second on the logic of 'exclusion *through* documentation and registration'. Policies in line with the first type of logic block migrants' access to official documents and registrations thereby excluding them from specific institutions. Policies that reflect the second type of logic actually attempt to document and register the migrant himself/herself, often in the early stages of the migration process, in order to exclude, or more specifically to expel, him or her at a later stage.

### Exclusion *from* documentation and registration

According to this logic, surveillance is deployed to exclude migrants from society's key institutions, such as the formal labour market, education, the housing market and the provisions of the welfare state. Migrants are prevented from obtaining certain documents or registration numbers on which access to specific institutions is conditional, the net result of which is that they are excluded from these institutions. Engbersen has asserted that the state is erecting a wall of documents and legal rules and requirements around its social institutions which it is 'patrolling' by means of modern identification and data systems (Engbersen 2001). It is a disincentive strategy applying rigorous social exclusion designed to undermine the legitimacy of, or even criminalize, the networks of people and institutions who can provide migrants with employment, accommodation and assistance. Its objective is to discourage illegal residency by means of social exclusion.

### Exclusion *through* documentation and registration

The second type of logic takes effect when the first does not work effectively and undesirable migrants are not discouraged but stay and live illegally. The focus then shifts to expulsion policy and to the undesirable migrants themselves. Policy in line with this logic does attempt to register and document migrants in order to use this information to exclude them. The focus also shifts to a different type of database, capable of tracing and identifying migrants. As a result, systems such as the SIS, Eurodac and the VIS come into play because they can re-identify apprehended irregular migrants and link them to a migration history and country of origin. As has already been pointed out, expulsion is only possible if identity and nationality are both known, as otherwise effective expulsion is prevented by legal safeguards and procedures and diplomatic resistance from the country of origin. In a number of EU member states, especially the Northern welfare states such as the Netherlands and Germany, politics are taking an increasingly serious interest in deportation policy. In recent years, these countries have seen a massive increase in the capacity of immigrant detention facilities for irregular migrants and failed asylum seekers with a view to expulsion (see Jesuit Refugee Service 2005; Welch and Schuster 2005; Broeders 2010). These are also the countries investing most in new database technologies and pushing for the development of EU migration databases (Aus 2006).

The development of the three EU databases actually reflects a shift in illegal migrant policies in which identification (exclusion through documentation and registration) will play an increasingly crucial role to supplement the first type of exclusion logic. The SIS was intended to be a genuine border tool, designed primarily to prevent migrants from crossing the border. The Eurodac system, intended to exclude asylum seekers from the procedure, was also given an important role in the implementation of the second type of logic following pressure from Germany. Eurodac is an important means of identifying irregular migrants without which it would probably remain impossible to expel them. The newer SIS II and VIS systems fully embrace both types of logic: exclusion from a visa and/or access to the EU (the first type of logic but on an EU-wide scale) and a high-tech system for biometric identification within the framework of the national expulsion policy as a means of realizing the second type of logic. Particularly for the second type of logic of exclusion with the help of documentation and registration, the application of biometrics on a European scale may be appropriately termed a 'killer application'.

## A digital and networked border under construction

How can we understand the creation of Europe's technological borders? This chapter has attempted to provide an answer to this question on the basis of the concept of surveillance. The analysis has shown that migration policies have two related functions on which technology has a significant influence: securing the border and categorizing the flow of migrants. Data systems are intended to close off the border to people who, according to these data systems, do not have a right of access, for example as a result of inclusion in a blacklist (previously expelled as an illegal alien, refused a visa on a previous occasion, etc.). It must also be possible to distinguish at, or preferably before, the border between the risky applicants and those who present less or no risk: who is entitled to access the asylum process and who isn't, who will be granted a visa and who will not? But the system goes further than this. Not all legally admitted migrants are subjected to the same level of scrutiny. Anyone who *needs* a visa is by definition already suspect and people travelling on a visa will soon be extensively documented and registered in the VIS, while migrants from the United States for example are treated with less suspicion. However, if the plans for the entry-exit system become a reality, detection and registration of travellers widen their scope further. Border surveillance will increasingly function as a *sorting machine* that separates and distinguishes the wanted from the unwanted migrants and creates and uses profiles to separate the two. Wherever possible it will fast-track the former and block the latter category. Secondly, border surveillance will function as an *identification machine*. The new data systems store personal information about migrants and link this to biometric identifiers such as a fingerprint or iris scan. Biometrics is expected to lead the authorities to information about the identity of individuals. The regime applied at the border has radically improved the function of sorting and distinguishing between migrants.

The new technology also drastically changes the *scale* on which the monitoring and recording of the migration movements take place. The European scale, with a system such as the VIS that will soon be capable of storing information on 70 million people, is only feasible as a result of new information and communication technology and only workable because the system of registration and documentation has become more Fordistic. It has become more specialized and standardized. This is a consequence of both technology and organization, although in this case it is difficult to distinguish between the two. As a result of the application of these systems, the personal/individual element in the migration process loses much of its relevance: this is the process of *double depersonalization*. Both the individual migrant and the individual immigration official have to deal increasingly with the system instead of, or more accurately, in addition to, each other. There is a little point in asking migrants who they are and what their background is, if their fingerprints can simply be entered into the computer to find the answer you need. Thinking twice about a migrant of whom the SIS indicates that he or she should be refused access at the border serves no purpose since it has already been decided what action should be taken. The authorities can call upon the system and need no longer rely on the discretion of the responsible official: the migrant becomes what the computer says he or she is. In itself, this is not an illogical development. The fact that it is impossible to identify and expel irregular migrants who refuse to speak or who lie (and the increasing awareness of the importance of not being earnest among illegal migrants) is ultimately why this kind of identification system was established in the first place.

These new systems of border surveillance raise questions about the hardware and the software, but also about their designer, in this case the world of politics. If decisions are increasingly delegated to the computer, this also imposes high demands on the reliability of the technology, among other things. Biometrics in particular is currently being included in the migration systems and hailed as miraculous. The body does not lie. The recent proposals for an entry-exit system and the introduction of the biometric EU passport are additional testimony of the member states continuing on the path of making biometric identification the cornerstone of EU policies on mobile populations. This proposed second generation of migration databases casts the digital dragnet out even wider and will take in data from nearly all travellers entering and exiting the EU territory. But every technology has a margin of error and at a scale of 70 million people in a single system, even a small margin of error can create a large number of errors and victims. New technologies create new risks of a technological (such as the reliability of biometrics) and a political nature. The politicians who 'design' the system are tinkering with a machine of which they have little technical knowledge but which promises to be a panacea for their policy problems. There is great faith in technology and new possibilities are embraced with enthusiasm. This is not the first time that politicians have shifted the parameters of specific technologies and data systems. The history of the development of the European immigration databases clearly shows that data collected for one specific purpose are also made available for other purposes if this is deemed to be opportune (function creep). The availability of large quantities of digital information is sometimes seen as a tempting invitation to use them more widely. It is possible to compile profiles from the data stored from which new information about groups and individuals can be extrapolated and later used in policy. Of course, a profile cannot answer back, which is especially significant against a background of depersonalization.

But essentially, the whole concept of digital border surveillance is already based on profiling and sorting. The first profile divides the migrant population into an unsuspicious and a suspicious component. EU citizens and the few Western countries that do not require a visa for entry into the EU find it easier to cross over the border. Everyone else is by definition slightly suspect. For this group, the filter is set to a more thorough sift. You will only be granted a visa if we are virtually certain that you will be leaving the country. You will only be given access to the regular asylum process if we, at the border, have ascertained during the 48-hour procedure that your application is likely to succeed. Even within these groups, the sorting continues: data systems are used to record and identify those who have broken the visa rules, those who have already applied for asylum and those caught attempting to cross the border illegally. Anyone with such a record in their digital dossier will initially not be allowed access to the country. The inner logic of the new data systems even requires that the identity characteristics and identity data of the whole group initially designated as suspect be permanently stored.

The digital and networked border under construction is a massive project in which millions of people are processed in order to ensure that an infinitely smaller group that becomes irregular at a later stage remains within the sights of state identification. If we remain within the framework of irregularity, we can establish that the group of suspect migrants is heavily over-classified. This is not completely illogical in view of the crucial importance of identification for migration policy but it does have unintended social repercussions. The classification of this group goes hand in hand with political and social distrust that has increased severely in Europe in recent times. Yet this distrust is completely non-existent for the unsuspicious group of the travellers that enjoys 'free' movement. However, anyone who thinks that there are no Americans living irregularly in Europe is profoundly mistaken. There are indeed plenty, but because we do not look for them, they remain unseen. James Scott's book about the emergence of the national state as a process in which the state makes its population legible, has the apt title: *Seeing like a State*. The state sees what it wants to see and in doing so creates the reality. The results are sometimes beneficial and sometimes less so. New systems of border surveillance increase the focus of what the government sees, but also make the selective nature of this vision all the more evident.

## Notes

1. With thanks to Corien Prins for her extensive commentary on an earlier version of this essay.
2. The 'Total Information Awareness' programme was a long-held dream cherished by the Pentagon that entered the realm of reality following a move

by the new Department of Homeland Security in 2002. It is a profile-based system that sifts through a mountain of information in order to filter out the 'potential' terrorists. The information originates from an extremely wide range of sources (Internet surfing behaviour, credit cards and banks, medical data, school data, etc.). As it is a military operation, the barriers between external and internal security in the TIA completely disappear (Lyon 2003: 94). In the wake of much criticism, the programme no longer exists under this name, but many of the activities have been continued.

3. See Broeders (2007) and (2009b) for a statistical overview of storage and use of the data in the SIS.
4. See House of Lords (2007: 20). There is an extensive analysis of this material in Chapter 4 by Van der Ploeg in this book.
5. See the article by Balzacq (2008) for an extensive analysis of access by security and information organizations to EU migration databases.

## Bibliography

Anderson, M. and D. Bigo (2002) 'What are EU Frontiers for and What Do they Mean?', in K. Groenendijk, E. Guild and P. Minderhoud (eds) *In Search of Europe's Borders* (The Hague: Kluwer Law International).

Andreas, P. (2000) *Border Games: Policing the U.S.–Mexico Divide* (Ithaca, NY: Cornell University Press).

Andreas, P. (2003) 'Redrawing the Line: Borders and Security in the Twenty-First Century', *International Security*, 28(2): 78–111.

Aus, J. (2003) *Supranational Governance in an 'Area of Freedom, Security and Justice': Eurodac and the Politics of Biometric Control*, DEI Working Paper no.72, Sussex European Institute.

Aus, J. (2006) 'Eurodac: A Solution Looking for a Problem?', *European Integration Online Papers*, 10(6): 1–26.

Balzacq, T. (2008) 'The Policy Tools of Securitization: Exchange, EU Foreign and Interior Policies', *Journal of Common Market Studies*, 46(1): 75–100.

Bauman, Z. (1998) *Globalization: The Human Consequences* (Cambridge: Polity Press).

Boyne, R. (2000) 'Post-Panopticism', *Economy & Society*, 29(2): 285–307.

Broeders, D. (2007) 'The New Digital Borders of Europe: EU Databases and the Surveillance of Irregular Migrants', *International Sociology*, 22(1): 71–92.

Broeders, D. (2009a) 'Add a Little Europe for Extra National Strength? The Europeanization of Justice and Home Affairs', in W. Schinkel (ed.) *Globalization and the State: Sociological Perspectives on the State of the State* (Basingstoke: Palgrave Macmillan).

Broeders, D. (2009b) 'Tracing, Identifying and Sorting: The Role of EU Migration Databases in the Internal Control on Irregular Migrants', in H. Fassmann, M. Haller and D. Lane (eds) *Migration in Europe: Threat or Chance* (Cheltenham: Edward Elgar).

Broeders, D. (2010) 'Return to Sender? Administrative Detention of Irregular Migrants in Germany and the Netherlands', *Punishment and Society*, 13(2).

Broeders, D. and G. Engbersen (2007) 'The Fight against Illegal Migration: Identification Policies and Immigrants' Counterstrategies', *American Behavioral Scientist*, 50(12): 1592–609.

Brouwer, E. (2002) 'Eurodac: Its Limitations and Temptations', *European Journal of Migration and Law*, 4: 231–47.

Brouwer, E. (2004) 'Persoonsregistraties als grensbewaking: Europese ontwikkelingen inzake het gebruik van informatiesystemen en de toepassing van biometrie', *Privacy & Informatie*, February: 4–11.

Caplan, J. and J. Torpey (2001) 'Introduction', in J. Caplan and J. Torpey (eds) *Documenting Individual Identity: The Development of State Practices in the Modern World* (Princeton University Press).

CEC (2003) *Communication from the Commission to the Council and the European Parliament: Development of the Schengen Information System II and Possible Synergies with a Future Visa Information System (VIS)*, COM (2003) 771 final, 11 December (Brussels: Commission of the European Communities).

CEC (2004) *First Annual Report to the Council and the European Parliament on the Activities of the EURODAC Central Unit*, Commission staff working paper, SEC (2004) 557, 5 May (Brussels: Commission of the European Communities).

CEC (2005) *Second Annual Report to the Council and the European Parliament on the Activities of the EURODAC Central Unit*, Commission staff working paper, SEC (2005) 839, 20 June (Brussels: Commission of the European Communities).

CEC (2006) *Third Annual Report to the Council and the European Parliament on the Activities of the EURODAC Central Unit*, Commission staff working document, SEC (2006) 1170, 15 September (Brussels: Commission of the European Communities).

CEC (2007) *Report from the Commission to the European Parliament and the Council on the Evaluation of the Dublin System*, COM (2007) 299 final, 6 June (Brussels: Commission of the European Communities).

CEC (2008) *Communication from the Commission to the European Parliament, the Council, the European Economic and Social Committee and the Committee of the Regions: Preparing the Next Steps in the Border Management in the European Union*, COM (2008) 69 final, 13 February (Brussels: Commission of the European Communities).

CEU (2002) *Presidency Conclusions*, Seville European Council, 21–22 June 2002 (SN 200/02) (Brussels: Council of the European Union).

CEU (2007) *Interinstitutional File: 2004/0287(COD)*, 9753/07, 19 June (Brussels: Council of the European Union).

Engbersen, G. (2001) 'The Unanticipated Consequences of Panopticon Europe: Residence Strategies of Illegal Immigrants', in V. Guiraudon and C. Joppke (eds) *Controlling a New Migration World* (London: Routledge).

European Data Protection Supervisor (2006) *Opinion of the European Data Protection Supervisor*, 20 January (Brussels).

Giddens, A. (1985) *The Nation-State and Violence* (Cambridge: Polity Press).

Gilliom, J. (2001) *Overseers of the Poor: Surveillance, Resistance, and the Limits of Privacy* (University of Chicago Press).

Guild, E. (2001) 'Moving the Borders of Europe', inaugural lecture, University of Nijmegen.

Guild, E. (2003) 'International Terrorism and EU Immigration, Asylum and Borders Policy: The Unexpected Victims of 11 September 2001', *European Foreign Affairs Review*, 8: 331–46.

Guild, E., S. Carrera and F. Geyer (2008) 'The Commission's New Border Package: Does it Take Us One Step Closer to a "Cyber-Fortress Europe"?', CEPS Policy Brief, no. 154, March.

Guiraudon, V. and C. Joppke (2001) 'Controlling a New Migration World', in V. Guiraudon and C. Joppke (eds) *Controlling a New Migration World* (London: Routledge).

Haggerty, K. and R. Ericson (eds) (2006) *The New Politics of Surveillance and Visibility* (University of Toronto Press).

Hampshire, J. and D. Broeders (2010) *The Digitalization of European Borders and Migration Controls.* Pilot study for the Migration to Europe in the Digital Age (MEDiA) project. www.mediaresearchproject.eu/reports/Report2_Borders.pdf.

Hert, P. de (2004) 'Trends in de Europese politiële en justitiële informatiesamenwerking', *Panopticon*, 25, January/February: 25–56.

Hobbing, P. and R. Koslowski (2009) 'The Tools Called to Support the "Delivery" of Freedom, Security and Justice: A Comparison of Border Security System in the EU and in the US', Ad Hoc Briefing Paper, European Parliament, Directorate-General Internal Policies, Policy Department C, Citizens' Rights and Constitutional Affairs, Committee on Civil Liberties, Justice and Home Affairs, PE 410.681, February.

House of Lords European Union Committee (2007) *9th Report of Session 2006–07. Schengen Information System II (SIS II). Report with Evidence* (London: The Stationery Office).

Jesuit Refugee Service (2005) *Detention in Europe: Administrative Detention of Asylum-Seekers and Irregular Migrants.* www.detention-in-europe.org (Brussels: Jesuit Refugee Service (JRS) – Europe).

Joint Supervisory Authority of Schengen (2004) *Activities of the Joint Supervisory Authority. Sixth Report*, January 2002/December 2003.

Justice (2000) *The Schengen Information System: A Human Rights Audit* (London: Justice).

Kohnstamm, J. and L. Dubbeld (2007) 'Glazen samenleving in zicht', *Nederlands Juristenblad*, 82(37), October: 2369–75.

Koslowski, R. (2002) 'Information Technology, Migration and Border Control.' Paper presented at the Institute for Government Studies, University of California, Berkeley, 25 April.

Koslowski, R. (2008) 'Global Mobility and the Quest for an International Migration Regime', in J. Chamie and L. Dall'Oglio (eds) *International Migration and Development: Continuing the Dialogue: Legal and Policy Perspectives* (Geneva: International Organization for Migration).

Leun, J. van der (2003) *Looking for Loopholes: Processes of Incorporation of Illegal Immigrants in the Netherlands* (Amsterdam University Press).

Lyon, D. (1994) *The Electronic Eye: The Rise of Surveillance Society* (Cambridge: Polity Press).

Lyon, D. (2003) *Surveillance after September 11* (Cambridge: Polity Press).

Lyon, D. (2004) 'Globalizing Surveillance: Comparative and Sociological Perspectives', *International Sociology*, 19(2): 135–49.

Lyon, D. (2005) 'The Border is Everywhere: ID Cards, Surveillance and the Other', in E. Zureik and M. Salter (eds) *Global Surveillance and Policing: Borders, Security, Identity* (Cullompton: Willan Publishing).

Lyon, D. (2007) *Surveillance Studies: An Overview* (Cambridge: Polity Press).

Marx, G. (2001) 'Identity and Anonymity: Some Conceptual Distinctions and Issues for Research', in J. Caplan and J. Torpey (eds) *Documenting Individual*

*Identity: The Development of State Practices in the Modern World* (Princeton University Press).

Marx, G. (2005) 'Some Conceptual Issues in the Study of Borders and Surveillance', in E. Zureik and M. Salter (eds) *Global Surveillance and Policing: Borders, Security, Identity* (Cullompton: Willan Publishing).

Mathiesen, T. (2001) 'On Globalization of Control: Towards an Integrated Surveillance System in Europe', in *Social Change and Crime in the Scandinavian and Baltic Region*, NSfK (Nordisk Samarbejdsråd for Kriminologi/Scandinavian Research Council for Criminology) Research Seminar Reports 43, Riga.

Monahan, T. (ed.) (2006) *Surveillance and Security: Technological Politics and Power in Everyday Life* (London: Routledge).

Ploeg, I. van der (2005) *The Machine-Readable Body: Essays on Biometrics and the Informatization of the Body* (Maastricht: Shaker).

Pluymen, M. and P. Minderhoud (2002) 'Access to Public Services as an Instrument of Migration Policy in the Netherlands', *Immigration, Asylum and Nationality Law*, 16(4): 208–23.

Prins, J. (2006) 'Variaties op een thema: van paspoort- naar identiteitsfraude', *Nederlands Juristenblad*, 81(1): 9–14.

Scott, J. (1998) *Seeing Like a State: How Certain Schemes to Improve the Human Condition Have Failed* (New Haven: Yale University Press).

Staring, R. (2001) *Reizen onder regie. Het migratieproces van illegale Turken in Nederland* (Amsterdam: Het Spinhuis).

Torpey, J. (1998) 'Coming and Going: On the State Monopolization of the Legitimate "Means of Movement"', *Sociological Theory*, 16(3): 239–59.

Torpey, J. (2000) 'States and the Regulation of Migration in the Twentieth-Century North Atlantic World', in P. Andreas and T. Snyder (eds) *The Wall around the West: State Borders and Immigration Controls in North America and Europe* (Lanham, MD: Rowman & Littlefield).

Welch, M. and L. Schuster (2005) 'Detention of Asylum Seekers in the US, UK, France, Germany and Italy: A Critical View of the Globalizing Culture of Control', *Criminal Justice*, 5(4): 331–55.

WRR (2003) *Slagvaardigheid in de Europabrede Unie*. WRR rapporten aan de Regering no. 65 (The Hague: SDU).

Zureik, E. and M. Salter (eds) (2005) *Global Surveillance and Policing: Borders, Security, Identity* (Cullompton: Willan Publishing).

# 4
## Migration and the Machine-Readable Body: Identification and Biometrics

*Irma van der Ploeg and Isolde Sprenkels*

### Introduction

Since time immemorial, migrants and travellers have been the subject of surveillance by governments and authorities. Wherever an authority's jurisdiction is delimited by territorial borders, those that cross the borders whilst travelling remove themselves from the authority exercised in the area they are leaving only to enter a new area where their status is as yet unclear. They do not belong to this local community so, initially, they fall outside the powers exerted by the local authority. That is why it is very important for the authorities to find ways to gain control over migrants and travellers. One of the most important means of doing this is establishing identities and issuing documents proving these identities and the associated status as a member/non-member of the community.

During the process of state creation, which took place mainly during the nineteenth century, national authorities assumed these powers.[1] More precisely, gaining a monopoly on the issue of the 'legitimate means of movement' (Torpey 2000) was an essential component in the state-creation process and involved the institutionalization of both territorial borders and the boundary between a country's subjects and any 'foreigners'.

This is how migration and identification have historically been associated with each other, culminating in the present-day development of gigantic national and international information systems for identifying migrants and travellers, that can be considered the central mechanism of the 'migration machine'. Identification – establishing who someone is and whether that someone is the person they claim to be (authentication) – plays a crucial role in government surveillance of migrants both during migration itself (crossing borders, requesting travel documents and residence permits, asylum procedures) and during the migrant's stay in a country of arrival (checking status and rights to stay, determining rights and obligations, participating in the life of the community).

In this chapter, we describe present-day developments and practices concerning the digitalization of identification in the context of migration and migration policy, together with the associated transformations of migrant surveillance practices. We focus in particular on the way migrants' bodies are increasingly at the centre of identification and surveillance practices through the fast proliferating use of biometrics.

In this introduction, we explain several elements of the context in which the present deployment of identification technology for migration management purposes should be placed. We then describe the identification methods and practices of present migration policy implementations. This will highlight, in addition to the considerable complexity of this policy area, the increasing importance of biometrics, prompting us in the next section to elaborate on the significance of this technology. We discuss the difficulties and tensions surrounding every application of biometrics, while indicating where, in the migration context, the socio-political and normative-ethical problems surrounding the application of biometrics can be expected, now and in the near future.

## The global context: convergence towards identification technology

Present-day 'migration management' is not an isolated process but exists in a complex force field that extends beyond the national level. Various social, economic, political and technological developments and factors converge to form a powerful engine for a global trend in which technological forms of identification, registration, storage and processing of personal data dominate. The most important aspects of this force field can be described in terms of closely related present-day developments such as globalization and mobility, the shift in political decision-making and policy development to the European level, digitization and use of information and communication technology (ICT), the coupling of migration and security policies, and the 'informatization' of the body. This context (described in more detail in the first chapter of this book) must form the background to any attempt to understand the present 'technologization' of migration policy and the central role of identification technology. Below, we look briefly at the three last mentioned developments.

## Digitization and the deployment of ICT

The globalization and flexibilization of production and labour markets come with an increasingly dynamic (illegal) labour migration (often associated with trafficking of people), with changes in policy and economy in the countries of arrival often resulting in reactive changes in migration flows. For this reason, migration policy is being included in bilateral and transnational consultation structures. Countries of arrival are active in the 'migrant- and refugee-generating countries' where they impose as many restrictions and selection procedures as possible. At the same time, international organizations such as the Organisation for Economic Co-operation and Development (OECD), the International Organization for Migration (IOM) and the United Nations are actively involved in shaping international policy and implementing it. This new level of complexity and cooperation provides a strong impetus for information sharing, intensification of communication and standardization of identification and verification procedures.

Globalization and the accompanying worldwide increase in mobility are significantly influenced and made possible by the information revolution, but information and communication technology (ICT) is regarded, at the same time, as the most important instrument in managing and controlling the migration flows. Of course, politics and legislation remain the primary determinants of immigration policy, but today it is as often the case that laws and regulations are formulated and adopted with the aim to enable the deployment of ICT in this context.

Some of the key developments in ICT over the past few decades have been primarily concerned with digitizing methods and techniques of identification and authentication, thus resulting in countless changes – some more, some less radical – in the ways of implementing government migration policy. Application procedures for visas and other entry documents, protocols for border crossing, the introduction of an identification requirement and even the specifications for photographs in travel documents are all examples of legislation to regulate migration. But the motive for introducing these particular requirements and the details of their formulation serve to a large extent to facilitate and regulate the deployment of ICT. Instead of ICT being instrumental in carrying out policy, the opposite is just as frequently true: laws and rules are formulated in order to utilize technological potential to its maximum. This applies at the global level of setting up databanks for international data sharing, right down to the detailed level of requirements for passport photographs that enable (future) application of facial-recognition technology.

The central role ascribed to ICT in migration policy, especially in dealing with illegal immigration, was recently clearly restated by the director of the International Organization for Migration, the Netherlands: 'In an effort to manage migration, governments try to prevent, hinder and reduce the parallel flow of illegal economic migrants. This is done by increasing border security, using biometric applications in documents, exchanging data files, etc. And this requires that a dialogue take place to ensure cooperation between the host countries and the countries of origin' (Migratie Info 2008). This quote indicates how international cooperation on migration can develop these days mainly into a 'dialogue' about implementing technology. Technology transfer, international standardization and the adaptation of practices and procedures in the 'countries of origin' to the demands of (the IT systems in) the 'host countries' are issues high on the agenda. It also serves to illustrate how the use of ICT in the migration context focuses mainly on identification and authentication. In addition to physically tracing people who illegally cross borders in freight lorries and containers etc. (also with the help of increasingly advanced technologies such as infra-red detectors and $CO_2$ detection apparatus), the control of illegal immigration is mainly sought in perfecting the system of issuing and verifying identity and travel documents and in mending the gaps in the international information networks (Van der Ploeg 2006).

At national levels, improving migration policy implementation, just as in many other policy domains, is often sought in 'chain computerization': (re)organizing the IT infrastructure to enhance communication, harmonization, cooperation and information sharing among the various agencies involved. 'Chain partners' such as (in the Netherlands) the Aliens Police, the Royal Netherlands Military Police, the Immigration and Naturalization Service (IND), the Central Agency for the Reception of Asylum Seekers (COA) and the Dutch Repatriation and Departure Service, all of which previously worked separately and independently, now hold meetings to agree on how they should harmonize their activities and information systems. Identification plays a crucial role here as well because all the files on individuals, kept by each of these organizations in their own, separate information systems, now need to be linked together. The key issue here is to find a mechanism which can bring together all the separately stored information about one person in the correct manner – another occasion where biometrics is among the most favoured solutions.

## Linking migration policy and security policy

The European Commission report of 13 February 2008 about the 'Border Package' includes the following statement: 'The increasing amount of passenger traffic is providing the European Union with a challenge: how can it ensure smoothly run border crossing procedures, and facilitate the influx of bona fide travellers *while at the same time tightening up security?'* (European Commission 2008, our italics). Here it seems to be taken for granted that migration policy and security policy are linked with each other. This was certainly not always the case. Of course, border controls have always aimed to hold back undesirable persons such as criminals and political enemies, but originally the new measures for reinforcing Europe's external borders, thought to be necessary for relaxing the controls at inner borders, were mainly aimed at securing economic interests, there being anxiety about a large influx of economic migrants and the loss of control over the import and export of goods.

In the present tense climate caused by wars and a fear of terrorist attacks, the way of thinking has changed. The checking and guarding of borders are now associated to an unprecedented extent with guaranteeing national security, and with searching for and arresting persons regarded as security risks. This has a number of direct and important consequences for the issues we discuss in this chapter.

In the first place, this means that governments are not only interested in the fact *that* people cross a border in a legitimate way, in other words, in possession of a valid travel documents, but they would also increasingly like to know *who* precisely has crossed the border and even who will be crossing *in the future*. More and more data on those who cross borders (especially air passengers to, for example, the United States) are being collected. This information, that may even have to be made available prior to travel, is subsequently stored in large quantities for future reference. In this way, it is hoped that anyone who could be a security risk can be identified with more precision.

Secondly, when 'national security interests' are deemed at stake, the European data protection regulations do not apply. In other words, the protection of personal data and the rules and laws that concern storage, access and exchange of this information can be ignored if security interests are involved.[2]

Other principles relating to legitimate deployment of information technology and registration of personal data may also come under pressure, examples being the proportionality and the purpose limitation principles. Of course it is very hard to argue that a particular measure is disproportionate (proportionality implying that the measure stands in some kind of a reasonable relationship to the goal to be realized) in situations where 'national security' is thought to be at stake, as the possibility of preventing gruesome terrorist attacks causes other interests to quickly fade into the background. The same applies to the purpose limitation principle, which states that data collected for a certain purpose should not be used for another, quite different one. This too will quickly seem less important whenever the spectre of terrorism is evoked and hangs over our heads.[3]

In light of the above, it would of course be more honest or even more practical to list 'fighting terrorism' and 'security' among the primary aims of any new measure involving identification and personal data collection. Then there will be even fewer barriers to the use of these data for security or crime-prevention purposes later on, since they do not appear as secondary or 'new' aims. This is, in fact, what happens today in all the announcements of measures and plans related to the identification of migrants and travellers, and to the central storage, linking and sharing of personal data.

## Informatization of the body

The increasingly extensive registration of migrants and travellers includes an increasing deployment of biometrics, the automated recognition of individuals by means of physical characteristics. The solution to the above-mentioned key issue in chain computerization, the correct linking up of all the separately kept files on a migrant, is increasingly being sought in biometrics. Moreover, the new generations of visas, passports, identity cards, driving licences, etc. are, with fewer and fewer exceptions, equipped with this technology. Travel documents, in particular, are required to be 'machine-readable' these days,[4] including the ability to verify automatically the relationship between the document and its holder. Where previously, and today mostly still as well, the border guard compares a passport photograph with the face of the person standing in front of him or her and holding the passport, in the future this verification process will increasingly be performed by means of an automated comparison of digitized fingerprints, facial photographs, iris scans and other such techniques.

This digitization of physical characteristics does not only take place in the context of migration and border surveillance but is part of what one could define as the informatization of the body (Van der Ploeg 2002). This is the phenomenon whereby the body is increasingly regarded and treated as information and is included as such in the world of digital files, information networks, databanks, software and search engines. Not so long ago, the information revolution was seen as a movement away from the physical, material world, thus creating a second, 'virtual' one, but now we can see that the contrast thus created was illusory. These days, software is 'embedded' and the physical world acquires 'ambient intelligence', while in an increasing number of instances it has really become difficult to distinguish the human body, that outstanding example of a 'material thing', from a dataset or an information-processing machine. Our DNA is a code, our medical history is an electronic patient record, our physical vulnerabilities amount to an ICT-generated risk profile and our identity is an algorithmically produced biometric template.

The use of identification technologies in general, and biometrics in particular, forms a key part of what are called 'technologies of surveillance' (see also Chapter 3 by Broeders in this book). For some time to come, full attention to the question of their socio-political and normative-ethical significance in terms of the relationship between state and individual, and of social categorization and discrimination, will be required. Especially where biometrics and the use of the body are concerned, issues such as a person's integrity and the emergence of new vulnerabilities and types of exclusion are of topical interest.

In the following section, we describe the identification processes of migrants, as currently carried out in the Netherlands, with specific attention to the role of biometrics. We will then consider a number of socio-political and normative aspects regarding this increasing role of biometrics in identifying and surveilling migrants.

## Identification and biometrics in Dutch migration management

Our discussion of current migrant identification procedures in the Netherlands and the use of biometrics to do so is divided up into three moments: the *request* (made in the country of origin) for travel and residence documents, the actual *border crossing*, and any surveillance or tracing activities during the period of *residence* within the borders. Before doing this, however, we should first briefly explain what biometrics is and how it works.

Generally speaking, biometrics technology comprises the generation of digital representations of physical characteristics that are unique to an individual, examples being fingerprints, the irises, the vein patterns in the hands or retina, the shape of the hands, the face, or the voice. It can also involve typical behavioural patterns such as key stroke patterns or the way a pen is held when writing one's signature. The digital biometric data are then algorithmically converted into what is called a template. This processing is in most cases irreversible, which means that the 'raw' biometric data cannot be retrieved from the template. These templates are usually stored in a database that is contacted as soon as a face, eye, hand, finger or voice is presented to the system in a particular identification or verification procedure. Once this second biometric image has been subjected to the same algorithmic transformation, an identical template is searched for in the database, and, if found, the individual is 'recognized' by the system. A second possibility is that the templates are not stored centrally, but on a chip card, in which case the user needs to show both the card and the required part of the body to 'prove' that they are the legitimate user of the card. This is comparable with a system of smartcards and pin codes, the important difference being that pin codes can be forgotten, or supplied to a third party. Biometric data stored on a chip card do not need to be kept in a database by the organization concerned, and could be deleted without loss of functionality.

This is why biometrics can sometimes be 'privacy-neutral', or even privacy-enhancing, which is what the supporters of biometrics like to emphasize, but an argument like this can only be used in precisely and carefully defined circumstances (Cavoukian and Stoianov 2007). Most of the current biometric systems fall outside this category, however, and the important applications of biometrics now in preparation or already implemented by national and European governments are associated with the construction of databases.

No biometric system is infallible; all the systems currently in use have error margins expressed in 'false acceptance rates' (FAR, in other words the system falsely recognizes someone as being the same person) and in 'false rejection rates' (FRR, the opposite case in which the system falsely reports that it is not the same person). These figures, expressed together as the 'equal error rate' or EER, suddenly become higher when the system makes the transition from laboratory conditions, with its relatively homogeneous group of test individuals, to the outside world with all the variable conditions. Facial-recognition systems, in particular, are still scarcely usable because of this problem. Another important problem is that, for each system, a percentage of the required target group does not possess the characteristics that have been requested (at least, not in a way the system can process them). Fingerprints may be impossible to read, body parts may be missing or damaged, and so on. In the case of fingerprints, for example, this applies to about 5 per cent of the population (Dessimoz *et al.* 2006). These 'failure-to-enrol rates' are often associated with certain categories of people such as young children, manual labourers and the elderly. In these people, the fingerprint ridge pattern is either undeveloped or no longer clear enough to be properly registered by the scanners. A large number of variables thus influence the performance of each biometric system. They include the quality of the scanners and software, the circumstances and situations in which the system has to function, the method of use and implementation, and the many variations in the human body, including all the changes it may go through during a person's lifetime.

### The request for entry and residence documents

As already indicated in this chapter, migration policy is currently on the agenda of both bilateral/transnational- and national-level meetings. The 'countries of arrival' are active in the 'migrant- and refugee-generating countries' in order to impose as many restrictions and selections there as possible. Bilateral cooperation on migration is today largely consisting of a 'dialogue' on the implementation of technology so that practices and procedures in the 'countries of origin' are adjusted to the demands (of the IT systems) in the countries of arrival.

At the stage of application for entry documents, the activity centres around the relevant embassy or consulate, which functions as the border-crossing point in advance, applying selection criteria, and dealing with visa requests for short (less than three months) and longer periods of stay.[5] (See Table 4.1.) This visa is a machine-readable sticker with a unique 'alien number' and is stuck in the travel document or passport.

*Table 4.1*  Types of visa

| Types of visa | Length of stay |
| --- | --- |
| Transit visa airports (A visa) | |
| Transit visa (B visa) | max. 5 days |
| Short-stay visa (C visa) | <90 days |
| Provisional Residence Permit (D visa) | >90 days |

Before this happens, however, the people applying for a Dutch visa have to be checked to see whether they fulfil a long series of conditions. They need to: have a valid passport or travel document, and prove they have travel insurance and health insurance as well as sufficient funds to survive (or someone providing financial guarantees for them). In addition, for the *short-stay visa*, the reason for travelling and for returning to one's own country needs to be made 'plausible'. For the *Provisional Residence Permit*, undergoing a tuberculosis check is required, as well as passing the controversial 'basic Civic Integration Examination'.[6] Finally, there is an investigation of whether the applicant is a potential danger to the public order, the health of the community, national security or international relations. To do this, searches are carried out in criminal and police databases and in the Schengen Information System (SIS) to see if the person is registered there and whether entry to the Schengen territory should therefore be refused.

The SIS, in operation since 1995, is the European information system to help maintain public order, security (to national level) and movement of persons within the member state territory. It contains information about persons and objects and consists of a central database, the C-SIS, and national databases, the N-SIS. Of all the data in the SIS, 90 per cent refers to persons, and, more precisely, to the group defined as 'foreigners or third-country nationals to be refused entry to the Schengen territory'.[7] Most of the objects entered in the SIS are lost and stolen identity documents or are otherwise related to migration (see Brouwer 2007).

National authorities enter data according to their own standards (that is to say there is hardly any harmonization) based on a decision declaring a particular person undesirable or refusing them entry. These authorities are also responsible for the accuracy of the data.[8]

Any parties that subsequently access the system are authorized to do so for a certain part of it only, and are only able to see whether there is a hit and what action to take (for example, 'arrest'). There may be an option to contact the country that entered the data to check whether they are still valid, but those consulting the system appear to trust the accuracy and legitimacy of the data information supplied without question.[9] The embassies where visas are requested do not in fact have direct access to the N-SIS, but receive the information on a CD-ROM, updated on a monthly basis.[10]

In the near future, the biometric data of anyone requesting a short-stay visa will be registered in the *Visa Information System*. This VIS is used at border entry to verify the authenticity of a visa and the identity of the person holding it. The idea is to ensure that visa requests are dealt with more rapidly, that fraudulent behaviour and 'visa shopping' are made much more difficult, while at the same time facilitating the application of the Dublin Convention (with regard to asylum requests) and the identification and return of illegal persons who have overstayed their visa.

The VIS, just as the SIS, comprising a central database CS-VIS, and national databases NI-VIS, is a European system containing information with regard to all visa requests and allowing this information to be available to all member states. All decisions regarding a request (including refusals, extensions or withdrawals of visas) and information about the migrants and their referent are kept for at least five years. *Biometric characteristics*, facial photographs and fingerprints are also recorded in the VIS.[11] That means that any migrant who requests a short-stay visa at a Dutch embassy has to supply these biometric data.[12]

Taking into account this 'biometrification' of a request for a short-stay visa (now possible with the VIS), it will become possible to include this new category of biometric data in SIS II.[13] For the time being, that will only apply to fingerprints and facial photographs. Initially, this biometric information allows the identity of a third-country national to be confirmed. Later, when technology allows, this information will be used as an 'identifier' (index or 'reference key'); in other words, without other information such as a name. This will turn SIS II into an intelligence system: beyond supporting the decision on how to act with regard to a particular person, it then becomes a search system enabling the linking of various data about a particular person.

Requests for a *longer stay* (Provisional Residence Permit) are already accompanied by the registration of biometric data when the Civic Integration Examination is taken at the embassy. There, candidates have to provide identity documents of which a copy is kept and, furthermore, a facial photograph and fingerprints are taken. All these data are subsequently registered in the *Civic Integration Examination Biometrics System* (IEBS). The system requires all ten fingers, one by one, to be scanned, which of course sometimes poses problems if there is a wound, no clear pattern or the person lacks one or more fingers. These are then registered as 'temporary trauma', 'permanent trauma' or 'unable to capture', respectively. However, fingerprints should be taken of at least two fingers (not the little fingers because they are the least 'reliable') and if that is not possible, there is a 'fall-back procedure'. With another embassy employee as witness, the fingerprints are taken once more and if this is still unsuccessful, the examination candidate is registered in the IEBS with the 'add person' function. This function is safeguarded with a password and can only be called up by a specially authorized employee. In addition, the identification documents are again checked and extra materials for proof of identity are requested (CINOP, LTS and Ordinate 2005).

All the data on applicants and their documents are not just registered locally (at the embassy) but also in the *Basic Facility for Aliens* using an allocated *aliens number*. This facility is a central database in which basic immigrant data for the Netherlands are recorded, generated by the systems of partners in the 'aliens chain'. For identifying and registering foreigners and changing and verifying personal data within this aliens chain, a standardized method has been developed, the *Protocol for Identification and Labelling* (PIL) (Dutch Ministry of Justice 2007). One of the basic premises of the PIL is that biometrics provides the surest identification and verification. Therefore, wherever legislation permits, biometric technology is applied.

Finally, the Visa Service, under the responsibility of the Dutch Ministry of Foreign Affairs, evaluates and grants requests for either a short-stay visa or a Provisional Residence Permit, depending on the travel destination. Only then can a label finally be stuck in the passport.

### The actual border crossing

The most important part of the actual border crossing is verifying or authenticating the documents presented (passport and visa). There are two aspects to this: the documents need to be checked for authenticity, and it is necessary to verify that the person showing the document is also the legitimate holder of that document, in other words, that it really was issued to this person. The central role played by the border officer in performing these two tasks is rapidly being taken over by machines, IT systems and automated identification and verification methods, which means that biometrics, in particular, is being deployed on a rapidly growing scale.

According to the Schengen Borders Code (European Union 2006), travellers with a short-stay visa (but also third-country nationals without visa requirement) have to be subjected to a thorough check at entry. Checks are made to see whether someone is a threat to the public order, internal security, public health or international relations involving the Schengen states. This means that, at the border, national databanks[14] and the N-SIS II are consulted to check whether entry should be refused, whether the person in question is being sought by the police or whether they need protection.[15] There are also questions about the purpose and length of stay, whether the person has sufficient funds and, of course, the validity of the travel documents is checked. A stamp is then placed in the travel documents with the date and location of entry as well as information on any plans for leaving the country.[16]

If third-country nationals do not satisfy the conditions, they will not be allowed to enter the Schengen territory unless they have a special right to asylum or international protection. The reasons for such a decision need to be substantiated; the third-country national is given a standard form that includes a statement of the reasons for refusal. It is possible to appeal against this decision, but in the meantime entry into the country is, of course, not possible.

In February 2008, the European Commission put forward a proposal to change the Schengen Borders Code so that it would become compulsory to consult the VIS at the border (European Union 2008a). After amendments to this Code, the VIS will also have to be consulted in order to carry out a thorough check of third-country nationals with a visa. This will involve a check of the visa number and fingerprint authentication. The VIS Convention does not at present include any provisions that make its use at the external borders compulsory or that make it possible to apply verification procedures when someone is exiting the country. There is simply an instruction to the effect that duty officers at the external borders *may* consult the VIS, making use of the visa label number and the visa holder's fingerprints, if they wish. Because the VIS contains data important for controlling the external borders, the Commission believes it is necessary to add the deployment of the VIS to the Schengen Border Code rules in order to strengthen the VIS Convention (European Union 2008b).

All checkpoints at the external borders should eventually have access to the VIS and be equipped with electronic passport readers and biometric readers. In the future, therefore, migrants with a short-stay visa will have their visas and identities biometrically authenticated by means of the VIS when they enter the country. The VIS will be introduced in stages, so initially there will be two ways of consulting it at border crossings: solely by means of the visa label using the visa number to call up the visa holder's information, or by means of the visa label plus verification of fingerprints.[17]

The European Commission's Border Package, mentioned above, contains the following, more far-reaching, computerized methods of identification and verification for use at external border checkpoints:

In the first place, it suggests making border crossing easier for certain *'bona fide third-country nationals'* (with or without visa obligation), EU subjects and other persons who have the right to free movement within the EU with an e-passport. An automated external border check is suggested for these persons. In addition, the status of *'registered traveller'* is being introduced for 'bona fide third-country nationals'. This status is granted in the country of origin at the embassy, on the basis of a set of criteria and prior checking of, for example, purpose of stay, risk to the public order, means of support, biometric passport and reliability of travel history. Thus, automated border checks are also possible for this group.

Secondly, it suggests investigating the desirability of an *entry and exit system* for third-country nationals with a short-stay visa and those who are exempt from the visa requirement (comparable with the American US-VISIT system). This would mean automatic registration of time and place of entry and exit, and the length of the permitted period of stay. If a person overstays the visa period, a warning would automatically be generated (*'overstayers'* are at present the largest category of illegal migrants). The visa application procedure will include recording biometric data. These will be registered at entry (for the third-country national without a visa requirement) or when the 'registered traveller' status is requested. This system would need to have the same technical architecture as SIS II and the VIS, which demonstrates the intention to link the various systems.

Thirdly, it suggests performing a feasibility study on setting up a *European Electronic System of Travel Authorization* (ESTA), a system for travel permits. Third-country nationals without a visa requirement would then need to request a travel authorization by making their travel and passport details (including the biometric data recorded in them) available electronically. As soon as these data have been compared with the various databanks, the authorization can be granted or refused.

### Surveillance within the borders

Migration policy and border surveillance are not limited to geographical borders. Just as the role of embassies in faraway countries amounts to an active part in border management, so too is the border performed *within* a country's territory by surveillance activities that enact and maintain the demarcation between those who are entitled to be there and those who are not. Within the practices of this surveillance of various groups of migrants within the borders an important role is reserved for the 'reporting requirement':

For example, travellers holding a short-stay visa should report to the Aliens Police in the place they are staying within three days, unless they are staying at a hotel or camping ground. They then receive a 'supervision' label in their passport as proof of 'legitimate stay'.

Migrants with a Provisional Residence Permit should request a Regular Residence Permit within eight days of entering the country: they do this at the front office of the Immigration and Naturalization Service (IND). The conditions for receiving such a Regular Residence Permit are the same as for a provisional one. An application form for the permit should be submitted together with documented proof of the purpose of the visit. The person concerned is then 'invited' to an identification procedure including an authentication and validation of the identity papers. All personal details are once more registered and checked against the 'aliens databank' (Basic Facility for Aliens), as well as police databases. The identity document is then provided with a residence label and an aliens number. Finally, these people have to register in the *Municipal Basic Administration* (GBA) database, which is also linked to the Basic Facility for Aliens database.[18]

This also applies to EU, EER (European Economic Area) and Swiss subjects who would like to stay for more than three months, even though in theory they are free to enter the Netherlands. This group is also 'advised' to register with the IND which then checks and verifies their identity papers, investigates any documents relating to the purpose of the stay, health insurance etc. and also any sign that the migrants may pose a risk to the public order, national security or public health. The IND registers the residence status, which is then sent to the Municipal Basic Administration and the Basic Facility for Aliens databases. This group is then also given an aliens number and a label declaring registration for the passport or identity card. The idea is to facilitate one's participation in society because documented proof of legitimate residence status makes things easier when dealing with various organizations such as banks and housing associations.

For people who wish to apply for *political asylum* in the Netherlands the story is entirely different. Once they have crossed the border in some way or other, they have to make their request for asylum in one of the two registration centres (Schiphol or Ter Apel). After filling out the application form (the first registration of personal data), the Royal Netherlands Military Police (Schiphol) or the Aliens Police (Ter Apel) starts an elaborate identification procedure during which the asylum seeker is searched (including all clothing and baggage) and a *facial photograph* is taken. Identity papers, tickets and diplomas are checked for authenticity and validity, and verified as belonging to the person in question.

Today biometric technology has become an essential tool in this process: *fingerprints* are recorded with the aid of an FIT device (*Fingerprint Image Transmission*), which involves rolling all ten fingers in ink and producing a fingerprint sheet, known as the '*dactyslip*', which is subsequently digitally scanned.[19] The original sheet goes to the *Dutch National Research Information Service* (dNRI). The scan, together with a digital facial photograph and all personal data, is sent to the Basic Facility for Aliens for verification and/or registration.[20] If the person is already known in the biometrics register of the Basic Facility for Aliens, that is, their biometric data have already been registered under an aliens number, then this number will be reported back. If the person is not known in this databank, he or she will be registered under a new aliens number and the biometric data (scanned dactyslip) saved.

The next step is to check whether the fingerprints have been recorded in the criminal database HAVANK or in one of several other police and law-enforcement databases.

Finally, the fingerprints are sent to Eurodac[21] to ascertain which country is responsible for dealing with the asylum request. As specified in the Dublin Convention, that is the country where the asylum seeker entered the European Union, or submitted a request for the first time (see Table 4.2).

Eurodac is a hit/no-hit system; you are simply informed whether there was a matching dataset in the system or not.[22] If no match was found, meaning that the person concerned has not been registered in Eurodac before, his/her fingerprints are recorded. However, if there is a preexisting entry for this person, the search is registered under a number, and the biometric data are sent to the 'Dublin office'. A hit in Eurodac

*Table 4.2*  Fingerprint categories

| Categories of fingerprints Eurodac | Period stored |
| --- | --- |
| 1) all asylum seekers from the age of 14 | max. 10 years |
| 2) migrants who crossed the border illegally | max. 2 years |
| 3) illegal migrants found in one of the member states | not stored; just compared with 1) and 2) |

means the person concerned has already been in another EU country and, according to the Dublin Convention, the country where the person first entered the EU is responsible for the asylum application. Such a 'Dublin procedure' can also be initiated if, for example, visa stamps in a passport indicate that the asylum seeker was previously in another EU country.

The crucial role of biometrics, fingerprinting in particular, is illustrated by evidence of self-mutilation of fingers by asylum seekers to avoid being enrolled in the various systems, or being recognized as a prior applicant, while, conversely, the very fact of failing to produce 'machine-readable' fingertips will influence the decision on the application negatively, despite the well-documented 'failure to enrol rates' of biometric systems themselves.

After this thorough identification procedure has been carried out, the asylum seeker signs a declaration of identity and nationality, and the registration centre gives him/her a *reporting pass* bearing the aliens number, passport photo, name, date of birth and the pass number. Only then does the 'first interrogation' with the IND take place; the person is now asked to provide details of identity, nationality and travel route, and a decision is made on whether this person has the right to a short or long application procedure.

Armed with this reporting pass, those who are to follow the long procedure go to an accommodation centre run by the Central Agency for Reception of Asylum Seekers (COA). While they are waiting for the decision, they are required to report in every week. When they report for the first time, the reporting pass is taken in and replaced by a *'W document'*. This requires fingerprint scans to be made, and the asylum seeker has to sign a statement to confirm receipt of this W document. (See Table 4.3 for an overview of the various aliens' documents.)

Since 2007, people can fulfil their reporting requirements by using standard reporting stations – self-service kiosks fitted with a card reader, screen and fingerprint scanner. Previously, one had to report to the Aliens Police (to comply with the Aliens Acts) and to the Central Agency for Reception of Asylum Seekers (to comply with the law concerning the latter) to have one's card checked. This card was compared with the passport photograph to see if it was the same person, stamped and provided with a new date and time for reporting the next time.[23] This manner of working was less than efficient, open to fraud (in cases of lookalikes) and time-consuming for the asylum seekers. It was therefore decided to make the reporting process at the Aliens Police and the Central Agency administratively more effective by combining both processes

*Table 4.3*   Document types

| Types of aliens' documents |
| --- |
| Type I residence permit for a definite period, regular |
| Type II residence permit for an indefinite period, regular |
| Type III residence permit for a definite period, asylum |
| Type IV residence permit for an indefinite period, asylum |
| Type EU/EER residence card for community subjects (e.g. those from new member countries) |
| |
| W document (pending asylum procedure/decision to request asylum for indefinite period) |
| W2 document (residing lawfully, not in possession of a cross-border or identity document such as a passport) |
| Privileged persons document |

and linking the systems, so the asylum seekers only had to report in at one location.[24] To this end, the project 'Reporting Requirement and Biometrics' was initiated (Aa 2007). The project team consisted of representatives from the Central Agency, the Aliens Police and a vendor of biometrics. On occasion, other parties were included such as, for example, the Director Coordination Aliens Chain, Immigration Policy officials and the Dutch Data Protection Authority. The starting point of this project, 'Reporting Requirements and Biometrics', was the Policy Document on Repatriation, written by a former Dutch Minister for Alien Affairs and Integration, whose profile consisted mainly of being a hardliner on immigration affairs (Dutch House of Representatives 2003–04).[25]

Reporting now takes place as follows. The asylum seeker enters his/her card (reporting pass or W document) in the station, which reads the aliens number on the card; a pictogram on the screen shows which finger has to be placed on the scanner and then the biometrics register of the Basic Facility for Aliens checks if the fingerprint matches the aliens number. If everything is in order, the asylum seeker gets his/her card back. If there are still matters to be dealt with in person, or if there is no match between the newly scanned fingerprint and the previously registered print linked to the aliens number, the card is 'swallowed'. The asylum seeker then has to report to the desk.[26]

An advantage of the automated biometrics reporting requirement is that it reduces the chance of identity fraud (using lookalikes), but this digital registration also expands surveillance, since it also gives more information about the asylum seeker's whereabouts and availability for activities related to evaluating the request for admission and a possible repatriation to the country of origin. Furthermore, the organization of accommodation facilities can be done more effectively because the facilities can be cancelled immediately if an applicant proves to be absent. On the whole, however, it is believed that the increased efficiency is advantageous to both parties: this procedure is quicker and easier for both the collaborating control authorities (they now operate from one location) and for the asylum seekers.

At the end of the application procedure (that is known to take years to complete), one particular group of asylum seekers, the ones who have exhausted all possible procedures but have finally been rejected, remains. This group is subjected to what is called the '*Repatriation Policy*'. Here, too, an in-depth identification procedure plays a crucial role, because without valid identity papers and without confirmation of being a subject of the presumed country of origin, repatriation is more or less impossible. Certain members of this group, especially those who entered the Netherlands before 2001, and who are now waiting to be repatriated while being housed in a so-called 'departure centre', are having to deal with the worst type of reporting requirement – the daily type. This policy is very much focused on preventing people, who have exhausted all procedures, from escaping surveillance and repatriation by disappearing into an illegal existence in the Netherlands.

The reporting requirements and procedures involving requests for asylum are not the only situations in which the identity of migrants is investigated inside the country borders. After all, there can be all sorts of reasons why the police stop somebody in the street and ask for identity papers; it could be anything from a minor traffic offence or a routine check, to being caught red-handed whilst committing a serious offence. The introduction of the identification requirement means that everyone of 14 years or older has to carry valid proof of identity. Anyone who cannot show this proof can settle the problem by paying a fine but, should there appear to be a reason for doing so, the person could also be arrested and taken to the police station where the identity would be fully investigated. Both the Royal Netherlands Military Police and the Aliens Police can stop someone if they have 'reasonable suspicion' of unlawful residence, or if they wish to prevent any potential case of unlawful residence immediately after the person has crossed the border.[27] On confirmation of this suspicion (for example if the person cannot identify themselves), they will be taken to the police station for a further identification.

There are highly detailed protocols for carrying out such *identity investigations* prescribing how to proceed in a wide variety of circumstances: which methods to use and how, what and where the information should be entered, registered, requested and investigated. The resources and instruments that can be applied include the 'holding' of the person (temporary arrest), the interview, devices for authenticating identity papers, searching luggage, clothing, mobile telephones, investigating social networks through acquaintances, magazine subscriptions and bank statements. Even an internal examination of the body is an option, and, if keys have been found, a search of premises. The terms used in this process are 'verification' (of any identity papers found), 'primary' and 'secondary' identity investigations (stages following on from one another if the previous stage has not supplied a decisive answer so that more and more resources may be deployed).

The quality of this secondary stage of identity investigation is becoming increasingly advanced, partly because of the availability of new organizational and technical adaptations. An example of this is the design of what is actually called an *'identity street'* at the police station. Here, all available technical resources are brought together and used for verifying and identifying the person concerned (see Boekhoorn and Speller 2006). The methods deployed include anything from the interview, dactyloscopy, and taking photographs to checking the authenticity of documents and consulting various databanks.

Thus, identification, and especially biometrics, has become absolutely central to migration policy in all its varieties. In particular this concerns taking and storing facial photographs and fingerprints, and checking these in an ever-growing series of national and international databases.

## The future of migration and identification: bodies at the centre

We have been deliberately elaborate in our description of identification and biometrics in relation to migration policy in order to convey the extensive nature of the bureaucracy, as well as the intense personal scrutiny migrants are facing these days. We also hope that this has put the complexity of this policy area in a new light. The simple terms 'migration' and 'migrant' conceal a huge number of people and categories, from Swiss tourists who are staying at a camping site to visit their relations in the Netherlands, to refugees from Somalia who, having resided here for eight years, are now waiting in a 'departure centre' to be deported. There are just as many stories as people, and the Dutch government wants to know exactly what each story entails. Identification, or establishing identity, can either be limited to looking at (and believing) the passport presented, or it can be an extremely complex, increasingly invasive process which really does deserve the name 'investigation'.

'Identity' is every possible answer to the questions 'Who are you?' or 'Who is this?' The answer can take on a number of different forms and can be obtained using a variety of sources, techniques and procedures. The idea that basic details such as the passport data, name, age, sex and nationality reveal the 'true' identity, the 'rock bottom' of identity, is a simplification. They are sufficient in some cases but mostly they are just the starting point of a process that goes much further.

Migration policy in Europe is characterized by a high degree of differentiation regarding assignment of rights and duties to various categories of migrants. To determine a particular individual's entitlements and obligations (for example regarding length of stay, freedom of movement, support), and what that person himself has to do to achieve this (what to request and where, who to report to, what documentary proof to provide, which languages to learn, when to depart), a thorough process of identification is required.

The process itself, which perhaps is best compared to a huge, complicated sorting machine, ultimately creates an extensive series of differentiated categories which are then ascribed to the person in question as 'labels'. These may literally consist of a stamp or label stuck in a passport, or, alternatively, an ID card of a particular type, or just a code or remark in a remote computer file or electronic dossier. All of these are then part of the identity of this person in the receiving country. The labels may sometimes be trivial, but all too often they signify the difference between having a future in the new country or not, between security and insecurity, certainty or uncertainty, freedom or incarceration, hope or despair.

Bearing all this in mind and making a list of all the identity categories our migration policy produces, we arrive at a staggeringly long provisional list containing the almost 90 different ways in which people can be categorized and classified after going through our migration sorting machine (see Table 4.4).

An interesting fact is that this proliferation of identities and categories has, to a large extent, actually only become *possible* with the availability of information systems' endless capacity for data handling. However, these systems do not only enable policy to become so highly differentiated and detailed, they can also be seen as one of the *causes* of that. The

*Table 4.4*  Migrant categories

- migrant or immigrant
- alien
- EU/EER/Swiss subject
- third-country national
- third-country national not requiring visa
- third-country national requiring visa
- third-country national requiring short-stay visa
- third-country national requiring long-stay visa
- third-country national requiring transit visa
- economic migrant
- with or without referee (e.g. employer/relations in the Netherlands or other referees)
- knowledge migrant
- student
- internship student
- au pair
- employee (labourer)
- entrepreneur
- relation/member of family for reunification
- future spouse or partner
- tourist
- leader of religious community
- patient
- healthy (TB)
- unhealthy (TB)
- insured (health insurance)
- uninsured (health insurance)
- can integrate (passed civic integration exam)
- cannot integrate (failed exam)
- has a command of Dutch
- does not have a command of Dutch
- sufficient funds
- insufficient funds
- possesses valid visa
- visa not valid
- possesses valid travel documents (biometric or otherwise)
- does not possess valid travel documents
- legitimate holder of documents
- not the legitimate holder of documents
- regular migrant
- regular resident for defined period
- regular resident for undefined period
- registered traveller
- recognized by SIS
- recognized by Eurodac
- recognized by HAVANK
- recognized by National Research Information Service
- recognized by Basic Facility for Aliens
- recognized by various national, international and European police databases
- unregistered
- identifiable
- not identifiable
- can be enrolled
- cannot be enrolled
- can be verified
- cannot be verified
- authorized traveller
- bona fide traveller/migrant/third-country national
- mala fide traveller/migrant/third-country national
- dangerous (national security and public order etc.)
- not dangerous
- sought by police/warrant for arrest
- refused entry
- admitted
- expelled/repatriated
- refugee
- asylum seeker
- asylum procedure pending
- regular procedure pending
- asylum seeker in accelerated (AC) procedure
- asylum seeker in full (OC) procedure

*Table 4.4* (Continued)

| | |
|---|---|
| • residence in asylum for definite period | • required to report |
| • residence in asylum for indefinite period | • in detention |
| | • has committed fraud |
| • solitary underage asylum seeker | • illegal |
| • age known | • illegal at the border |
| • age dubious | • illegal within a member state |
| • underage according to bone scan | • overstayer |
| • adult according to bone scan | • migrant = aliens number |
| • rejected | • migrant = biometric profile |
| • has exhausted all possible procedures | • migrant = PNR (person – name – record) |

notion that identities are *produced* by and within this technologically enhanced practice is nicely exemplified in the aforementioned 'identity street', located in police stations, where, with the aid of a wide range of machinery, 'input' is processed to produce a verified 'identity'. Also, the mere fact of being registered in one databank (or not) may generate a comment, a code, an attribute, a piece of information that may be added to one's file in yet another databank. The very process of registration of more and more details, together with the increasing number of searches in ever more databanks, supplies new information that is generated by the system itself (e.g. the dactyslip or the comment 'hit in Eurodac' in the Basic Facility for Aliens). This information is sent back and forth between organizations and their systems, and causes the *'digital identity'* of migrants to become increasingly comprehensive, widely distributed and thus even more difficult to process.

It should therefore come as no surprise that resources and techniques are being sought to make things simpler and to bring all the widely distributed bits of identity data back together again. The allocation of an aliens number is one way of doing this. However, the method increasingly used to fulfil this function is biometrics; this technology forms the basis of the proposed simplification of border management in the European Union. As recent plans (discussed in this and other chapters in this book) demonstrate, future policy will be focusing on reducing that large number of categories and the way they have to be processed at the border to three main categories: the *trustworthy, bona fide, desirable traveller*; the *non-trustworthy, undesirable traveller*; and the 'misfits' or '*special categories*' for whom the systems (and especially biometrics) do not work well and for whom exceptional procedures need to be organized (until the people ultimately take their place in one of the first two categories).

The 'front office' of automated identity checks and border cross-ing will depend to a large extent on making not only the travel documents machine-readable, but also the people themselves – the *'machine-readable body'* (Van der Ploeg 2005). The 'back office' will con-sist of the various European and national systems and databanks such as VIS, SIS II, Eurodac, an entry and exit system (still to be developed) and ESTA, made interoperable and linked, and including the databases of law enforcement, intelligence and counterterrorism; biometrics will be the key technology to link them all.

Because biometrics is thus increasing in importance, we will devote this last section to a more in-depth discussion of the socio-political and the normative-ethical aspects involved in the design, implementation and use of such systems.

Within the range of available systems for automated identification of human beings, biometrics is a special case. It is special because it uses the human body itself to identify a person, as opposed to something a person knows or has, like a pin or a document.

To be sure, using the human body for identification is quite com-monplace in itself: in ordinary social interaction, once we have become acquainted, we all identify each other by our bodily appearance and unique features; and if we do not know each other, we use all kinds of bodily clues to at least categorize the strangers that we meet. Even for administrative purposes, using the human body to identify and register individuals is not entirely new: branding, tattooing and using primitive forms of fingerprinting, for example, have already been used in ages long gone (Cole 2001; Caplan 2000). Also, to use ICTs to image, pro-cess and store features of our bodies is being done in medical settings for diagnostic and therapeutic purposes as well, and in ways far more intrusive than any biometric system for identification.

To have automated human identification through biometrics, how-ever, is quite something else. To transform the human *body* into a *machine-readable identifier*, as biometric systems have done for or to us, is in important ways different from any of the above.

To use the body, instead of a pin or document, is, whatever perspective one takes on this, using part of the person themselves. This, of course, is fraught with risks and dangers to basic personal freedom that need to be articulated and controlled. Moreover, biometric systems today are being used in settings and by agencies that, unlike the medical setting, are not precisely geared to helping and curing a person with bodily problems, nor bound by professional confidentiality, but, instead, aim at checking and controlling a basically distrusted person, sharing the information as widely as is legally allowed, and beyond. In other words, the interests served by biometric identification are generally not coinciding with the interests of the person whose body is used, one could say, as a witness for or against itself.

Because of this situation it becomes all the more urgent to inquire into the particularities of what it is that biometric systems do, and how they impact on social and ethical values.

That is why it is even more important to ask ourselves what these biometric systems actually do and what the social and normative implications are. In trying to articulate what might be at stake in widespread use of biometrics – as an aside, a further widespread use of RFID tagging would have to be taken into account here as well – a general feeling persists that the notion of 'privacy' may not quite cover it; bodily integrity, human dignity and social justice should at least be considered as well. It is not sufficient to consider only 'privacy'; the discussion around biometrics is then limited to privacy regarding *information* and data protection. In other words, the discussion is limited to the data generated by biometrics, to the fact that a person is represented simply by data and to whether that person has any control over the data.

Biometrics transforms the physical characteristics of a person into electronic data; in other words, into information that can be processed digitally and that refers to the body of that person. Often a distinction is made between the body itself and the information about that body. The information about the body seems to belong to the domain of privacy (regarding information) while the body itself belongs to the domain of bodily integrity. However, in the case of biometrics, the 'body itself' is treated as information, so the distinction is no longer unequivocal. How can the integrity of the body be respected if, at the same time, it is also a piece of information? Beyond which limits can one say violation is taking place? An additional problem is that we are talking here about *digital* information, meaning that the digital body can be searched remotely – in both time and place. In other words, without the person being present or knowing what is happening.

The question of whether biometrics violates bodily integrity is asked now and again but in doing so attention is only paid to the method of *generating* the biometric data (for example a finger making contact with a sensor). This method would not be regarded as invasive as the investigation is 'on' and not 'in' the body. The data are collected and the biometrics template is then solely regarded as information to be protected, so the more fundamental question regarding bodily integrity is not under discussion here.

Questions relating to social justice are also hardly ever addressed. Practices such as searching databases, profiling and classifying all affect certain groups more than others, which means that they are more vulnerable to social categorization, exclusion and automated decisions, with all the risks that may be attached. Once given a certain label (rightly or otherwise), it is difficult or even impossible to shed this label, and this applies to an even greater extent when biometrics – regarded as infallible – is involved (Van der Ploeg 2002, 2008).

Because of the potentially far-reaching significance of biometrics, we should be looking at it from many different perspectives. In general, we can assume that biometrics – as a technique, as a concept and as a practice – is imprisoned in a number of paradoxes and dualities that make it unavoidably controversial. We describe below the most important of these. As a whole, they pose a real dilemma and this means that biometrics may only be applied after very careful consideration.

## Identification: establishing unicity and category

An interesting thing about the concept of identification is that it is always dual: it is about both determining one's unique identity and assigning into categories – these two aspects are intrinsically interwoven. For example, your unique identity, as testified by your passport, is 'proven' by virtue of the passport being part of a series issued by a government and proclaiming you to be a citizen of a particular country, that is, a member of a particular category. Similarly, a facial image or fingerprint in a police database may help in identifying a particular suspect, but simultaneously defines the person in question as belonging to the category of registered deviants.

This duality should be kept in mind in regard to biometrics' potential for profiling, categorical surveillance and discrimination (Norris and Armstrong 1999; Lyon 2003). Historical examples abound of identification and registration schemes that subsequently enabled all too efficient exclusion of large segments of the population from basic civil rights; in some of the worst instances of 'ethnic cleansing' and genocide in the previous century, national identification schemes are believed to have played such facilitating roles (Longman 2001).

Today, many countries have introduced, or at least discuss the possibility of introducing, national identity cards which now generally are designed to include biometric data. Such national identity card schemes cannot function without central registrations. While preventing identity fraud and improving public services are mentioned as major reasons for this, justifications generally include references to the more systematic interception of certain types of behaviour and surveilling certain categories of people. Central registration of individual identities will always also allow categorization, and with that the possibility of differential targeting is created.

### The two faces of surveillance

It cannot be denied that biometrics is part of surveillance networks. Taking peoples' biometric data, storing, checking and cross-matching them, has the undeniable effect of rendering people more visible, and their movements and actions better known and, ultimately, more controllable.

One of the key issues in all discussions of biometrics is the creation of large, even population-wide databases, such as we are witnessing today in border management and national identification schemes. In terms of surveillance this constitutes the nightmare scenario, and the tendency today is indeed to shift from specific-purpose databases to general monitoring and (pre-emptive) law enforcement.

In addition, it must be noted that these databases will probably prove to be goldmines for data miners with various agendas. 'Knowledge discovery in databases' (KDD) will very likely be practised on biometric databases; associations between biometric and medical characteristics or other traits may be discovered, and new forms of (bio-)profiling could emerge.

However, the question is whether increasing levels of surveillance are inherently negative. Against too bleak views, it is good to remind ourselves constantly of the two sides of the coin. Surveillance is both empowering and subjecting, a condition for distributing rights as well as a means of control.

Besides increasing control over people, creating the possibility of a registered identity is also an acknowledging act: it can be an acknowledgement of citizenship and all its connected entitlements that many people in this world still are deprived from. In this context, the figures provided by UNICEF are enlightening. UNICEF states on its website that some 50 million births go unregistered every year – that is, over 30 per cent of all estimated births worldwide – and explains that, apart from being the first legal acknowledgement of a child's existence, registration of births is fundamental to the realization of a number of rights and a number of basic practical needs, including access to healthcare, immunization, education, and protection from underage forced marriage, employment, conscription or military service. Beyond the individual level, having access to correct demographic data is also instrumental in designing various social programmes and policies aimed at the advancement of particular groups in society (UNICEF 2010).

On the other hand, however, it could be argued that the controlling function of identification practices is produced precisely by making so many rights and entitlements contingent upon them.

Moreover, if practices of surveillance always have this dual nature of being both empowering and subjecting, this should not be taken to mean that the net result is neutral. There needs to be ongoing, careful investigation into the question of 'who gains and who pays', and how exactly groups or individuals are positioned in specific socio-technically mediated practices.

### Security versus privacy and liberty

This theme resonates most with the 'mainstream' debate on biometrics. There is a widely recognized tension between the quest for security on the one hand, and civil liberty and privacy rights on the other. More security (in the form of more accurate and more frequent identification) means less privacy and, hence, less liberty, and vice versa.

The question should be raised to what extent the often used metaphor, in this context, of striking a 'balance' is actually adequate. More security can also mean more privacy and more liberty, of course, since it is hard to imagine what enjoying one's freedom could mean if there is no security and safety in the first place. It may not be necessarily the case that you lose on the one side what you gain on the other.

Perhaps the more relevant question to ask is what and whose security is at stake, and against what and whom exactly protective measures are designed. State security may not be equivalent to citizen security, personal security something entirely different from organizational security. With regard to the question of informational security and the issue of securing access to information, the issue of who may be given authorization to legitimately access data may be more salient in determining impacts on privacy and liberty than database security as such.

Moreover, these questions repeat themselves when security/liberty between same-level entities is concerned: one person's security may mean the end of privacy for another; one state's security policy can mean air-raids on another.

Although in debates on biometrics 'security versus privacy and liberty' usually refers to the relation between state security and civil liberties, even this opposition needs to be deconstructed and concretized in any given situation – who is securing whom against what exactly, and whose and which particular liberties are at stake? When attempting to gain meaningful insight into ethical and social impacts of particular technologies and applications, highly politicized rhetorical terminology and blanket terms need to give way to concrete and specific analysis and diagnosis. That way, chances that the potential for synergies – rather than oppositions and perceptions of the inevitability of trade-offs – are discovered, could increase.

### Technocracy versus democracy

The final theme we wish to highlight is the matter of control over developments and implementations. The main question here is to what extent current developments in biometric identification practices are the result of technology-push and expertocracy, as opposed to being subject to democratic control, and characterized by transparency of the decision-making processes involved.

It can be safely assumed that the average citizen who gets issued a new e-passport with biometric and RFID features will be little aware of when, where or how exactly the information on it will be registered, processed or stored, let alone what this implies for their traceability and basic freedoms. They will trust their government and democratic institutions to take care of proper safeguards that their civil rights are being respected and protected. Mostly, in democratic countries this will be justified, but, of course, democratic governments can be trusted precisely because, and to the extent that, they are held accountable, are checked by parliaments and other overseeing bodies, and required to operate transparently.

There are, however, several factors operative today that preclude full transparency and accountability in decision-making regarding implementation of biometric systems.

First, many decisions concerning the larger, government-implemented biometric applications are presented as part of policy areas such as state security, anti-terrorism and preventive law-enforcement – the so-called third pillar of EC policy – and as such largely exempt from the requirement for full openness to democratic scrutiny, or from the application of data protection and privacy regulations. With the Lisbon Treaty coming into effect, this pillar structure is to be abolished, but what this will do for accountability concerning the migration technologies discussed in this chapter, remains an open question for now.

Next, in the European Union in particular, political and democratic structures are still less than optimal. The European Commission has, for example, the power to issue 'Regulations' that do not require parliamentary approval. Also, many policies and proposals are decided by councils consisting of the assembled national ministers of a particular policy area, far removed from the field of vision of the average citizen, who is still largely focused on national politics. Moreover, some of the relevant overseeing bodies, like the European Data Protection Office and the Article 29 Working Group on Ethics, appear to feel that their assessments, though officially an obligatory passage point, all too often appear to make little difference. Again, with the Lisbon Treaty, this is expected to improve significantly, but many of the policies and technology implementations discussed in this chapter have been decided prior to it coming into effect.

Finally, there is a tendency to present certain aspects as 'technological', thus conceptually closing these matters off from ethical or political debate and scrutiny. What is, and what is not, 'essentially technical' is, however, more often than not, a matter for debate. Something may look like a purely technical matter only by virtue of a lack of ability or willingness to think through societal and ethical consequences, or, conversely, because of a relative technical 'illiteracy'. Thus, debates about central storage versus token-based storage of biometric data, or the use of templates as opposed to 'raw' biometric data, may sound technical to an averagely informed citizen, but their outcomes will have far-reaching ethical and socio-political implications. Similarly, issues like standardization and interoperability, defining the range of what a system will present as a 'match', or the frequency at which an RFID tag emits its signal, are all too often considered technical, whereas such issues are perhaps better understood as examples of the truism *'technology is politics by other means'*.

## Conclusions: issues regarding the machine-readable body

In this chapter, we have shown how biometrics is becoming increasingly important in the identification and verification procedures relating to migrants. The range of uses includes everything from visa requests, e-passports, checking asylum applications in Eurodac (which has been operational for years) and the recently announced EU entry-exit system, to the local implementation of a reporting requirement for asylum seekers. In the context of an already considerable emphasis on digital identification, biometrics is becoming increasingly dominant.

There are many practical advantages to biometric identification; in addition to the aforementioned ones, one can also think of the reduction of cases of mistaken identity caused by the variety of ways of spelling, for example, Asian names, or the much-needed improvement in supervising underage asylum seekers exposed to the risk of being kidnapped by sex-industry exploiters. Despite these advantages, it is still extremely important to keep in mind that every form of identification is fundamentally unstable: neither biometrics nor any other identification technique provides 100 per cent positive, reliable identification. Nevertheless, the champions of biometrics all too often claim just that: in contrast to the unsafe, fallible and fraud-sensitive identification methods based on paper documents, pin codes, passwords, passes and keys, or self-identification ('flight accounts'), biometrics is supposedly objective, safe and fraud-proof. The 'body itself' is used and that body does not lie (Van der Ploeg 1999).

This depiction of the facts should be recognized for the myth it is: the idea that the 'body itself' can be directly consulted is absolutely mistaken. As we have already indicated in our description of the technique (see above), every biometric identification or verification procedure comprises a whole series of steps. Starting with an input signal generated from a physical characteristic, this digital signal is subsequently subjected to a whole series of translations and transfers. Scanning (or the deployment of another input device) is followed by an algorithmic transformation into a (sometimes encrypted) template, which is then sent back and forth through networks (some well protected, others not; some wireless, some not) to be subsequently matched, by using pattern-recognition software, with a previously stored file that was created by a similar series of transformations. Finally, this generates a probabilistic result which is then visually represented on some computer screen. If the body really is 'speaking' here, it is only via a long series of 'translations' like this, based on a 'dictionary' that no one completely understands. In theory, an error can arise at every one of these steps and any data flow runs the risk of being intercepted – fallibilities illustrated by the existence of a rapidly expanding literature on 'spoofing': the technique of leading a biometric system astray by, for example, deploying fake input signals. Moreover, every error margin, however small, very rapidly leads to an extremely large number of errors in systems that are going to be rolled out on a large scale, like the ones discussed in this chapter.

The consequences of all this could be serious for any travellers who may be subjected at the borders to wrongful accusations or refusals, time-wasting fall-back procedures and extra checking, without access to adequate means to defend themselves. It could also become costly for border-management organizations themselves, who will need to spend a lot of time and money on checking and correcting, with the result that the hoped-for increases in efficiency and effectiveness will not materialize. If the importance attached to biometric identification continues to increase in the way it is doing now, the results of these unavoidable system errors will be dramatic for migrants and asylum seekers in particular, for whom so much is at stake.

Another highly relevant point when considering migration and the surveillance of borders is that certain ethnic groups (as well as certain age groups and gender categories) relatively frequently experience problems when biometric systems involving fingerprints, hand shapes and facial characteristics are used (Dessimoz *et al.* 2006). The idea that biometric systems make use of universal and stable physical features (features that *everyone* possesses and that over the years remain *unchanged*) is premised on the fiction that there is such a thing as '*the* human body'. In many situations, this fiction may be relatively unproblematic, and even be of theoretical or practical use. It is a different story, however, when it concerns international migration, family reunification, refugees, asylum seekers and border controls all over the globe. These phenomena, after all, involve the greatest possible diversity of people from all corners of the world, so it is here that we can expect to come across the biggest problems with acquiring 'usable' biometric data and successfully matching them with previously stored ones. This is all the more serious since it is precisely in relation to these groups, for whom so much is at stake, that authorities tend to put a disproportionate amount of faith in biometrics, while often hardly understanding the way it functions.

Despite, or perhaps thanks to, this lack of transparency, a shift is taking place in the power balance between individuals and all sorts of authorities. A shift that, although it does not affect every individual in the same way, is becoming more and more difficult to object to or to resist. The public servant with his finger scanner and computer screen is backed, after all, by the power created by countless network connections, watch lists, search engines, algorithms and enormous numbers of files, profiles and dossiers in faraway databases. The person in front of him, by contrast, only has a story, perhaps some travel documents, and their fingertips, with the credibility of the former two increasingly regarded as inferior to that of the latter.

Now that the informatization of the body has extended to the body of migrants, a group that is often quite vulnerable anyway, proper thought should be given to the way these new forms of control, far removed in place and time from the persons they affect as they may be, are coming ever closer to the skin.

## Notes

1. Previously, regional and local authorities such as landowners (often titled) and town councils exercised these powers.
2. As defined in European Parliament and Council (1995).
3. For a thorough legal analysis of these principles in relation to migration and technology, see Chapter 6 by Brouwer in this book.
4. Officially MRTDs (machine-readable travel documents).
5. This refers to requests for a short-stay visa (C visa) or for a Provisional Residence Permit (D visa). In addition to these two, there is also the transit visa for airports (A visa) and a transit visa for up to five days (B visa).
6. The Civic Integration Examination applies to all those aged 16–65 years who come under the Provisional Residence Permit regulation and who wish to join their future spouse/partner in the Netherlands, or to be reunited with family already living in the Netherlands or to lead a religious congregation. The exam tests basic knowledge of the Dutch language and society and is held at the embassy, using a telephone line connected up to a computer.
7. The number of hits pertaining to this group is, however, relatively small.
8. In the Netherlands, it is the National Police Services Agency (which comes under the Ministry of Home Affairs) that is responsible for the storage and use of data in N-SIS. The IND, that comes under the Ministry of Justice, is responsible for registration of 'third-country nationals'.
9. There seems, for example, to be an automated decision for the purpose of Art. 15, paragraph 1 EC Directive on protection of personal data (95/46). This states that everyone has a right 'not to be subject to a decision which produces legal effects concerning him or significantly affects him and which is based solely on automated processing of data'.
10. This was the method used in 2006 (more recent information not available); the information used to make a decision regarding the issue of a visa could therefore be out of date.
11. The VIS will be introduced gradually; recording of biometric data will be started up at different times in different regions. The expectation is that the VIS will not be fully operational before 2012 (European Union 2008b).
12. Data to be recorded according to ICAO (International Civil Aviation Organization) standards; the same applies to biometric data in passports.
13. Due to the expansion of the EU, a second-generation Schengen Information System (SIS II) is being developed to include the Commission's wish to increase functions, add information categories, link up various observations and give more organizations access.
14. National databanks that are searched include the Dutch police Investigation Registration System (OPS) which contains national tracing and arrest warrants and also those arrest warrants issued by non-Schengen countries.
15. Regarding refusal – a person who is found in the SIS has his/her visa cancelled by the border-control agent who places a 'CANCELLED' stamp on the travel document.

16. This stamp also contains the first letter of the country involved, the border office, date, serial number and a pictogram indicating the type of border (land/sea/air).
17. If the visa holder is exempt from providing fingerprints (diplomats, young children and people from whom it is physically impossible to take fingerprints), no fingerprints are available in the VIS and this will be reported.
18. According to the Protocol Identification and Labelling (PIL), the Municipal Basic Administration (GBA) data determine the standard method for indentifying and registering aliens, and amending and verifying personal data; thus, they cannot be changed by parties in the aliens chain.
19. If it is not possible to take fingerprints of a suitable quality, the best possible results are used and labelled either 'temporary trauma', 'permanent trauma' or 'substandard fingers'.
20. With children of 4–12 years old, an analogue fingerprint sheet is sent to the Dutch National Research Information Service (dNRI) and stored in a card-index system; their biometric characteristics are not scanned and verified.
21. Eurodac (European dactylographic system), operational since 2003, is a European databank containing the fingerprints of asylum seekers, 14 years and older, and of migrants who have crossed the border illegally or were discovered leading an illegal existence in one of the member states. There are thus three categories of fingerprint. Firstly, all asylum applicants (stored for up to ten years); secondly, migrants who crossed the border illegally (stored for up to two years); and thirdly, illegal migrants discovered in one of the member states. The fingerprints of this last category are not stored but merely compared with those in the other two categories. Data are deleted from Eurodac as soon as an asylum seeker has been granted the nationality of a member state. Apart from that, it is necessary to mask the data of asylum seekers who have received a residence permit for asylum for an indefinite period or from refugees that have received a residence permit for asylum for a definite period (Brouwer 1999).
22. For the rest, Eurodac contains only limited information: place and date of requesting asylum, sex, fingerprint data, date fingerprints taken, date sent to the Eurodac central unit and the reference number of the member state which supplied the data.
23. People have to report to the Aliens Police (they function as an enforcement agency) and to the Central Agency for Reception of Asylum Seekers (COA) to check whether reception facilities are being supplied rightfully or whether they should be stopped (referred to as 'in-house registration').
24. The COA is now responsible for ensuring the reporting requirement is carried out. However, the Aliens Police are still responsible for legal enforcement.
25. One of the measures in this policy document in relation to aliens who have to leave the Netherlands because of the asylum procedure is 'ensuring the alien remains available for identity or nationality checks by linking the reporting requirement with in-house registration'. This policy document suggests that both processes, being very labour-intensive and difficult to perform consistently, should be merged and supported by automated systems that make use of biometrics.
26. This could be because the person who reports in has to be issued with a document or because this person is not the one to whom the pass was

issued. But there is also the possibility of 'false rejection'; in other words, something went wrong when scanning, processing and comparing the fingerprint. Perhaps the finger was placed on the scanner too slowly or the finger had been damaged by physical labour, or errors occurred during data processing; biometric systems are not at all infallible and all show either a 'false acceptance rate' (FAR) or a 'false rejection rate' (FRR).

27. The Aliens Police are responsible for supervising aliens within the country borders; they supervise procedures such as the reporting requirement for asylum seekers and holders of a short-stay visa, but also have the task of checking for illegal aliens and asylum seekers, tracing them and expelling them, preventing any trouble and ensuring illegal persons are not misused. The Royal Netherlands Military Police focus on the surveillance of the external borders of the Schengen territory (i.e. airports and harbours – except in Rotterdam where this is the task of the Harbour Police) and on providing a 'mobile surveillance of aliens' involving random checks at the Belgian and German borders, in trains, aeroplanes and boats.

# Bibliography

Aa, H. van der (2007) 'Project Meldplicht en Biometrie. Van complexe meervoud naar eenduidige enkelvoud.' Paper presented at the Nationaal Biometrie Congres, Utrecht, 20 September.

Boekhoorn, P. and T. Speller (2006) *Vreemdelingenpolitie in transitie. Een nadere verkenning van het operationeel vreemdelingentoezicht* (Nijmegen: Bureau Boekhoorn Sociaal Wetenschappelijk Onderzoek).

Brouwer, E.R. (1999) 'De Eurodac Conventie', *Privacy & Informatie*, 2(1): 15.

Brouwer, E. (2007) *Digital Borders and Real Rights: Effective Remedies for Third Country Nationals in the Schengen Information System* (Nijmegen: Wolf Legal Publishers).

Caplan, J. (ed.) (2000) *Written on the Body: The Tattoo in European and American History* (London: Reaktion Books).

Cavoukian, A. and A. Stoianov (2007) *Biometric Encryption: A Positive-Sum Technology that Achieves Strong Authentication, Security AND Privacy* (Toronto: Information and Privacy Commissioner Ontario).

CINOP, LTS and Ordinate (2005) *Verantwoording Toets Gesproken Nederlands* ('s-Hertogenbosch: CINOP).

Cole, S.A. (2001) *Suspect Identities: A History of Fingerprinting and Criminal Identification* (Cambridge, MA: Harvard University Press).

Dessimoz, D., J. Richiardi, C. Champod and A. Drygajlo (2006) *MBioD: Multimodal Biometrics for Identity Documentation: State-of-the-Art*, Research Report, University of Lausanne. http://danishbiometrics.files.wordpress.com/2009/08/90_264_file.pdf.

Dutch House of Representatives (Year 2003–04) 29 344, no. 1.

Dutch Ministry of Justice (2007) *Protocol Identificatie en Labeling*, 8 March (The Hague: Stafdirectie Coordinatie Vreemdelingenketen).

Dutch National Ombudsman (2008) 'Man dertien jaar slachtoffer van identiteitsfraude', Press Release, The Hague, 23 October. www.nationaleombudsman.

nl/nieuws/persberichten/2008/Mandertienjaarlangslachtoffervanidentiteits fraude.asp.

Engberg, S.J., M.B. Harning and C.D. Jensen (2004) 'Zero-knowledge Device Authentication: Privacy and Security Enhancing RFID Preserving Business Value and Consumer Convenience.' Paper presented at the Second Annual Conference on Privacy, Security and Trust, New Brunswick, Canada.

European Commission (2008) Communication from the Commission to the European Parliament, Council, the European Economic and Social Committee and the Committee of the Regions. *Next Steps in Border Management in the EU*, 13 February (Brussels).

European Parliament and Council (1995) *Directive 95/46/EG. On the Protection of Individuals with Regard to the Processing of Personal Data and on the Free Movement of Such Data* (Brussels).

European Union (2006) *Regulation (EC) No. 562/2006 of the European Parliament and of the Council of 15 March 2006 Establishing a Community Code on the Rules Governing the Movement of Persons Across Borders (Schengen Borders Code)*. PbEU, 13 April, L105/1.

European Union (2008a) *Regulation (EC) No. 296/2008 of the European Parliament and of the Council of 11 March 2008 Amending Regulation (EC) No. 562/2006 Establishing a Community Code on the Rules Governing the Movement of Persons Across Borders (Schengen Borders Code), as Regards the Implementing Powers Conferred on the Commission*, PbEU, 9 March, L97/60.

European Union (2008b) *Regulation (EC) No. 767/2008 of the European Parliament and of the Council of 9 July 2008 concerning the Visa Information System (VIS) and the Exchange of Data between Member States on Short-Stay Visas (VIS Regulation)*, PbEU, 13 August, L218/60.

Longman, T. (2001) 'Identity Cards, Ethnic Self-Perception, and Genocide in Rwanda', in J. Caplan and J. Torpey (eds) *Documenting Individual Identity: The Development of State Practices in the Modern World* (Princeton University Press).

Lyon, D. (ed.) (2003) *Surveillance as Social Sorting: Privacy, Risk, and Digital Discrimination* (London and New York: Routledge).

Migratie Info (2008) Interview with Chief of Mission Joost van der Aalst: 'Migratiebeheer vraagt om dialoog', no. 1. www.iom-nederland.nl/nieuws/ migratie_info_categorie.asp?miaId=176.

Norris, C. and G. Armstrong (1999) *The Maximum Surveillance Society: The Rise of CCTV* (Oxford: Berg).

Ploeg, I. van der (1999) ' " Eurodac" and the Illegal Body: The Politics of Biometric Identity', *Ethics and Information Technology*, 1(4): 37–44.

Ploeg, I. van der (2002) 'Biometrics and the Body as Information: Normative Issues in the Socio-Technical Coding of the Body', in D. Lyon (ed.) *Surveillance as Social Sorting: Privacy, Risk, and Automated Discrimination* (New York: Routledge).

Ploeg, I. van der (2005) *The Machine-Readable Body: Essays on Biometrics and the Informatization of the Body* (Maastricht: Shaker).

Ploeg, I. van der (2006) 'Borderline Identities: The Enrollment of Bodies in the Technological Reconstruction of Borders', in T. Monahan (ed.) *Surveillance and Security: Technological Politics and Power in Everyday Life* (London and New York: Routledge).

Ploeg, I. van der (2008) 'Machine-Readable Bodies: Biometrics, Informatisation and Surveillance', in E. Mordini and M. Green (eds) *Identity, Security, and Democracy: Social, Ethical and Policy Implications of Automated Systems for Human Identification*, NATO Science Series: Human and Societal Dynamics, vol. 49 (Amsterdam: IOS Press).

Stratton, A. (2008) 'Personal Data on Thousands of Prisoners Is Lost', *The Guardian*, 22 August.

Torpey, J. (2000) *The Invention of the Passport: Surveillance, Citizenship and the State* (Cambridge University Press).

Turk, A. and F. Pizzetti (2008) *Comments of the Article 29 Data Protection Working Party and the Working Party on Police and Justice on COM(2008) 29, COM(2008) 68 and COM(2008) 67* (Brussels: Article 29 Data Protection Working Party).

UNICEF (2010) *Birth Registration: Child Protection from Violence, Exploitation and Abuse*. www.unicef.org/protection/index_birthregistration.html. Accessed 31 January 2010.

Unisys and European Biometrics Portal (2006) 'Biometrics in Europe', *Trendreport 2006*, Brussels: 1–113.

## Websites consulted

www.coa.nl, most recent search July 2008
www.identiteitsdocumenten.nl, most recent search June 2008
www.ind.nl, most recent search July 2008
www.justitie.nl, most recent search May 2008
www.kmar.nl, most recent search July 2008
www.minbuza.nl, most recent search May 2008
www.politie.nl, most recent search June 2008
www.regering.nl, most recent search June 2008
www.szw.nl, most recent search May 2008
www.vluchtelingenwerk.nl, most recent search June 2008
www.vrom.nl, most recent search May 2008

# 5
# Migration Technology and Public Responsibility

*Albert Meijer*

## Using powerful technologies responsibly?[1]

As stated in many other parts of this book, information systems are crucial for implementing migration policies. Information systems play a key role in the admissions procedure as well as in tracing illegal aliens. In addition, these systems are of great importance for the cooperation among the different administrative levels, different countries and different organizations involved in these policies. The features offered by information technology are deployed in many ways. According to the proponents of the use of information technology, this technology contributes to the effectiveness and legitimacy of migration policies. They also argue that information systems can facilitate an objective assessment of asylum requests and improve the coordination among the various parties involved.

However, it also appears that the use of these technologies is not without risks. The most significant risk is that using technologies can affect the precision with which individual decisions are taken and actions carried out. Opponents of the use of information technology emphasize that migrants who have been wrongly registered may not be dealt with correctly and therefore run into problems. The incorrect use of information from these systems when tracing migrants can lead to them being treated wrongfully. Furthermore, if the information provided by migrants is insufficiently protected, third parties will have access to extremely sensitive information.

Beyond the debate between proponents and opponents of the use of information technology in migration policies, lies a fundamental debate about the instruments governments should be allowed to use in the implementation of migration policies. Winner (1986: 52) stresses: 'What appears to be merely instrumental choices are better seen as choices about the form of social and political life a society builds, choices about the kinds of people we want to become.' An analysis of the choices involved in the implementation of information technology in migration policies is needed to feed a debate about these choices. This chapter aims to contribute to these choices by highlighting new patterns of government responsibility.

Information systems give governments access to powerful resources and it is essential that they use these resources responsibly – both to deploy all the available features properly and to minimize risks. The creation of guarantees for correct usage is paramount here. Of course, a responsible approach does not only mean that governments need to be careful in their use of technology but also careful with regard to *not* using technology. Responsible usage means ensuring that new technology is used if it can help to ensure that better decisions are taken. The theme of responsible use of technology is a key theme in the philosophy of technology, and various philosophers have warned against irresponsible use of technology. More specifically, Winner (1977) calls our attention to the risk of 'technics-out-of-control' and Galbraith (1968) warns us of the danger that technology will develop its own logic which may run counter to the intentions of the users and the common interest.

This chapter explores how exactly the use of information technology affects government responsibility. This will not be a legislative exploration of responsibilities but rather an organizational and administrative analysis. Thus, it is not so much an analysis of the formal rules as an account of what actually happens in practice.[2] It should also be said that this chapter does not claim to be exhaustive: a comprehensive exploration of this issue demands a whole book and not just one chapter. The aim of this chapter, therefore, is to generate critical questions regarding government responsibilities for using information technology.[3]

In each member state, many parties are involved in implementing migration policy and each party has its own responsibilities. The diversity is enormous. To enable an analysis of mechanisms and patterns, this chapter will focus on the Netherlands. A case study of the Netherlands will highlight mechanisms and patterns which will arguably also exist, in some form, in the other member states. The objective of this analysis is to stimulate more responsible practices of technology use in line with Winner's (1986) argument that technology criticism is not about rejecting technology but rather about stimulating better technological practices.

## Responsibility: administrative interpretation

The concept of 'responsibility' is one that is often and easily used in discussions about politics and administration. Members of Parliament often emphasize that the relevant minister is responsible and, if something is unclear, the responsibilities require a crystal-clear definition. An unambiguous definition of responsibilities is generally regarded as an essential prerequisite if a government is to function both effectively and legitimately.

In fact, however, the concept of responsibility can embrace a multitude of opinions. It is an 'essentially contested concept' in that there are many ways of interpreting it, all of which could be plausible, but which do not always tolerate each other well (Bovens 1990: 29). I will use the concept 'responsibility' to evaluate whether governments use technology in the proper manner. Responsibility is regarded here as a combination of a task and a virtue (Bovens 1990: 34, 40–7).[4] An example of interpreting 'responsibility' in this way is a statement such as: the Justice Minister bears his responsibility for migration policy well. This means it is clear the minister is responsible for migration policy and, what is more, this minister takes his tasks and duties seriously.

Does a particular authority have sufficient information about what is happening in order to assume its responsibility? Does the authority have the means to shoulder this responsibility? My empirical focus here differs from the legal perspective in which the emphasis is on the liability that becomes an issue whenever laws or rules are not obeyed. A legal interpretation of responsibility is not necessarily a guarantee for responsible actions in complex organizations if the latter pay no attention to all the possibilities for acting in a responsible manner. If one takes things from a cybernetics point of view, therefore, one can stipulate extra conditions. 'Acting responsibly' also implies that it may be possible to influence how an organization acts and that there is sufficient information available to know how and when action will be taken. Control instruments and information sources are important additions to the legal perspective on responsibility.

When exactly can one say that technology is being used responsibly? First of all, there are the demands arising from the responsibility to perform tasks. Strom demonstrates how a parliamentary democracy can be regarded as a succession of delegations: from voter to parliamentarian, to public administrator, to public sector employee (Strom 2000). In order to analyse the political, administrative and public sector responsibilities, it is important to look at the three links, namely, parliamentarians, public managers and public sector employees and to investigate their responsibilities.

- *Political responsibilities*. It is the responsibility of those who are chosen by the people to represent the interests of the people ('acting for the people') and in addition to take decisions for the general good ('standing for a particular idea'). They should relate to technology in such a way that it is deployed in the interests of the people. Furthermore, the decisions taken on technology should be made carefully.
- *Management responsibilities*. Public managers are responsible for ensuring an adequate implementation of decisions: the technologies should be used in such a way that they lead to the desired effect. What is more, undesirable side effects should be prevented.
- *Responsibilities of public sector employees*. Public sector (or government) employees are required to make the right decisions about using technology in individual cases. These considerations should be based on general rules laid down by those politically responsible. These general rules should be applied in specific situations and should also do justice to the characteristics of the individual situation.

Even if tasks are clearly assigned at these three levels, the question still remains as to whether public officials then interpret these tasks in the proper manner. The following criterion is crucial:

- *A serious and autonomous interpretation of performing one's role*. Using technology responsibly means doing so in the way that is expected of someone performing the duties of a public servant or someone in a particular position. In order to be able to use technology responsibly, the acting public servant or organization needs to have a certain amount of autonomy and to act according to their own observations and norms. Public sector employees and organizations should have a level of autonomy that matches the role they have been given, as defined by legislative rules.

Dutiful behaviour implies more than a serious and autonomous interpretation of performing one's role. In addition, the following criteria apply to 'responsibility as a virtue' (Bovens 1990: 40–7):

- *Adequate perception of and attention to any possible violation of standards.* The use of technology should be accompanied by an awareness of the possible dangers and by a consideration of conflicting norms and interests. Will the technology lead to undesirable results for the individual? The possible consequences of using technology and more especially the consequences for others should be taken into account.

- *Assessment of behaviour using a consistent code.* Technology can only be used responsibly if a moral code (and not an emotion) is used as the ground rule. Anyone should be able to assess the manner of using that technology and to find it understandable. Naturally, these codes apply mainly to the behaviour of public managers and public sector employees.

I will use this normative model to analyse the use of technology in migration policies. Are tasks defined in such a way that the political-administrative system can use the migration technology in a responsible manner? Can those involved interpret the tasks they have been entrusted with in a proper manner? Through interviews and document study, I have investigated the problem areas associated with (1) the use of technology in one policy-implementation agency, (2) the use of a technological system in the chain of responsible organizations and (3) technological systems that facilitate international collaboration. In all these situations, I will assess changes in political, management and civil servants' responsibilities. On the basis of the findings I will describe shifts in patterns of government responsibility. This analysis does not pretend to be exhaustive and only focuses on one member state. This chapter will, however, show which problems can arise and thus demand the attention of government, politics and society to prevent the risk of 'technics-out-of-control'.

## Responsible use of technology in policy implementation agencies?[5]

The Dutch Immigration and Naturalization Service (IND) is a large administrative government organization that deals with large numbers of requests from aliens. INDIS is the IND Information System which processes these requests. The system comprises various components such as a database with information about all aliens and the Decision Support System (DSS) which contains knowledge about all formal rules and regulations concerning requests from aliens.

First of all, I would like to consider the political responsibilities for INDIS. Are these interpreted properly? A responsible manner of using ICT demands that political decisions be taken with care to avoid technology being deployed in a careless or incorrect way. Recent events at the IND indicate that political responsibilities are not always met. In 2005, the Dutch Court of Audit was very critical about the use of information technology within the IND, stating that systems were not well coordinated and that databases were contaminated (Netherlands Court of Audit, 'Immigration and Naturalization Service IND', Dutch House of Representatives, Year 2004–05, 30 240, nos. 1–2). This critical report did not come as a surprise to the IND: 'In the years previous to that report, the IND had got themselves into difficulties. There was nothing new in that report from the Court of Audit' (Interview IND, 8 April 2008). The problems that occurred in 2004 were, according to the IND and also to the Court of Audit, mainly due to political decisions with regard to transferring tasks from the police to the IND (Interview IND, 8 April 2008; interview Netherlands Court of Audit, 11 March 2008). All the information from the police was transferred to the IND in just two nights. The IND received boxes full of information from the police and had to take on another new and heavy task. 'Our system could not cope with this and neither could our method of thinking' (Interview IND, 8 April 2008). This just goes to show that political decisions, taken with insufficient consideration of the problems of implementation, lead to irresponsible use of technology. In a strongly politicized area such as migration policy, this is certainly not surprising. The interviewees at the Court of Audit: 'We also looked at the implementation of new information systems. We noticed that warnings of incorrectly functioning systems were ignored. When one is under political pressure, one has to carry on' (Interview Netherlands Court of Audit, 11 March 2008).

Political pressure as a reason for using technology irresponsibly and with insufficient regard for the consequences of certain choices is a given fact in the literature on crisis situations. Romzek and Dubnick described in a classic article how the Challenger space shuttle disaster could be ascribed to political pressure on NASA to carry out sufficient launches (Romzek and Dubnick 1987). The emphasis on the number of launches was more important than professional quality and this led to warnings about possible problems with the launch being ignored. The political pressure on the IND has not led to such visible disasters but the insidious influence was enormous and led to many problems in implementing migration policy.

An aspect directly related to political responsibility is the responsibility held by civil service management. The expansion of information systems over the years had led to information-management problems within the IND. The present facilities consist of many different databases that are not directly linked to each other. The Dutch Court of Audit report also demonstrated that the IND made incorrect estimates regarding the implementation of information technology; this was probably due to the reorganizations that were taking place (Dutch House of Representatives, Year 2004–05, 30 240, nos. 1–2; Interview Netherlands Court of Audit, 11 March 2008). A new system was put into place while the underlying data structure was still incomplete. 'The new system was like a Ferrari on a muddy road' (Interview IND, 8 April 2008). A link was also made to the Municipal Basic Data Administration even though insufficient information about the underlying coding was available. These findings indicate that management responsibilities could not be exerted properly since technological possibilities were overestimated and the difficulties of implementing such systems underestimated.

At the bottom level of public sector organizations, officers within the IND take decisions – within limited discretionary powers – about requests from aliens to be admitted to the country.[6] The role of INDIS, or more specifically the Decision Support System (DSS), in this decision-making is important. Officially, the DSS simply advises the decision-processing officers, but in practice it has a controlling nature. 'The advice indicated by the DSS is often compelling. You are immediately placed in the correct decision pathway. The decision-processing officer is then presented with the question: do you wish to deal with this matter in the DSS? Everyone then says "yes".' The official decision is also made using INDIS/DSS. The DSS even has some influence on the recording of transcriptions of interviews and of minutes. 'The minutes are written using information from the dossier but they also coincide with the questions that will be asked by the DSS' (Interview IND, 8 April 2008). The decision-processing officers are not familiar with the structure of the DSS: 'Decision-processing officers have never seen the decision tree. The DSS has seven levels and is rather complicated' (Interview IND, 8 April 2008). The use of such systems raises questions with regard to the responsibility held by individual public servants. Are they able to take decisions in a responsible manner if they do not know how the decision has been made? Van den Hoven talks in such cases of 'epistemic dependence' (Van den Hoven 1998), meaning that users of the system are not so much dependent on technological systems for their behaviour as for their observations. They can no longer think outside the system.

Bovens and Zouridis indicate – in a theory that can also be applied to the DSS – that the responsibility of the individual for performing tasks is being replaced by the responsibility of the 'system level bureaucrats' (Bovens and Zouridis 2002). These researchers believe that problems arise if the new responsibilities are insufficiently embedded in the task. One wonders whether there really is a problem in this case. The DSS is basically made up of 'aliens circulars', which are changes to the legislation and thus come under parliamentary control. At least 50 are produced every year. By directly linking the decision tree to parliamentary control, the responsibility of the 'system level bureaucrats' would seem to be clearly defined. In practice, however, this link is not always straightforward. Certain legal forms of reasoning are unsuitable for incorporation into a decision tree. Systems developers then have to take the initiative to make the legislation more precise, to fit in with the system. The task responsibility of these system-level bureaucrats is then raised to a higher level and can interfere with the task responsibilities of parliamentarians.

There is another, more optimistic, way of looking at how migration policy is implemented at the level of the individual: systems can provide a guarantee that expertise is present in the organization. At the beginning of the twenty-first century, the IND had to take on several hundred new employees to deal with additional tasks. This meant that, for a while, employees with relatively little expertise were issuing the decisions (Interview Netherlands Court of Audit, 11 March 2008). That led to problems, but these could be solved to a certain extent by using information systems. In other words, knowledge can be stored in a system and technology can guarantee an adequate implementation of a policy.

## Responsible use of technology throughout the chain of organizations?[7]

Establishing responsibilities for the use of technology at the level of the policy-implementation agency poses many questions, but shaping the responsibilities for technology used in the whole chain of organizations is even more complicated. The chain of responsibility for Dutch migration policy is large and complex. A lack of management and coordination can lead to various types of problems such as missed deadlines (Interview Netherlands Court of Audit, 11 March 2008). When Court of Audit employees were interviewed, they indicated this could mean that one organization had to compensate for the errors made by another: 'The IND is tackled about the errors made by others who use the information provided by municipalities and posts abroad' (Interview Netherlands Court of Audit, 11 March 2008).

An essential technology for bringing about collaboration within the policy chain is the Aliens Information Interface (Dutch abbreviation: BVV) (see also Chapter 4 by Van der Ploeg and Sprenkels in this book). Any discussions about responsibility and technology in the chains of organizations will mainly be focused on this facility. Questions regarding responsibility can refer to decision-making about technological systems as well as their use. Both aspects are discussed here. I will also specifically address collaboration with private parties because this type of collaboration raises questions regarding the interpretation of public responsibility for technology.

The aim of the BVV is to make it easier to exchange information about aliens.[8] Information exchange is, after all, only possible if an alien has an identity that remains the same. If someone has more than one identity, the system cannot function. The focal point in the BVV is therefore the unique aliens number that all aliens are allocated when they first come into contact with the government in order to obtain a work or study visa, during an asylum procedure, or if arrested as an illegal person. This means that four organizations can enter an alien's details in the BVV: the Ministry of Foreign Affairs, the IND, the Royal Military Police and the Aliens Police. Various organizations in the chain can request information from the system. The BVV can be represented as shown in Figure 5.1.

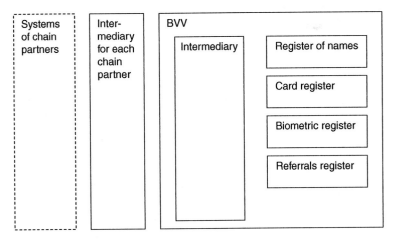

*Figure 5.1*   Aliens Information Interface (BVV)

The development of the BVV can be regarded as an attempt to use technology in a responsible manner. For example, the National Ombudsman noticed in 2002 that the chain partners all used their own registration systems and that these were not linked to each other. This meant there could be no automatic check of any erroneous personal details (National Ombudsman 2003).[9] The National Ombudsman concluded this was one of the reasons so many citizens had complained. The BVV was a reaction to this conclusion and a manner of solving the collaboration problems.

Chain collaboration raises questions about the division of political and management responsibilities. Which politician is able to take responsible decisions about collaboration within the chain? Which administrator within this complex collaborative situation is able to interpret their responsibilities adequately? In this cooperation, we see complexity both in the number of actors involved and in the multilevel aspects of governance. The coordination of collaboration for alien affairs centres around the Coordination Group for Alien Affairs (CGV). The principal members of the CGV are the Ministry of Foreign Affairs, the Central Agency for Reception of Asylum Seekers, the Royal Military Police, IND, Aliens Police, Seaport Police Rotterdam and the Dutch Repatriation and Departure Service. The partners are the Council for the Judiciary, Legal Aid Council and the Custodial Institutions Service. The coordination group is a consultation group but also a steering group for large computerization projects. 'There is no single rule regarding decision-making. It is mainly a question of common interests. Computerization deals, by its very nature, with common interests' (Interview Ministry of Justice, 22 April 2008). Because decisions have to be taken at different levels, it becomes increasingly complex. In addition to the above-mentioned strategic level, decision-making also takes place at functional and operational levels. At the functional level, the chain partners within the Steering Group for Chain Computerization consult each other; operational management is the responsibility of the Facility Organization of the Dutch Police Force.

This complexity involved in decision-making and in shaping the BVV raises the question as to what extent the parties involved have sufficient insight into the choices made about the BVV. Or is the link between technical matters at an operational level and the management choices made at a strategic level too complex? It is possible to discover the consequences of various actions by monitoring the quality of the information system. The quality of the BVV is checked by regular trend reports on the quality of the information. An auditing process has also been agreed: the correct application of the protocol is audited every two years. This form of monitoring and auditing allows attention to be paid at a systematic level to the consequences of breaking the norms.

When there is collaboration on using technological systems within a policy chain, the implementation of migration policy can also lead to problems for the responsible managers. The following example clearly demonstrates the dilemmas posed by collaborating on technical systems. The Dutch Court of Audit noticed that the length of time required to process requests from aliens was being insufficiently monitored because each chain partner was only concerned with their own timing. 'Then, the municipality front offices were removed and this had a positive effect. Now [the IND] are in charge.... An advantage of this change is that more expertise is present at the enquiry desks, which is better for dealing with difficult cases. A disadvantage of the front offices being removed from the municipalities is that travelling time has increased. Some people now have to travel [a long distance] for matters previously dealt with by their own municipality.... This can be regarded as a considerable deterioration in service' (Interview IND, 8 April 2008). In this example, the pros and cons of working in chains are clear: working in a chain can lead to coordination problems but the integration of functions into one single organization leads to a lack of flexibility.

One specific question that arises for members of a chain is the involvement of private parties, in, for example, various aspects of granting visas at the diplomatic posts abroad. In the future, all the personal details of those requiring a visa will be entered into the system, even for short-stay visas. This leads to a discussion of outsourcing in its various gradations; extensive forms can lead to resistance. 'Parliament is not in favour of this. One gets the idea that a travel agency in Lagos can enter data into the BVV' (Interview Ministry of Justice, 22 April 2008). The only alternative is to send Dutch personnel to all the posts, and that would be too expensive. This is the problem of shifting responsibilities for public tasks over to private parties. The Dutch Scientific Council for Government Policy states that an adequate combination of guarantees is necessary when public tasks are transferred to private agencies. The question in this case is whether, in light of the distance, there can be sufficient guarantees against inadequate implementation of the public tasks related to migration. Can a Dutch minister ensure that private parties in faraway countries use IT in migration policies correctly?

## Responsible use of technology in international collaboration?[10]

Due to the Schengen Treaty, a great deal of coordination on migration policy takes place between the member countries. The development and use of information systems is one way of streamlining and enhancing this collaboration. However, the use of these systems does raise questions about responsibilities that are partly to do with European decision-making and partly with the character of new technologies. This chapter contains discussions of the most important European systems and, with these as examples, of the issue of responsibility and technology.

The Schengen Information System (SIS) was developed to support the implementation of the Schengen Treaty of 1985 (Kroon 1997). This treaty provided for the discontinuation of internal border controls between the member countries and raised the question of how the controls at the external borders could be coordinated. That is why the SIS was developed and in 1995 implemented. The SIS consists of a large database in Strasbourg, with separate systems in the member states. In the Netherlands, the National Police Services Agency manages the N-SIS register. The SIRENE Office is responsible for daily data-traffic exchange. The N-SIS and the SIS are linked up permanently.

The SIS contains entries which enable the detection of goods (especially stolen or missing vehicles and stolen identity documents) and persons. The Schengen countries enter these data but there are no specific criteria on who/what should be entered except the broad provisions in Articles 95–100 of the Schengen Implementation Agreement. In general, for persons, this refers to: persons who should be arrested and extradited, aliens who should be refused admission, missing persons, persons sought in relation to criminal procedures (witnesses) and persons who should be allowed admission as part of discreet checks (e.g. drug smuggling). In other words, the SIS mainly contains data on aliens who should be refused admission by the border-control officers. In the Netherlands, this system refers to the entry 'ONGEW' (declared undesirable according to Article 67 of the Aliens Act) or to 'OVR' (undesirable alien). When visas are requested at the external border, a check is made of whether the alien has been entered as ONGEW or OVR and, if this proves to be the case, he/she is generally refused admission to the country (Aliens Circular 2000 (A), 9.2.1 and 9.2.2).

At present, the successor of the 1995 version of the SIS is being developed, SIS II. It is basically a modernized version of the old SIS and will be more accessible for a larger number of states. One important difference is that biometric data are being added to SIS II, to be ready for identification and verification. Another difference is that links will be made between different entries, for example between persons and goods.

The SIS has led to a great deal of discussion and criticism among academics, refugee organizations and others. Moreover, the Dutch National Ombudsman has received various complaints about the system and its effects, and various cases have been brought to court. Tables 5.1 and 5.2 present an overview of these cases.

It is clear that registrations in the SIS can lead to problems.[11] One might take the view that this number of cases is not particularly high, considering the extremely large number of registrations and the amount of processing. The conclusion would then be that the use of the SIS leads to relatively few problems. Another interpretation is, however, that this is just the tip of the iceberg and that most of the cases involving problems with the SIS do not reach the National Ombudsman or the Administrative Court for one reason or another.

The EU Visa Information System (EU VIS) is currently under construction. Since the Schengen Treaty, the policy relating to visas has become one of the most harmonized of EU matters. All the countries have the same visa, and a uniform policy and a uniform issue (sticker in the passport) were already in place. A uniform system of registration would then make this system watertight and it would prevent 'visa shopping'. In June 2008, the Agricultural Council agreed to the wording of the Council Regulation,[12] but the European Parliament has still to agree to this Regulation. There is still political discussion, particularly on data protection and the use of personal details. The design of EU VIS has largely been thought out. It contains personal details, visa information and biometric characteristics (fingerprints). The European Commission requested the development of the system and a private party did the development work. EU VIS, although meant to resemble the SIS, will have a much larger database. All the countries have their own information intermediary to link the system to national systems.

Which questions about responsibility are raised by the SIS and EU VIS? A well-known problem for those assuming political responsibility for European decision-making is the complexity and the multitude of parties involved. This problem has certainly arisen in making decisions about the EU VIS through a 'co-decision' procedure which requires the approval of both the Council (in this case the Justice and Home Affairs Council) and the European Parliament. The initiative to create the EU

*Table 5.1* Matters relating to the SIS handled by the National Ombudsman

| Report | Complaint | Role information system | Decision |
|---|---|---|---|
| 1997/304 | Information from IND not correct | Necessary information was inaccessible | Allowed. Request for Provisional Residence Permit took too long |
| 1998/164 | Wrongfully entered in OPS and arrested | Incorrect registration in OPS and SIS | Allowed. Data should have been removed |
| 1999/300 | Not informed soon enough about entry in SIS | Entry in SIS prevented accused from travelling | Allowed: information too limited |
| 1999/420 | CRI refused to remove registration from SIS | Requester believed registration to be unlawful | Proper. Registration is not the responsibility of CRI |
| 2002/078 | Granting of Provisional Residence Permit refused | Incorrect name entered in OPS | Allowed: incorrect information entered and insufficient checking |
| 2002/087 | Granting of Provisional Residence Permit wrongfully delayed | No entry in SIS | Allowed: information too limited |
| 2003/023 | Time required to grant Provisional Residence Permit; no information from SIS | Requester wished to see information in SIS | Procedure to obtain information from SIS carried out correctly |
| 2003/388 | Delay to granting Provisional Residents Permit; not well informed | Entry in SIS done in Germany | Dismissed: correct procedure. Allowed: information provision |
| 2007/199 | Held by Military Police too long | Linking of information with the wrong person | Dismissed: correct procedure. Allowed: information provision |

OPS = Investigation Registration System; CRI = Criminal Investigation Information Service.

*Table 5.2* Cases at the Administrative Court relating to the SIS

| Court case | Request | Role information system | Decision |
| --- | --- | --- | --- |
| LJN: AW2424 | Remove entry in SIS | Entry in SIS | Allowed |
| LJN: AA6557 | Remove entry in SIS | Entry in SIS | Dismissed |
| LJN: AR7219 | Remove entry in SIS | Entry in SIS | Italy decides |
| LJN: BB6132 | Spain appealed against request to remove entry from SIS | Entry in SIS | Dismissed |
| LJN: AU3548 | Remove entry in SIS | Entry in SIS | Dismissed |
| LJN: BA1316 | Remove entry in SIS | Entry in SIS | Dismissed |
| LJN: AR3286 | Unlawful arrest at Schiphol | No entry in SIS, but arrested | Allowed |
| LJN: BA3547 | Accused wants to remain in the Netherlands, despite SIS entry | Entry in SIS | Dismissed |
| LJN: AT9961 | Unlawful arrest | No entry in SIS, but arrested | Allowed |
| LJN: BA3169 | Remove entry in SIS | Entry in SIS | Dismissed |
| LJN: BA2132 | Remove entry in SIS | Entry in SIS | Allowed |
| LJN: AW2427 | Remove entry in SIS | Entry in SIS | Allowed |
| LJN: AA5370 | Remove entry in SIS | Entry in SIS | Dismissed |
| LJN: BC3296 | Entry to the Netherlands unlawfully refused; in transit | Entry in SIS | Allowed |

VIS came from the Commission and this was subsequently discussed in both the Council and the EP. Prior to the discussion in the Council, there was a discussion in the Netherlands to determine the country's standpoint; a working group was set up to look at the financial consequences and to decide which organizations would be affected by the proposal. The working group's standpoint was discussed by the relevant ministers. During the meeting in Brussels to decide on the EU VIS, the Ministry of Foreign Affairs supplied the spokesperson, but representatives of Foreign Affairs, Justice (Immigration Policy directorate) and the IND were also present. Before the meetings, preliminary consultations took place in which the Royal Military Police and the director of the Immigration Coordination Department at the Justice Ministry were also present. Prior to meetings of the Council working group, Foreign Affairs prepared instructions that were presented to the departmental heads. This meant there was no political involvement during the discussions on the EU

VIS (except where there were points at issue between member states or ministries). However, all topics for the Justice and Home Affairs Council were discussed in a General Consultation of the Dutch House of Representatives in order for parliamentarians to give their views to the Justice Minister. Within the Council, the proposal was discussed in the Council Visa Working Group and, parallel to the decision-making in the Council, decisions were taken in the European Parliament. By means of contact among those involved, a proposal was sought which was acceptable to both parties. This complex decision-making process raises the question: who can take the final decision in a responsible manner?

The complexity of implementing European policy also raises questions about the responsibilities of the administrators and public employees. An important issue here is decontextualization: disconnecting the context in which information is entered into systems from the context in which it is used. In the case of the SIS, the entries to allow detection raise questions. Entry of data is often done in one country (context) and used in another context. The link between contexts is limited: the SIS contains no information other than personal details and registrations with reference to the Article in the Schengen Implementation Agreement on which the registration is based. A national government decides to include an entry using its own criteria and these differ per country. Furthermore, the countries do not know what the others' criteria are. The context of use is often the border control. If a match is found in the database entries, this may be why an alien is refused admission at the external border, but the meaning of the registered entry differs per country. A country that refuses admission can in theory ask for extra information from the country responsible for registering the person, but this does not happen in practice. This means that decontextualization causes the Dutch government to rely on information of which the meaning is unknown.

Another point related to the complexity of implementation is the sharing of administrative responsibilities. In the Netherlands, the entries in the SIS are managed by the National Police Services Agency (general management) and the responsible authorities (specific registers). For example, the IND is responsible for managing the register with Article 96 entries. 'One then wonders who exactly is responsible for the quality of the information, as the responsibilities of the Police and the IND overlap partly' (Interview IND, 15 May 2008). In the case of the EU VIS, too, there are issues regarding the distribution of responsibilities; for this system, a central control organization will be set up and managed in Strasbourg, but the system will be filled with data in the various participating countries.[13] This problem is partially a repeat of the earlier mentioned problems of sharing responsibilities in policy chains. Four different authorities grant visas (Foreign Affairs Ministry, IND, Royal Military Police and the Seaport Police), and in order to carry out its monitoring function, the police force may also view the EU VIS. In addition, the EU VIS is used by Schengen member countries and thus also, within countries, by a multitude of organizations. At the moment, it is not clear how to guarantee that identification and verification take place in the same way everywhere. 'In fact, I don't know how they are going to do this. Perhaps the European Commission will supply a manual, but I've heard nothing so far' (Interview IND, 6 May 2008). There is a measure of standardization in the use of the form in which the reasons for refusing a visa request have to be filled in. However, there is no standard form for indicating why a visa *can* be granted. The numbers are simply too great in the case of the EU VIS to allow contact to be made with the relevant country. An IND employee said about the use of the SIS: 'In implementing policy you have to rely on the information supplied by other countries' (Interview IND, 15 May 2008). On the other hand, the police trade union recently said that since the Eastern European countries joined the EU, there is not much confidence in how other countries deal with the SIS (Smits 2007).

Specific questions about responsibility become an issue when migration policy tasks are contracted out to others. Various levels of outsourcing can be distinguished, such as making appointments with people who wish to request a visa and carrying out administrative procedures required for the implementation of certain steps such as taking fingerprints. In fact, the procedure can never be completely covered by outsourcing. 'Ultimately, a civil servant has to sign somewhere.' An important barrier for the EU VIS is that it is linked with discussions about the Council Regulation that enables embassies to take fingerprints. This regulates the possibility to use outsourcing – third parties taking fingerprints – and there is a lack of agreement on this. The questions about outsourcing are, of course, not new. At the Dutch Embassy in Moscow, a private company, VFS, is already recording fingerprints (Interview IND, 6 May 2008). Certain parts of the visa procedure have been outsourced to VFS.[14] Technological development is therefore not necessarily related to outsourcing, but technology does seem to be making it increasingly easy to use outsourcing because it is now easier to control processes remotely.

## Shifting and complex responsibilities

The discussion of responsibility and technology at three different levels – policy-implementation agencies, chain of organizations and international collaboration – has demonstrated that the practice is richly variegated. In this account, I will evaluate all the practices that have developed and are still developing using criteria that I introduced earlier, namely a serious and autonomous interpretation of performing one's role, an adequate perception of and attention to any possible violation of standards and an assessment of behaviour using a consistent code.

Firstly, the findings of the analysis have shown that 'serious and autonomous interpretation of performing one's role' is a problem. To follow up on what Bovens has said, I would like to make this clear by considering a number of *shifting responsibilities* (Bovens 2000). These responsibilities shift on three levels, which is why the interpretation of responsibilities is a problem:

- *Political responsibility.* The political responsibility for choices about migration policy is increasingly becoming a problem because choices that are in fact political ones are being made in a technical arena. As the rules in technical systems increase their influence, politics moves from formal political arenas into systems design. During the development of the DSS, for example, the designers noticed it was possible – in some cases – to set up a good link between system development and formal political control. The discussion of European collaboration has also shown how this can lead to increasing interdependence between countries. The complexity of the political decision-making pathway (involving information, interests, rules and the people who take action) leads to a situation in which it becomes difficult for the parliamentarians to carry out the tasks they have been given: taking responsible decisions about European information systems. Migration policy is becoming increasingly European in character, and this problem leads to the fundamental question: how should political responsibilities for technology be interpreted in a united Europe?
- *Management responsibility.* Even within organizations it is possible to see a shift of control towards the system developer. Managers are insufficiently able to understand the complexity of technological systems and thus cannot direct (with any degree of responsibility) the actions of system developers. In addition, the responsibility is

shifting from the organization that was given the responsibility to a network of organizations. Information plays a key role in migration policy, and information collection and exchange takes place in a network of organizations. The organization that has been granted responsibility is often unable to discover the origin of the information. Because of the large number of links between information systems, one small error during data entry can have enormous consequences. The networks create a complexity that makes it extremely difficult for managers to keep sight of the desirable and undesirable effects of deploying technology in migration policy. Referring to this, Thompson talks of the 'problem of many hands': the multitude of people involved makes it extremely difficult to make sensible decisions (Thompson 1980).

- *Public sector employee responsibility.* In the discussion of the IND as a policy-implementation agency, we saw that the responsibility is shifting from the decision-processing officer to the one who built the system. The officer taking decisions has to do so using systems which he/she does not understand and cannot possibly be expected to do so. The fundamental problem here is that public servants are less and less able to use their own judgment in individual situations. They find themselves in a limited 'epistemic space' that has been constructed by technology; the space for individual applications disappears as a result. Public servants have to look through a 'technological lens' in order to view a specific situation, while unable to estimate to what extent this lens is distorting the situation. The shifting of responsibilities can be characterized as a movement from an individual level (the decision-processing officer) to a system level (the algorithm). This means that mechanisms for social sorting become less personal while, at the same time, these mechanisms also become more difficult and more abstract. The responsibility also shifts from the decision-processing officer to the person who enters information into the system. This information is then used to take decisions even though the background of this information may be insufficiently clear. In particular, the use of international systems such as the Schengen Information System leads to situations where the distance between entry and usage of this information is too great because the person entering the data is in another country with another political and legislative context. The decision-processing officer often has few possibilities to verify this information and just has to assume that it is accurate.

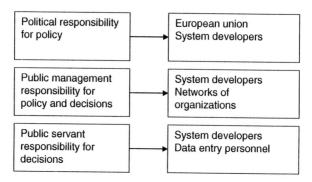

*Figure 5.2* Shifting responsibilities

The whole picture of shifting responsibilities is represented in Figure 5.2.

These shifts take place in order to increase the effectiveness of migration policy. Large numbers of collaborating organizations are necessary to make the development and use of complex European information systems a success (Kroon 1997). These shifts do, however, make one wonder about the responsible usage of technology, which is why this is a dilemma for governments and parliamentarians.

Secondly, the analysis at the three levels has shown that an adequate perception of and attention to potential breaks with the norm is a problem. Various reasons for not being able to meet this criterion have been offered in this analysis. One group of reasons can be placed under the heading of *increasing complexity*. The complexity of migration policies is growing because of the use of technology. A good example of this can be found in the decision trees in INDIS which cannot be understood by decision-processing officers (or only after a great deal of effort). It should be noted that the link between decision trees and Aliens Circulars is a good way of coupling the interpretation of these systems and political supervision. In addition, the complexity is increasing because technology makes it easier to form new collaborative ventures. Administrative complexity has thus increased considerably both in the form of collaboration within the chain and of collaboration internationally. This enormous complexity means that governments are no longer able to see the consequences of this use of technology. It thus becomes clear that the criterion 'adequate perception of and attention to potential breaks with the norm' cannot easily be achieved: increasing complexity seems to be necessary for an effective migration policy but at the same time raises questions about a responsible use of technology.

Another set of reasons for not being able to meet the criterion of adequate perception of and attention to any potential breaks with the norm is *political pressure*. I have demonstrated that, particularly at the level of the policy-implementation agency, political pressure has led to problems in the design of information systems and in policy implementation that is supported by information technology. Responsible use of information technology in migration policy requires a political system that recognizes the possibilities offered by technology, but also the limitations. There should be awareness of both the potential and the limitations of the technology when political decisions are taken. This is difficult because it requires political autonomy to be limited but it is absolutely essential if technology is to be used responsibly and without all manner of problems developing. Nevertheless, the description shows that recently more attention has been given to the implementation of policies and the accompanying use of technology. More recently, the necessary degree of political restraint can be observed more clearly.[15]

Thirdly, can one speak of behaviour based on a code that can be assessed and which is consistent? In fact, one could assume that information technology offers many possibilities here. Codes have been developed at national level – for example, for entering information into the SIS – but these are not publicly available. Much more of a problem is the use of codes for international collaboration as they either do not exist (EU VIS) or are inconsistent. The development of clear, checkable codes is a necessary development if the use of technology is to be responsible; and does not cause the same problems as the other two criteria. Guaranteeing responsible entry of information by using a clear coding system should be an important point of discussion. The system developed for entering information in the National Schengen Information System (N-SIS) is an example of how such a guarantee can be specified.

The evaluation of large-scale computerization in migration policies only seems to result in criticism, but it should be pointed out that this critical assessment is mainly based on the fact that the new 'migration machine' is challenging the old system of responsibilities. The migration machine does not only have a dark side; it also offers all sorts of possibilities for enhancing the effectiveness and efficiency of migration policy, as well as to ensure justice at an individual level. The complexity of technology reflects the complexity of the policy system in which the machine is used. Policy efforts over the past few years have focused on further developing this complex machine. There also appears to be more empirical support for the positive effects: effectiveness and efficiency, better coordination and independent evaluation. The negative effects such as wrongful registration, infringement of privacy and unlawful treatment seem to be relatively limited. However, shaping responsibilities adequately seems to have been given a lower priority. It is precisely in the area of migration policy that the interpretation of political and public service responsibilities is of extra importance, because the target group is one which cannot put up much opposition. Migrants often have a weaker position than citizens in terms of their relationships to governments, even if one just takes into account the lack of voting rights. They have some legislative possibilities to express any disagreements but their political influence is limited because they are not part of the electorate. When asked why the information systems set up by the Social Insurance Bank work better than those of the IND, the Court of Audit employees who were interviewed stated the following: 'The Social Insurance Bank has far more customers; if there are problems, then 20 to 30 per cent of the country citizens have a problem too. That is why the Social Insurance Bank has ICT specialists test new systems many times. A system must and will work properly. This demand is the result of huge pressure from outside, but it costs a great deal of money to do things well. The Court of Audit knows about this from previous research carried out on the Social Insurance Bank' (Interview Court of Audit, 11 March 2008). Furthermore, it should be noted that the administrative logic used by organizations such as the above-mentioned Social Insurance Bank cannot be applied to migration policy just like that; there are greater and more far-reaching differences between 'customers'.

## Uncontrollable machine?

The shifts in political and management responsibilities can have enormous consequences. Because of these shifts, individual migrants have less understanding of why a decision has been taken. The information used by decision-processing officers comes from anonymous information systems. The complaints the National Ombudsman receives from migrants demonstrate how difficult it is for them to get to grips with the migration machine. But these shifts also have important consequences for Dutch citizens. There are only limited possibilities for exerting one's influence by voting or protesting. Decision-making in Brussels and the decisions made by system developers are completely outside a citizen's field of vision and influence. The migration machine would seem to be uncontrollable, and Winner's dystopia of 'technics-out-of-control' seems to come near.

Modern information technology is an enormous challenge to the present-day political and administrative system which – as Frissen so aptly phrased it – goes back to the era of the steam engine (Frissen 1998). Such challenges mainly involve the growing complexity and the shifting of responsibilities towards the implementing personnel who are physically a long way from the decision situation. Shifts in task responsibilities make it difficult to deal with technology in a sensible manner. Winner (1977: 284) speaks of 'manifest social complexity': 'The technological society contains many parts and specialized activities with a myriad of interconnections.' Nobody is capable of forming a coherent, rational picture of the whole. In this situation, the concept of responsibility becomes 'as slippery as a squid in a fish market' (Winner 1977: 302) and hence the notion of moral agency dissolves in technological complexity (Winner 1977: 303).

The challenges will probably increase rather than decrease in the future. A recent Dutch study about the future effects of various technologies can be used to reflect on the future of applying information technology to migration policy (Teeuw *et al.* 2007). The report highlights the increasing epistemic dependence. The report mentions a number of times that the degree of dependence information systems require in terms of obtaining information about 'the world' continues to increase. It also indicates that there will be more polycentric governance in the sense that there are more and more links to all sorts of other systems. The report also shows that the technological complexity of systems continues to increase and that is why it is becoming even more difficult for decision-makers to take responsibility for the development of information systems.

This discussion of trends demonstrates that many of the problem areas discussed in this chapter will only get more urgent in the future. The image arises of a machine that is out of control: the system functions but no one understands it any more, neither can anyone regulate it in a responsible manner. To find an answer to the problem, it will be necessary to think about a re-evaluation of the responsibilities. This will require a clear vision of the responsibilities for large-scale policy implementation to be set out in detail.

A source of inspiration for seeking solutions for a policy system out of control is to think about complexity. The complex links between information systems cause responsibilities simply to evaporate. The problem of too many people being involved has become even more extreme: no one is responsible for the outcomes any more. This is a problem if viewed from the classical point of view of responsibility. Sharing out responsibilities *ex ante* is, after all, a way of guaranteeing that there is control over the system. The arguments against this could be that a lack of *ex ante* responsibility is a characteristic of advanced technical systems: the choice of advanced technologies always leads to more complex systems without clear responsibility structures. The question is, then, how it can be ensured that the controls over the system are sustained. *Ex post* guarantees, where responsibilities take form after the event rather than beforehand, would seem to be a possible solution. This solution can be embedded in a more general incrementalist approach to policy change (Lindblom 1959): small steps are taken and each step is carefully evaluated.

The possibilities for *ex post* guarantees can be further investigated in order to obtain an answer to this increasing complexity. A crucial factor here is learning from one's experiences. The fact that SIS I was not sufficiently evaluated before SIS II was developed is definitely a missed opportunity (Brouwer 2008: 527). On the other hand, the distribution of responsibilities for evaluating the EU VIS could well be an important opportunity for *ex post* guarantees. Furthermore, error detection appears to have a very limited role in the use of systems (including the design of information-system chains) at the moment. It should be clear to whom errors can be reported. This regulatory authority should also check the functioning of the system regularly. It is possible to check the quality of information systems by comparing them. It is important that someone is responsible for the quality of the information. This responsibility should not lie with the technical department but with the department responsible for the subject matter. American companies make a distinction between a Chief Technology Officer and a Chief Information Officer.[16] At the level of the public servant, this type of guarantee of responsibilities can be made more explicit by including competing information in the decision-making process.

The increasing complexity of techno-policy systems that focus on implementing legislation relating to aliens also results in the situation becoming increasingly opaque for those involved. The many links between organizations and systems make it very difficult for external parties to understand how it all works. What information is entered into the system by whom and when? Which considerations and analyses have been used in the process? In theory, this does not have to be a problem, as the functioning of the system can be tested in terms of the output. Does the system result in actions and decisions that comply with the law? There are mechanisms for output control and they are in the form of internal and external complaints procedures and the possibility to appeal. The lack of transparency in the system means, however, that these output controls remain extremely important and can even be used to make adjustments to the system in some way. Complaints and appeals can play a key role in the *ex post* guarantee of responsibility.

This chapter has shown how the use of information technology in migration policy is associated with growing complexities and substantial shifts in the actual way in which responsibilities are allocated. Technology plays an important role in shifting responsibilities because information is increasingly being decontextualized, combined and reassembled in order to be used in trading and decision situations. A high degree of fragmentation is the price one pays for dealing with the international complexity of migration policy. In addition, technological systems create a form of system coercion against which it is very difficult for human actors to offer resistance. As a result, new practices have arisen in migration policy. In many cases, the institutional framework has not yet adapted to this situation, which means a conflict arises between technological practice and the rules that hark back to the steam age or perhaps, rather, the old customs booths. Governments and parliamentarians are faced with the difficult task of looking for a new way of interpreting responsibilities in migration policy, one that suits modern information technology. The answer to the question as to who is the boss of the border-control officer in his/her booth is no longer sufficient. We must now ensure a correct interpretation of our responsibilities for the complex international information system with which the border-control officers work and on which they base their decisions.

## Notes

1. This chapter builds upon the same empirical work as Meijer (2009) but the data and arguments are analysed and structured differently within the context of this book.
2. This empirical analysis comes from a qualitative investigation consisting of interviews with employees at the IND, Netherlands Court of Audit and the Justice Ministry. A large number of documents were also studied. In addition, there was a systematic analysis of complaints investigated by the National Ombudsman and court proceedings at the Council of State.
3. The distribution and specification of responsibilities in migration policy can be analysed in many ways. This chapter deals only with the responsibilities

for the manner of using information technology. The discussion about responsibilities for implementation is much broader and leads to important questions. An interesting point is, for example, the description Walters (2006: 194) gave of the responsibility of truck drivers in relation to illegal immigrants who hide in their trucks. Such cases are not considered in this chapter because they have nothing to do with responsibility for managing information technology.

4. Bovens (1990: 32, 33) distinguishes in addition to 'responsibility as a task' and 'responsibility as a virtue' another three types of responsibility: 'responsibility as liability', 'responsibility as cause' and 'responsibility as power'. The focus on 'responsibility as task and virtue' means that the question of whether governments are liable ('was the minister responsible for the failure of the implementing organization?') is not so important here.

5. This section contains material from interviews with the IND (15 October 2007 and 8 April 2008) and the Netherlands Court of Audit (11 March 2008). Also the following documents were studied: Dutch House of Representatives, Year 2004–05, 30 240, nos. 1–2; IND 2008; Appendix to the letter of 3 November 2006 (DDS 5444981/06/SCV) from the Minister for Immigration and Integration and the Minister of Foreign Affairs, Report on Immigration Chain for the period May–August 2006 (October 2006).

6. Theoretical research has shown that decision-processing officers at the IND deal with this discretionary freedom in different ways. Public employees mainly differ in the way they deal with information supplied for asylum requests (Mascini 2004).

7. This section was written using interviews with the IND on 6 May 2008. Also the following documents were studied: National Ombudsman (2003), Ministry of Justice (n.d.).

8. The BVV will also be linked to the European information systems. The chain partners now have access to SIS I. The BVV is the national interface with the European chains (EU VIS, Eurodac and possibly SIS II). In future, people requiring visas (even on short-stay) will be allocated an aliens number.

9. National Ombudsman (2003) is a public report of research initiated internally into the implementation of tasks related to admitting aliens and carried out by different government organizations (especially the Immigration Services of four police forces, the Secretary of State for Justice and the Minister of Foreign Affairs). The report is available at: www.ombudsman. nl/rapporten/grote_onderzoeken/vreemdelingendiensten/rapport_vreemde lingendiensten.pdf.

10. This section contains material from interviews with the IND on 15 October 2007 and 8 April 2008 and with the Netherlands Court of Audit on 11 March 2008. In addition, the following documents were studied: Aliens Circular 2000 (A) (about entries for detection purposes), Schengen Implementation Agreement (1990); draft regulation VIS (PE-CONS 3630/07). Nicole Kroon's thesis (1997) was also used. There was also research into statements made by the National Ombudsman and the Council of State with reference to European information systems. A search was performed on the National Ombudsman website (www.ombudsman.nl) on the term 'SIS' (31 March 2008). Similarly on the website Rechtspraak.nl (www.rechtspraak.nl) (9 April 2008).

11. The SIS has the closest relationship with the affairs of the National Ombudsman and the Administrative Court. No cases for the Ombudsman were found in the other information systems; for the Administrative Courts, four were found for Eurodac and one for INDIS.
12. The EU VIS is in fact a subject for the Justice and Foreign Affairs Council, but documents may also be approved by another Council than that of Justice/Foreign Affairs, provided no further discussion on the content is necessary.
13. Draft Regulation of the European Parliament and the Council concerning the visa information system (VIS) and the exchange of information about short-stay visas with other member states (2004/0287, PE-CONS 3630/07).
14. More information: www.vfsglobal.com. This is a large international company that organizes administrative procedures for a large number of countries. The website states the following: 'VFS Global serves diplomatic missions by managing all the administrative and non-judgmental tasks related to the entire lifecycle of a visa application process, enabling diplomatic missions to focus entirely on the key tasks of assessment and interview.'
15. In interpreting political responsibility, the guidelines of the Netherlands Court of Audit can be of help (Dutch Court of Audit 2007). The Court states politicians should be realistic; in other words, ICT is not a 'quick fix' for any problem, political deadlines can be deadly for a project, there is always a gap between policy and implementation in the ambitions of ICT organizations, reconsiderations during implementation are often unavoidable and an exit strategy prevents people muddling through. The Court also states that to get to grips with ICT projects, it is imperative the minister is fully involved in discussions with both the Dutch House of Representatives and the ICT supplier. Also important: decision-making takes place in phases, decisions are taken using well-founded plans, projects are evaluated in terms of the whole project portfolio and reconsideration remains possible.
16. Guarantees for the quality of information are, in practice, more related to technology than to the subject matter. For example, the SIRENE Office (Supplementary Information Request at the National Entry) guarantees the technical quality of information in the SIS. The content is however less strictly controlled. SIRENE does not look at this aspect. This can be ascribed to a technological way of viewing information; it is regarded as 'bits' with a certain format and not as semantic symbols that can reduce uncertainty (Interview IND, 15 May 2008).

## Bibliography

Bovens, M. (1990) *Verantwoordelijkheid en organisatie: beschouwingen over aansprakelijkheid, institutioneel burgerschap en ambtelijke ongehoorzaamheid* (Zwolle: Tjeenk Willink).

Bovens, M.A.P. (2000) 'De vierde macht revisited. Over ambtelijke macht en publieke verantwoording.' Inaugural address, Utrecht University.

Bovens, M. and S. Zouridis (2002) 'From Street-Level to System-Level Bureaucracies: How ICT is Transforming Administrative Discretion and Constitutional Control', *Public Administration Review*, 62(2): 174–83.

Brouwer, E. (2008) *Digital Borders and Real Rights: Effective Remedies for Third-Country Nationals in the Schengen Information System* (Leiden and Boston: Martinus Nijhoff Publishers).

Dutch Court of Audit (2007) *Lessen uit ICT-projecten van de overheid. Deel A* (The Hague).

Dutch House of Representatives (Year 2004–05), 30 240, nos. 1–2.

Frissen, P.H.A. (1998) *De virtuele staat. Politiek, bestuur, technologie: een postmodern verhaal* (Schoonhoven: Academic Service).

Galbraith, J.K. (1968) *The New Industrial State* (New York: The New American Library).

Hoven, J. van den (1998) 'Moral Responsibility, Public Office and Information Technology', in I.Th.M. Snellen and W.B.H.J. van de Donk, *Public Administration in an Information Age: A Handbook* (Amsterdam: IOS Press).

Immigration and Naturalization Service (2008) *De IND belicht. Jaarresultaten 2007* (The Hague).

Kroon, N. (1997) *Europese informatiesystemen: grensverleggen? Een verkenning naar barrières in de bouwfase van het Schengen Informatie Systeem en het Social Security Network* (Delft: Eburon).

Levitt, S. and S.J. Dubner (2005) *Freakonomics: A Rogue Economist Explores the Hidden Side of Everything* (New York: William Morrow/HarperCollins).

Lindblom, C.E. (1959) 'The Science of Muddling Through', *Public Administration Review*, 19: 79–88.

Mascini, P. (2004) 'De wisselvalligheid van de twijfel: ongelijkheid in de uitvoering van het asielbeleid verklaard', *Amsterdams Sociologisch Tijdschrift*, 31(1): 113–46.

Meijer, A.J. (2009) 'Complex Responsibilities: An Empirical Analysis of Responsibilities and Technological Complexity in Dutch Immigration Policies', *Public Management Review*, 11(6): 771–90.

Ministry of Justice (n.d.) *Kila en Kali en het PIL* (The Hague).

Ministry of Justice (2006) *Naar een modern migratiebeleid. Notitie over de herziening van de reguliere toelating van vreemdelingen in Nederland* (The Hague).

Mulder, R. de (1998) 'The Digital Revolution: From Trias to Tetras Politica', in I.Th.M. Snellen and W.B.H.J. van de Donk, *Public Administration in an Information Age: A Handbook* (Amsterdam: IOS Press).

National Ombudsman (2003) *Onderzoek Vreemdelingendiensten.* Report no. 2003/160 (The Hague).

Romzek, B. and M. Dubnick (1987) 'Accountability in the Public Sector: Lessons from the Challenger Tragedy', *Public Administration Review*, 47(3): 227–38.

Smits, H. (2007) 'Politie bezorgd over Schengen', *Financieel Dagblad. Economie & Politiek*: 4.

Strom, K. (2000) 'Delegation and Accountability in Parliamentary Democracies', *European Journal of Political Research*, 37(3): 261–89.

Teeuw, W., A. Vedder, B. Dorbeck-Jung, B. Custers, E. Faber and R. Leenes (2007) *Impact of Converging Technologies on Future Security Applications* (Enschede: Telematica Instituut).

Thompson, D.F. (1980) 'Moral Responsibility of Public Officials: The Problem of Many Hands', *The American Political Science Review*, 74(4): 905–16.

Walters, W. (2006) 'Border/Control', *European Journal of Social Theory*, 9(2): 187–203.

Winner, L. (1977) *Autonomous Technology: Technics-Out-Of Control as a Theme in Political Thought* (Cambridge, MA: MIT Press).

Winner, L. (1986) *The Whale and the Reactor: A Search for Limits in an Age of High Technology* (University of Chicago Press).

WRR Dutch Scientific Council for Government Policy (2000) *Het borgen van publiekbelang* (The Hague).

# 6
# Legal Boundaries and the Use of Migration Technology

*Evelien Brouwer*

## Introduction

What are the legal boundaries in the use of databases and biometrics in border surveillance and migration policy? This chapter aims to reach a better understanding of the standards that are frequently neglected against the backdrop of current developments or whose importance is all too easily trivialized: the right to privacy, the principle of non-discrimination and two substantive standards relating to data protection law: the purpose limitation principle and the prohibition on automated decision-making.

The decision to focus specifically on these rights and principles is related to four significant trends in information policy. Firstly, the increased use of central databases and the application of RFID chips and biometrics have enabled the ever closer and more systematic tracking of individuals' movements. The question arises as to whether this new form of monitoring or 'electronic tracking' of individuals can be reconciled with the right to a private life as protected in Article 8 of the European Convention on Human Rights (ECHR) and elsewhere. There is also doubt as to whether the conflict between security and privacy as two equal individual rights often cited in political debate is actually justified.

A second trend is the desire on the part of policy-makers to use information systems for multiple purposes. Although this development is not limited to information about migrants, a series of proposals have been made, with particular reference to these people, and also at European level, to provide access to personal data originally collected for one specific purpose for other purposes as well. An important example of this is the proposal to give law-enforcement authorities access to data stored into Eurodac, which was originally established as a means of determining which state is responsible for an asylum application. The Visa Information System, used to store details of both positive and negative decisions relating to visa applications, has also been clearly designed for multifunctional use. When it becomes operational, the system will be used to combat illegal immigration, to monitor whether migrants in the EU on a visa stay are here for the legally allotted period, to facilitate the return of unlawful immigrants and also to combat terrorism. This development creates an obvious tension between multifunctionality on the one hand and the purpose limitation principle on the other. According to the purpose limitation principle, one of the central tenets on which data protection law is based, data may exclusively be collected for specific purposes described in advance and in principle may only be used for such purposes. In this chapter I shall examine the limits of information policy that arise from this principle.

A third trend is the automation of the decisions made in migration law: government agencies increasingly act, or are deemed to act, on the basis of information from a range of databases, irrespective of the origin of these data. The most significant example of this is the proposal by the European Commission relating to new border-control measures ('Border Package') which envisages the use of electronic gateways or e-borders as a means of distinguishing more rapidly between bona fide travellers and those who are unknown and may have illicit intentions. A second obvious example is the Schengen Information System (SIS). This system is based on the reciprocal recognition of decisions made at national level (and recorded within it) by the authorities of the Schengen member countries (see also Chapter 3 by Broeders in this book). What role does the aforementioned ban on automated decision-making play in the light of these developments?

A fourth and final trend is the increasing use of profiling. Profiling is a classic instrument by which law-enforcement authorities compare a range of information sources to identify the characteristics of a specific target group. Based on these characteristics, specific groups can be monitored more closely and subjected to specific measures. Although the use of profiling is not limited to migrants, the technique has increasingly been used by government agencies within the framework of migration and border controls. An important example of this are the existing EU rules relating to the exchange of passenger information in which profiling is used to subject specific travellers to closer monitoring (Scholten 2008; Brouwer 2009). However, profiles based on information provided in advance will also be used in the processing of these applications and the Commission's proposal for 'e-borders'. This use of data profiling, which selects on the basis of information on race, origin or nationality, also raises the question of the extent to which this practice is reconcilable with the non-discrimination principle enshrined in international law.

The thrust of my argument is based on the assertion that policymakers and politicians who do not take account of the legal boundaries at an early stage will inevitably find themselves confronted by them when implementing these measures. This will occur as a result of the decisions made by independent supervisory authorities, such as the courts and data protection authorities, or because of an increased unwillingness on the part of individuals and legal persons to cooperate with government. Prevention is better than cure. In my conclusion I shall make a number of recommendations to protect the rights of those individuals who are the subject of this research: migrants.

## The right to privacy

### Data surveillance and the scope of Article 8 of the ECHR

Article 8 of the ECHR reads as follows:

1. Everyone has the right to respect for his private and family life, his home and his correspondence.
2. There shall be no interference by a public authority with the exercise of this right except such as is in accordance with the law and is necessary in a democratic society in the interests of national security, public safety or the economic well-being of the country, for the prevention of disorder or crime, for the protection of health or morals, or for the protection of the rights and freedoms of others.

The collection and storage of personal data does not always entail an interference with the right to a private life, as protected in Article 8 of the ECHR. Indeed, in most cases of data processing, it is quite normal for a specific body or government authority to store personal data and use it in exercising a specific task or duty. In certain situations, however, the collection and use of personal data do constitute a clear infringement of the right to a private life. Examples of this include the breaching of medical privacy laws, the revealing of sensitive information about someone's religious beliefs or health, or the covert collection of information about an individual by means of video surveillance or wire- or

Internet tapping. The question is whether it is possible, in the light of these developments in migration technology – such as the use of central databases, information sharing and the application of biometrics – to identify an infringement of Article 8 of the ECHR.

From the case law of the European Court of Human Rights (ECtHR), it is possible to identify those situations in which Article 8 of the ECHR applies to the collection and storage of data by government.[1] The italicized names included in brackets below refer to case law; references to these are included at the end of this chapter. Among other things, these situations related to the use of secret files by police or internal security organizations (*Leander, Segerstedt-Wiberg, Rotaru*); the use of files held by public organizations irrespective of the nature or sensitivity of the data included within them (*Amann*); the storage of medical data (*Z v. Finland*); files relating to juvenile care (*Gaskin*); the recording of video images (*Perry*), voices (*Peck*) or photographs (Commission: *Lupker* and *Friedl*); the use of administrative data relating to telephone conversations (*Malone*); the issuing or refusal to issue birth certificates, identity cards and driving licences (*Goodwin*), and passports (*Smirnova* and *Íletmiş*). In the judgments cited, the Court took account of the following aspects in order to determine whether there was indeed any interference in the individual's right to a private life: the systematic collection and storage of personal data by government (*Rotaru, Amann, Segerstedt-Wiberg*); information about an individual's past (*Rotaru*); when information was not provided voluntarily (*Perry*); and when the later use of the information exceeds what is normally foreseeable (*Peck, P.G. and J.H.* and *Perry*). In *Amann* the ECtHR also determined that it is not always relevant whether or not the data stored have actually been used: the mere fact that data have been stored, in this case by the security services, can be sufficient to determine that there has been interference in someone's right to a private life.

Within the context of this subject, migration technology and the European Commission's proposal for an 'entry-exit system', there can be little doubt about the applicability of Article 8 of the ECHR. Firstly, there is systematic collection and storage of personal data within the framework of systems such as Eurodac, the Visa Information System (VIS) and the inclusion in travel documents of biometrics. The measures presented by the European Commission in February 2008 concerning 'An integrated vision for border management' include the introduction of a so-called entry-exit system that may be used to monitor the legality and validity of visas held by non-EU citizens staying in the EU.[2] According to the Commission, if fingerprints and possibly at a later date also biometric data are taken from all non-EU citizens (third-country nationals) and a so-called alert system is installed, it will be easier to identify those persons who have exceeded their authorized period of residence. Moreover, an increasing number of measures used in migration technology involve the processing of sensitive data, such as ethnicity and health, as part of the passenger information provided for visa or asylum applications. Biometric data such as fingerprints, facial recognition and iris scans may also in some cases be regarded as sensitive information which may be used to extrapolate other information about the health of the person concerned.[3]

In several of its judgments, the ECtHR has made a direct link between internal security controls and the right to privacy (*Perry, Peck, Rotaru, Klass*). Clearly, the use of the databases referred to, the exchange of data and the accessibility to the systems for national security organizations and others will lead to surveillance measures. These will involve interference in the right to a private life if the individual involved is systematically subjected to additional controls such as being taken aside, interrogated and physically searched.

It is important to note, as the ECtHR acknowledged in the case *İletmiş* v. *Turkey,* that the right to a private life can also include freedom of movement. In the case cited, it involved the seizure by the Turkish authorities of the complainant's passport as a result of which this person was no longer able to travel in and out of the country. In its judgment, the ECtHR was unanimous in deciding that the seizure of his passport represented an infringement of his right to a private life, arguing as follows: 'in an age when the freedom of movement, especially across borders, was considered essential for the full development of private life, especially for people like the applicant, having family, occupational and economic ties in more than one country, denial of that freedom by the State without any good reason constituted a serious failure on its part to discharge its obligations to those under its jurisdiction' (§ 50). It is quite conceivable that the intensive border controls and controls on the territory of EU states in which various databases are compared and biometrics is used, will be designated as interference in migrants' right to freedom of movement and thereby also in their right to a private life.

### Exceptional conditions

Pursuant to Article 8, Section 2 of the ECHR a restriction on the right to a private life is permitted under certain conditions. According to ECtHR case law, any such restrictions must meet certain specific substantive and procedural conditions. In a nutshell, these restrictions entail that the interference in this right must be provided for within the law (knowledge and foreseeability requirements), must be necessary in democratic society and be in the interest of a legitimate goal as described in the exception clause. Article 8, Section 2 cites the following legitimate objectives or target criteria for which the right to a private life may justifiably be restricted: the interests of national security, public safety or the economic well-being of the country, for the prevention of disorder or crime, for the protection of health or morals, or for the protection of the rights and freedoms of others.

Article 8, Section 2 also states that the interference must be necessary in a democratic society. The ECtHR has ruled that this restriction in the right to a private life must be compatible with the principles of proportionality and subsidiarity. According to the principle of proportionality and subsidiarity there must be a reasonable relationship between the chosen means and the intended (legitimate) end: the measure must go no farther than is required in order to achieve this goal. According to the subsidiarity principle, the chosen measure is justified if no other, less far-reaching, means are available to achieve the same goal.

Within the framework of this subject, the use of migration technology and more specifically the use of databases and biometrics, the following criteria formulated by the ECtHR are of relevance. Firstly, the relevant legislation must include the following information in relation to data processing. It must contain a clear description and restriction of the authorities to collect and store data (*Leander, Rotaru*). The legislation must also define the type of data that may be stored (*Leander, Rotaru*); the category of persons against whom surveillance measures such as the collection and storage of data may be taken (*Kruslin-Huvig, Rotaru*); the circumstances in which these measures may be taken and procedures to be followed (*Leander, Rotaru*); and the situations in which it is permissible to provide the information (*Peck*). The legislation must also incorporate restrictions on the time period for which data can be stored (*Rotaru, Segerstedt-Wiberg*); adequate safeguards against actions which contravene Article 8 of the Data Protection Convention (*Z v. Finland*); and safeguards to protect the quality of data and sensitive information (*Z v. Finland*). Finally, the individual involved must be informed in advance that data is being stored (*Perry*), unless it is being collected by the security services.

An assessment of current trends in the use of databases and biometrics at the border leads one to conclude that in many areas the relevant legislation does not meet the standards described above. One of the most important problems is that individuals in most cases remain completely uninformed of the situations in which information is being stored and by which government agency. As we will see below, the regulations in question often include far too general descriptions of the purpose for which data are being collected and also permit information to be provided to third parties, such as the governments of other EU member states and even non-EU countries.

This lack of transparency is not only an issue within the framework of Article 8 of the ECHR. In a judgment issued on 11 March 2008, the highest German constitutional court (*Bundesverfassungsgericht*) ruled that the legal regulations applied by police in relation to the automatic recording of vehicle number plates in the federal states of Hessen and Schleswig Holstein represented an infringement of the vehicle users' constitutional right to the protection of their personal life (Kraftfahrzeugkennzeichen 1 BvR 2074/05; 1 BvR 1254/07. 1 BvR 256/08). The *Bundesverfassungsgericht* examined the issue in response to constitutional complaints about the measures in question made by several vehicle owners. It decided that the relevant rules in the federal states referred to did not meet the constitutional preconditions of clarity and transparency ('*Normenbestimmtheit*' and '*Normenklarheit*') because they failed to define either the reason for collecting and comparing these data or their purpose in crime detection. According to the *Bundesverfassungsgericht*, these rules permit far-reaching infringements of the right to informational self-determination ('*informationelle Selbstbestimmungsrecht*') of data subjects without clearly defining the required legal parameters or thresholds for the automatic collection of data. This judgment shows that the powers of the police and other authorities with regard to information are being subjected to rigorous legal scrutiny also at national level.

### Independent supervision

In various judgments, the ECtHR has highlighted the need for an independent control mechanism to protect the right to a private life. In doing so, the Court has also made it clear that this is necessary, not only in order to ensure that the rights of the individuals involved are weighed against the interests of the authority collecting the information but also to prevent the abuse of power by government.

With regard to covert surveillance measures in particular, the ECtHR emphasized the need for an independent supervisory authority to protect the right to a private life enshrined in Article 8 of the ECHR (for example *Klass*, *Leander* and *Rotaru*). In other cases, the ECtHR saw the need for an independent control mechanism when specific and sensitive data or a claim for access to such data was involved, for example medical data or information about a person's youth (*Z* v. *Finland* and *Gaskin* v. *the United Kingdom*). In these cases, the independent supervisory mechanism was emphasized not only as a means of protecting the right of the data subjects to a private life but also to ensure that the different interests involved are carefully weighed against each other. In its judgments, the ECtHR shows a clear preference for access to a judicial authority, because this gives the best guarantees of 'independence, impartiality and a proper procedure' (*Klass* § 56). In some judgments, however, the presence of a non-judicial authority was considered to be adequate (for example in *Gaskin, Leander*). The general requirement is that the legal recourses must be practical and effective, as established in the judgment *Segerstedt-Wiberg and others* v. *Sweden*. In this case, which involved the collection of data by security services, the Court explicitly examined the practical significance of the Swedish data protection authority which citizens involved could turn to in order to submit complaints. This judgment is examined in more detail below.

In the judgment on *The Association for European Integration and Human Rights and Ekimdzhiev* v. *Bulgaria*, the existence of an independent control mechanism within the framework of surveillance by security organizations was also subjected to rigorous scrutiny. In this case, the ECtHR concluded that the Bulgarian government offered inadequate safeguards against the risk of the abuse of data 'inherent in any system of secret surveillance'. This conclusion was based in part on the lack of independent supervision of compliance with the maximum storage periods for the data acquired. The ECtHR referred explicitly to the wide-scale application of secret surveillance systems in Bulgaria during the period under assessment (1991–2001). In a single year more than 10,000 orders were said to have been issued for the secret monitoring of individuals by means of telephone taps, video surveillance and bugging, which did not include the tapping of mobile telephones. In only 267 or 269 of these cases, did it ultimately prove possible to use these data in a criminal procedure. According to the ECtHR, this information showed that 'the system of secret surveillance in Bulgaria is, to say the least, overused, which may in part be due to the inadequate safeguards which the law provides'.

### Right to damage compensation

Whenever an infringement of Article 8 of the ECHR is identified, the individual involved may be entitled to damage compensation. In the case of *Rotaru* v. *Romania*, for example, the right of individuals to financial redress for damage caused by data collection by the Romanian authorities was acknowledged. The fact that Romanian law did not offer the individual involved a procedure which they could use to claim this damage compensation through the courts also represented, according to the ECtHR, an infringement of their right to a fair trial as protected in Article 6 of the ECHR.

In *C.G. and others* v. *Bulgaria*, the ECtHR awarded the complainant a significant sum in compensation partly as a result of the infringement of Article 8 of the ECHR caused by the deportation of the first complainant. This involved the protection of this individual's right to a family life since he had already been living legitimately in Bulgaria over a long period and had built up a family there. The complainant was deported based on secret information from the security service acquired by the use of covert observation. The ECtHR asserted that this involved a contravention of ECHR Article 8, Article 13 and Article 1 of the seventh protocol of the ECHR. The most important reason cited for this conclusion was the lack of any independent controls on the use of information by the security services.

### Privacy versus security?

In May 2007, the so-called Future Group, an organization established in 2007 to advise the EU presidency on issues relating to Justice and Interior Affairs, issued a memorandum in which 'security, mobility and privacy' were proposed as a new paradigm for cooperation within the EU (Future Group 2007). Although this memorandum explicitly states that security and privacy should not be considered to be mutually opposed, it does consider one of the most important challenges for policy-makers to be what it calls 'finding the right balance'. There have also been several publications in the Netherlands on finding the right balance between security and privacy (Muller *et al.* 2007). This duty on the part of policy-makers appears at first glance to be completely clear and uncontroversial. Who could fail to agree with a policy that places security, mobility and privacy at its forefront? Thus far, however, the discussions on this subject do not appear to have provided any additional clarity on the existing conditions and legal boundaries. Such discussions often tend to become bogged down by an emphasis on the interests of security and the need within this to occasionally focus less on what may be termed 'privacy issues'. Within this context, it is interesting to note that government ministers increasingly invoke an opposition between the right to security and the right to privacy. In the debate in Europe and in the Netherlands, there is an increasing tendency to present the concepts of 'security' and 'basic rights' as being equally worthy of protection. For example, in a memorandum issued by the former Slovenian EU presidency on terrorism, security and basic human rights, security is referred to as a fundamental human right (Dutch Data Protection Authority 2007). Moreover, when presenting his report, *Veiligheid en privacy. Een zoektocht naar een nieuwe balans* (*Security and Privacy: Finding a New Balance*), the Dutch Justice Minister Hirsch Ballin also cited 'security' as one of the basic rights. In this, the minister asserted that 'the ECHR also equates the rights to security and privacy and codifies these alongside each other in Articles 5 and 8 respectively' (Hirsch Ballin 2007).

Both the concept of 'security' as a legal right and the use of this concept to put the right to privacy in perspective deserve closer critical examination. Indeed, it is incredible that there were no additional questions from the Dutch Parliament on the minister's reference to Article 5 of the ECHR as a basis for the 'right to security'. It is clear that Article 5 of the ECHR was cited inappropriately in this context, if not actually misused. The minister would appear to base his argument on the opening clause of Article 5, which states: 'Everyone has the right to liberty and security of person.' However, this clause does not offer individuals the right to freedom in the general sense, nor does it impose on the state the duty of protecting the security, or safety, of citizens. The clause cited must be interpreted within the framework of the primary objective of Article 5 of the ECHR: to protect citizens against government intervention relating to arrest and detention. Pursuant to Article 5 of the ECHR, it is the duty of *government* to take account of certain rules, such as informing the individual involved of the reasons for his or her arrest or detention. Article 5 also includes important safeguards for the protection of the individual, such as the right of an individual to be brought promptly before a judge, and the right to compensation in the event of unlawful detention. None of this has anything to do with a general right to security or safety.

The characterization of 'security' as a basic right actually paves the way for further limitations on citizens' 'real' basic rights and freedoms. The notion that citizens can claim the right to security as a basic right is a misunderstanding perpetuated by politics. Security and protection of citizens' safety is the role of government (Muller *et al.* 2007: 17). Of course, the government must do all in its power to safeguard the security of people within its territory, whether the threat be from hostile foreign powers, terrorist attacks or natural disasters. It is clear however that no government can ever vouch for the safety of an individual from the cradle to the grave. Anyone who in the wake of a terrorist attack invokes a breach of his or her right to security in the courts is highly unlikely to be successful. The most important function of Article 5 of the ECHR, and indeed of other basic rights, is the protection of citizens' liberty vis-à-vis the government. When the politicians mentioned above invoke the 'the right to security', this is actually a misnomer. Indeed, in order to effectively protect this so-called right against often unknown third parties, governments would need to be given even greater powers of intervention.

The idea of setting privacy and security against each other has in any case little purpose as it can quickly lead to the conclusion that policy-makers or lawyers must always make a choice for one or the other. As a result, the participants in the ongoing security debate are often portrayed as being either in the privacy camp or in the security camp. This opposition fails to take account of the fact that the right to privacy as protected in Article 8 of the ECHR already contains inherent conditions. As highlighted earlier, Section 2 already allows for the right to privacy to be restricted in the interests of national security or public safety. Case law from the ECtHR shows that in the framework of security, the government is permitted to take far-reaching measures and the judge is also allowed to apply a more marginal assessment in general. There is therefore no question of there being too far-reaching privacy issues affecting the work of the security services, as is so often argued. Nevertheless, in the event of interference in the right to a private life, this restriction must be subjected to substantive scrutiny as elaborated in ECtHR case law. This means, as outlined above, that the interference must be necessary in a democratic society, that it must be proportional and subsidiary with a view to a legitimate goal and the interference must be regulated by law.

## The right to data protection: substantive requirements

The developments in migration technology are to a large extent covered by data protection law. Since its inclusion in Article 8 of the EU Human Rights Charter, it is clear that data protection is to be protected as a separate basic right alongside the right to privacy. Article 8 of this Charter states:

1. Everyone has the right to the protection of personal data concerning him or her.

2. Such data must be processed fairly for specified purposes and on the basis of the consent of the person concerned or some other legitimate basis laid down by law. Everyone has the right of access to data which has been collected concerning him or her, and the right to have it rectified.
3. Compliance with these rules shall be subject to control by an independent authority.

In addition to national legislation, the principles of data protection were previously incorporated in the binding Data Protection Convention from the Council of Europe in 1981 and the EC Data Protection Directive 95/46 (see *European Treaty Series (ETS)*, no. 108, Strasbourg 1982 and *OJ* L 281, 23 November 1995). These binding regulations include important procedural safeguards for the individual, such as the right of access to and correction of personal data, the protection of sensitive data, security regulations and supervision by independent supervisory authorities. In its so-called Border Package, proposing far-reaching measures for automated border controls, the European Commission asserts that 'systems must comply with EU data protection rules including the requirements of necessity, proportionality, purpose limitation and quality of data' (COM (2008) 69, 13 February 2008, p. 9 respectively). In addition, several of the instruments referred to earlier also include references to the standards laid down in EC Directive 95/46 or the Data Protection Convention of 1981. The question remains however as to whether clear references to existing data protection rules do sufficient justice to the protection of the persons involved.

At this point it is relevant to refer to the case of *Österreichischer Rundfunk* (C-465/00) in which the Court of Justice underlined the importance of a broad interpretation of EC Directive 95/46 on the protection of personal data and the relationship between this directive and the right to a private life as protected in Article 8 of the ECHR. This case concerned the question of whether the obligation enshrined in Austrian legislation for legal persons to provide information about the salary and pension of their employees to the Austrian Court of Auditors was actually in accordance with the EC Directive. According to the Court of Justice, whenever national judges establish that national legislation relating to the processing of personal data contravenes Article 8 of the ECHR, such legislation would automatically also contravene the proportionality principle set out in Articles 6(1)(c) and 7(c) or (e) of Directive 95/46. Equally, according to the Court of Justice, this means that any restriction on data protection rights (as authorized in Article 13 of Directive 95/46) must meet the proportionality requirement in terms of the general interest it aims to achieve. In the case of the *United Kingdom and Ireland* v. *the Council* (C-137/05), the Advocate General of the Court of Justice, Trstenjak, issued a remarkable warning on the use of biometrics. This case concerned *Regulation 2252/2004 on standards for security features and biometrics in passports and travel documents* (OJ L 385, 29 December 2004). The central legal issue in this case was not related to data protection, but concerned whether it was legally possible for the United Kingdom and Ireland to participate in this regulation. Despite this, the Advocate General deemed it necessary in her conclusion to express her concerns about the consequences of this biometric passport for the basic right to data protection. In the final section of her conclusion, she referred explicitly to the problems that may arise in the implementation of Regulation 2252/2004 in terms of the fundamental right to data protection as enshrined in the EU Charter.

In the following sections I will discuss two key principles in data protection law, which are both extremely important yet rarely examined in any detail: the purpose limitation principle and the right not to be subjected to automated decision-making. In my view, these principles entail significant substantive restrictions on the application of wide-scale data systems as discussed in this chapter.

## The purpose limitation principle: a specified, explicit and legitimate objective

The purpose limitation principle is just one of the principles in data protection law and is a fixed component of both national and international rules relating to data protection. Pursuant to Article 6.1(b) of EU Directive 95/46, personal data must be acquired for specified, explicit and justified purposes and must not be subsequently processed in a manner which is incompatible with these purposes. Article 7 of EC 95/46 describes legitimate purposes: data processing is legitimate when the data subject has given his or her unambiguous consent or if it is necessary for the performance of a contract or to meet a legal obligation. Data processing is also legitimate if it is necessary for the performance of a task in the general interest or if it is part of the performance of a public law duty imposed on the agency responsible for the processing or the third party to whom the data are made available. A legitimate purpose may also include the protection of the vital interests of the data subject or if processing is necessary to protect the legitimate interests of the agency responsible for the processing or the third party to whom the data are made available, providing that the interest does not prejudice the fundamental rights and freedoms of the data subject.

The purpose limitation principle offers several layers of protection. Firstly, it prohibits the collection of personal data for unknown or unspecified purposes: in Germany this is known as the *Verbot 'pragmatiklose Datensammlung'*. Secondly, the purpose limitation principle prohibits the use or making available of personal data for purposes other than the specific end for which the data were collected. Thirdly, the purpose limitation principle entails that the data may not be stored for longer than is necessary for the intended purpose. In this sense, purpose limitation is closely related to purpose specification: the latter implies that the governments or organizations processing the data must make clear and transparent the purpose of the data processing in advance. Both the purpose limitation and the purpose specification principle reflect the principle that data processing must be foreseeable for the data subject and must not go further than he or she may reasonably expect (Elgesem 1999). As we saw earlier in the discussion of case law relating to Article 8 of the ECHR, the ECtHR has explicitly emphasized the importance of foreseeability in terms of the processing of personal data by government. But the purpose limitation principle also applies when there is no direct interference in the right to a private life. It gives individuals the right to know when, in what circumstances and by whom information is being collected and stored about them.

When discussing purpose limitation and the related question of whether a specific form of data processing is legitimate, it is useful to bear in mind the classic purposes of data protection. If one looks at the primary purpose of information files or databases, the classic distinction made is that between administrative, information or statistical databases (Enschedé 1974: 1025 ff.). The most important characteristic of administrative databases is that they come about as a result of the performance of policy. However, the registration of information is merely a means used for the performance of the task in question. In the case of information or intelligence registers, however, the provision of information to government authorities or third parties is a goal in itself.[4] The various proposals put forward at EU level for the processing of data (SIS, VIS, the provision of passenger data) show that databases originally established for purely administrative purposes increasingly take on the character of intelligence files. An important feature of information registers is that it is not always clear in advance what and by whom the data can be used.

The purpose of intelligence files is to contain as much data as possible which may be of benefit for later purposes or use.

## Migration technology and purpose limitation: multifunctional use or function creep?

The purpose limitation principle has been sidelined by current developments. On the one hand, systems such as information registers have been established without any specific or clearly described purpose. On the other hand, systems originally established for purely administrative purposes have been made accessible to government authorities with a wide range of tasks. An important example of the former is the VIS which was set up as a general information system from the outset. But as a result of the inclusion of biometric data, the Schengen Information System II will also take on the character of an information register. An example of the second development is the proposal to allow detection agencies access to Eurodac.

The fact that, especially since the attacks in the United States in 2001, politicians increasingly make a direct link between immigration and security policy has further contributed to the sidelining of the purpose limitation principle. This link has been justified by the German government in its assertion that: 'asylum seekers and foreigners who stay in the EU illegally, are regularly involved in the preparation of terrorist attacks'.[5] At a national level, the distinction between purposes relating to migration law and crime detection has become increasingly blurred. For example, in a letter of 12 November 2007, the Dutch Minister of Justice proposed broadening the use of fingerprints taken for the purposes of alien registration by allowing them to be automatically compared with fingerprints taken for the purposes of criminal enquiries (Dutch House of Representatives, 2007–08, 19 637, no. 1176). Since the introduction in 2001 of the Dutch Data Protection Act (WBP), such a comparison of fingerprints is only permissible if the suspect is also thought to be a suspect alien, or if the case involves the investigation of 'a serious crime' that 'seriously shocked social order'. As a result, according to the Minister of Justice, 'the number of matches between fingerprints identified from unsolved crimes and the fingerprints of aliens has decreased proportionally'. It is interesting to note, that in order to justify this proposal, the minister referred to developments at EU level, which also plans to allow crime-detection agencies to access the upcoming Visa Information System. According to the minister, this extended use will make a significant contribution to improving the crime detection and cooperation with other EU states 'taking account of the safeguards relating to the protection of the personal data of aliens'. In making this assertion, the minister is firstly indicating that the Dutch legislator clearly does not need to make its own judgment on the rights and wrongs of interfering in the fundamental rights of asylum seekers but can simply look at decision-making at EU level and follow suit. Secondly, this reference to cooperation with other EU member states would appear to imply that foreign governments will also be allowed access to this asylum data as well as Dutch crime-detection agencies.

### Prohibition on automated decision-making

Within administrative law and criminal law, the power of authorities to base their decisions on automated data processing is already subject to legal restrictions. For example, in accordance with general principles of administrative and criminal law, administrative authorities are obliged to provide written reasons for their decisions and in criminal cases judges must provide reasons for their rulings and tailor their individual decisions to the circumstances of the actual case in question. It is only in a number of areas of law, such as taxation law or traffic law, where a large number of individual decisions are made with regard to the payment of tax returns or traffic fines, that more or less automated decision-making has occasionally been adopted.

Against the backdrop of the developments described above where decisions are increasingly being made on the basis of joint EU data systems, it is useful to examine the background to and meaning of this principle more closely. The prohibition on automated decision-making was first established in one of the pioneers in national legislation on data protection: the French Data Protection Act. Based on this French clause, a similar clause on automated individual decisions was included in Article 15 of EC Directive 95/46. According to this, everyone has the right 'not to be subject to a decision which produces legal effects concerning him or significantly affects him and which is based solely on automated processing of data intended to evaluate certain personal aspects relating to him, such as his performance at work, creditworthiness, reliability, conduct, etc.'.

This ban on automated decision-making is however not an absolute prohibition. Article 15.2 of the EC Directive contains various restrictions; for example, an automated decision is permitted if such a decision 'is taken in the course of the entering into or performance of a contract, provided the request for the entering into or the performance of the contract, lodged by the data subject, has been satisfied or that there are suitable measures to safeguard his legitimate interests, such as arrangements allowing him to put his point of view forward' or 'is authorized by a law which also lays down measures to safeguard the data subject's legitimate interests'. With regard to administrative decisions, this last exception plays a significant role and it is regrettable that the EC Directive does not provide a clearer definition of 'measures to safeguard the data subject's legitimate interests'.

The legitimacy (and the proportionality) of automated decisions will often depend on the sort of decisions made on the basis of automated data processing. In this, a distinction can be made in the use of data processing for what may be termed positive or negative measures. Positive measures are records kept in order to promote or reward positive discrimination. Indeed, the aim of keeping records based on specific characteristics is primarily to improve the legal, social or economic situation of persons sharing those characteristics, for example a particular ethnic background, nationality or religion. Registration or data processing with a 'negative purpose' includes databases used primarily or exclusively in order to make decisions that have negative consequences for the data subject: for example, deportation, denial of access, control or prosecution. In this context, one could detect a switch in policy with regard to ethnic minorities in the Netherlands (Prins 2006). Whereas the original aim of the Employment of Minorities Act (*Wet Samen*) was to register minorities for a 'positive purpose', the current 'Civic Integration Information System' and the 'Database of potential persons requiring civic integration' proposed for the Civic Integration Act (*Wet Inburgering*) have far more negative consequences in terms of compulsion for third-country nationals. From the outset, the SIS involved negative decisions about non-EU subjects: on the basis of decisions made at national level as to whether someone should be defined as an 'undesirable alien', the individual involved is denied further access to the entire Schengen zone. Although the VIS will register all positive visa decisions and the data about people who have been granted a visa, this information will not automatically result in their being allowed access to EU territory. On the contrary, the *Visa Code* adopted on 13 July 2009 (Regulation 810/2009) specifically states that a visa issued does not automatically entitle its holder to access to the EU. This gives the national border-surveillance authorities the discretion to refuse access to a person regardless of the fact that they hold a valid visa.

## Migration technology and the prohibition on automated decision-making

The regulations concerning the SIS, the VIS or Eurodac do not include any references to the prohibition on automated decision-making. The SIS is even based on the opposite principle: the reciprocal recognition of decisions made at national level. The French and Dutch authorities (including the Dutch Immigration and Naturalization Service or IND) and others have repeatedly made reference to the obligation to implement in their own countries any findings in the SIS that originate from other Schengen partners (Brouwer 2008a: 1–18).

However, the significance of the ban on automated decision-making in the framework of the Schengen Information System has been clarified by the Court of Justice in its ruling on the case of the *Commission* v. *Spain* (C-503/03, 31 January 2006, *OJ* C 86, 8 April 2006). This case concerned the registration of non-EU subjects in the Schengen Information System and the fact that they had been refused access to and/or a visa for Spain on the basis of this. The complainants, both of Algerian nationality, were married to Spanish subjects and therefore had a stronger entitlement to stay in the EU states. The EC Court ruled that Spain had violated EC law by refusing access or a visa to the individuals involved without investigating whether they actually constituted a threat to public order. In doing so, the Court indicated that national authorities are not permitted to base their negative decision solely on data stored in the SIS system. Even if the system in question is based on the principle of mutual recognition of national decisions, the authorities will still need to assess whether any refusal violates rights protected by European law. In this case it involved the right of EU subjects and their families to free movement, but it is clear that the Court's reasoning also applies to other rights protected in EC or EU law, including human rights.

Another important reason why member states are not permitted to use the information stored in the European systems unchecked is the possible unreliability of these data. Firstly, this is because, as indicated earlier, biometric identification has been seen not to be infallible, in view of the current level of technology available. It has also been shown that the personal data in the current SIS and also in Eurodac, for example, is not always deleted within the statutory terms or in accordance with the legal conditions (Brouwer 2008b: 378, 427, 483). As a result, data about people may remain in such a system despite the lack of any legal justification for this. In accordance with Article 12 of the Eurodac Regulation, for example, the data of people acknowledged as refugees must be deleted. This has proved difficult to achieve in practice. In

February 2007, the Dutch State Secretary for Justice said in response to questions from Parliament that four years after Eurodac had been taken into use, the government still had no mechanism to ensure that fingerprints were deleted.[6]

Referring to Eurodac, a British immigration judge formulated an important precondition for the decision-making based on this system.[7] Based on Eurodac, asylum seekers can be returned by the authorities of one member state to another member state if a comparison of the fingerprints of the individual in question with fingerprints in Eurodac reveals that this person has already resided in the latter member state. This case involved an asylum seeker from Eritrea who was to be deported to Italy by the British authorities solely on the basis of a fingerprint match in Eurodac. The asylum seeker disputed the fact that he had previously claimed asylum in Italy protesting that he had been carrying out his military service in Eritrea at the time he was alleged to have been in Italy in 2005. In his judgment, the senior judge stated that when assessing whether a person has submitted an asylum application in another member state, an immigration lawyer must not only take account of fingerprint matches but also consider other information which might be used to determine whether a previous asylum application had been made, such as: a photograph, age, name and the claims made by the person involved. The judge must also admit information on how Eurodac functions and its reliability. At the core of this ruling is the judge's judgment that a court involved in alien issues must apply a fair system and assess whether the asylum seeker has received sufficient information about the allegations being used against him and whether he has had the opportunity, if he so wishes, to carry out forensic enquiries to present his side of the case. The British judge also pointed out that an asylum seeker is of course free to dispense with the option of such an enquiry if for example the fingerprint match is accurate and further evidence could jeopardize the case for him. However, in the judge's view, 'it is therefore the availability of the facility rather than the take-up that is needed in a fair system'. A similar entitlement to a reappraisal could also be an important precondition for the use of biometrics in migration and border controls.

The dangers of automated decision-making have been acknowledged by the European Parliament, suggesting the inclusion of a clause in the *Community Visa Code* to stipulate that a visa refusal must in no way influence any future visa decision and that every visa application must be judged on its own merits (see the report of the European Parliament 18 April 2008). This would mean that national authorities would be explicitly prohibited to refuse a visa to a third-country national based on previous negative visa decisions as recorded into the VIS. Unfortunately, when adopting the final text of the Visum Code (Regulation 810/2009), the Council decided, contrary to the advice of the European Commission, to delete the proposed clause.

### The supervisory role of data protection authorities

Many instruments used for data collection refer to the role of national data protection authorities as a safeguard for ensuring compliance with the relevant conditions and the protection of the rights of data subjects. The numerous developments at both national and international level have led to an enormous increase in workload for these supervisory authorities in recent years. There is therefore some doubt as to whether these organizations actually have the financial resources and legal powers they need in order to effectively exercise control.

In several countries, including the Netherlands, the data protection authorities have indicated that they are indeed suffering from a lack of sufficient resources, financial or otherwise. In 2007 the Dutch Data Protection Authority (*College Bescherming Persoonsgegevens* – CBP) announced that it could no longer process individual requests for advice because of insufficient resources. Forced as it was by this lack of resources to make certain choices, the CBP issued a memorandum entitled Enforcement Requires Resources (*Handhaven vereist middelen*), announcing that it was to focus more on compliance with legislation and less on its advisory role. According to its chairman Jacob Kohnstamm, the CBP now found that budget constraints made it impossible: 'to focus on the privacy issues faced by individuals since this detracts from our supervisory role over a range of developments which potentially affect all citizens'. He also referred to the development of the new Citizen Service Number (BSN), the public-transport chip card in the Netherlands and the provision of passenger data and proposals to combat terrorism in Europe. Other important issues such as the increased use of video surveillance and the application of biometrics were to receive minimal or no attention at all. In a series of press releases, the French data protection authority, CNIL, also announced that it was forced to make choices on the areas on which it could focus. It would require additional financial resources if it were to exercise its powers more effectively in practice and better meet the expectations of citizens.[8] The policy choices adopted by the CNIL even led in December 2007 to the occupation of the CNIL headquarters by civil-society organizations expressing their concern about the CNIL's failure to play an active role in the face of government measures relating to data processing (CNIL 2007).

The *Segerstedt-Wiberg* ruling issued in 2006 and mentioned above already highlights the need for an effective and well-equipped supervisory authority within the framework of Article 8 of the ECHR. In this ruling, the ECtHR explicitly examined the effectiveness of the powers of the relevant authorities in this area charged with monitoring the use of personal data by the Swedish secret police. With regard to one of the five complainants in this case, the Court ruled that there had been a violation of the right to effective legal recourse as protected in Article 13 of the ECHR in combination with Article 8 (*Segerstedt-Wiberg v. Sweden*, §§ 118–22). This conclusion was primarily based on the fact that the Swedish parliamentary ombudsman, responsible for supervising the operations of the secret police in general, lacked any effective powers to take decisions that were binding on government. The Court also determined that the Records Board, an institute specifically responsible for monitoring data processing by the secret police, had no powers to enforce the destruction, deletion or correction of stored data. Perhaps even more important are the ECtHR's pronouncements on the way in which the Swedish Data Inspection Board operated. The ECtHR determined that no information had been submitted to show that the procedure accessible to citizens to request removal of their data had actually provided an effective legal recourse (§ 120). Although the Data Inspection Board does have the power to impose financial sanctions in the event of irregular data processing and compel the organization to cease data processing or block the relevant data, this body did not have the power to compel the authorities to delete the irregularly stored data. Its only recourse was to submit a request to the local Administrative Court. More generally, the ECtHR determined that no information had been provided in this case 'to shed light on the effectiveness of the Data Inspection Board in practice'. On the contrary, the Court concluded that the procedure had revealed that the Data Inspection Board had never conducted a substantial investigation into the Swedish secret police databases at any point in its 30 years of existence.

With regard to the functioning of national data protection authorities, the European Court of Justice published, not only for Germany, a far-reaching judgment on 9 March 2010 in the case of *European Commission v. Germany* (C 518-07). Dealing with the interpretation of Article 28 (1) of the EC Data Protection Directive 95/46 on the role and requirements of national supervisory bodies, the EC Court gave a very broad interpretation of the requirement of 'independence'. Concluding that the data protection authorities of the different *Länder* were still subject to the scrutiny of their political governments, the Court found that the German law failed to meet the condition of 'complete independence'.

## The advisory role of data protection authorities

In addition to controls, data protection authorities also have an advisory role. It is however doubtful whether the advice provided by the data protection authorities highlighting issues with various proposals relating to data surveillance is sufficiently heeded by national and European policy-makers. Indeed, various national and European data protection authorities have repeatedly expressed their concerns about the use of and central storage of biometric data. In 2004, the French data protection authority CNIL rejected a proposal made by the French government for the biometric data of visa applicants to be registered centrally. According to the CNIL this proposal was neither legitimate nor proportional and this registration could also lead to the stigmatization of asylum applicants (CNIL 2004). The European Data Protection Supervisor (EDPS) has highlighted the technical drawbacks of biometric recognition in several reports. For example, it pointed out that 5 per cent of all individuals are not suitable for fingerprint recognition because their fingerprints are either damaged or insufficiently clear. The EDPS has also repeatedly highlighted the fact that a margin of error of between 0.5 and 1 per cent is normal for biometric recognition but unacceptable in view of the wide-scale storage of data at EU level. More recently, the EDPS has also expressed its concern both about the proposed entry-exit system and the use of profiling.[9]

To cite a Dutch example, the Minister of the Interior sidelined the negative advice issued by the CBP on draft legislation to extend the powers of the information and security services to collect the data of private individuals.[10] In its advice, the CBP indicated that although the data streams 'may have been set up with the best of intentions', the combination of the sheer size of the files and the far-reaching application possibilities of information technology would lead to disproportionate tracking and monitoring of citizens. The CBP also highlighted the lack of necessity and transparency of these measures and the fact that it is unable to supervise the relevant data processing because of an exclusion clause in the Dutch Data Protection Act. Despite these fundamental objections, the government announced to Parliament that it did not share this criticism and intended to pursue the proposed measures.

An important problem in the current advisory function of data protection authorities is the fact that the advice they provide is not binding. Despite this, politicians would be well advised not to systematically ignore or sidestep the warnings issued by these organizations if only as a means of securing additional legitimacy for their proposals.

## The right to non-discrimination[11]

### Data surveillance and the ban on discrimination

This study relates to information-technology instruments used specifically on migrants or third-country nationals (non-EU subjects). So far, policy-makers and legislators would seem to have failed to see the necessity of establishing whether the measures in question actually contravene the right to non-discrimination as protected in various parts of European legislation. In accordance with Article 14 of the ECHR, the states must ensure that all individuals are entitled to have the rights enshrined in this convention protected 'without discrimination on any ground such as sex, race, colour, language, religion, political or other opinion, national or social origin, association with a national minority, property, birth or other status'. In addition, Protocol number 12 of the ECHR offers a general prohibition on discrimination that is not limited to the human rights stipulated in the ECHR itself.[12]

EC law also includes additional conditions relating to compliance with human rights and the prohibition on discrimination. For example, Article 4b of the modified *Regulation laying down a unique format for residence permits* (Regulation 380/2008) stipulates that the recording of biometric data must be in line with the conditions outlined in the ECHR and the UN Convention on the Rights of Children. In accordance with the *Schengen Border Code* (Regulation 562/2006) border guards are obliged to conduct their border controls without discriminating on the grounds of gender, race, ethnic origin, religion, belief, disability, age or sexuality.[13] The preambles to the *Family Reunification Directive* (Directive 2003/86), the *Directive concerning the status of third-country nationals who are long-term residents* (Directive 2003/109) and the *Directive on the free movement of Union citizens (*Directive 2004/38*)* expressly stipulate that member states must apply these directives without discrimination on grounds such as race, colour, ethnic or social origin, language, religion, or membership of a national minority. Nationality is not included here as a prohibited grounds for discrimination. However, as has been highlighted previously by Groenendijk and others, within the scope of community law the general prohibition on discrimination on the grounds of nationality included in Article 12 of the EC Treaty (now

Article 18 of the Treaty of the Functioning of the European Union, TFEU) also applies for migration law (Groenendijk 2006b: 231–7; Boeles 2005: 500–13). This is also established in Article 21 of the EU Charter on Human Rights (OJ EC C 303/1, 14 December 2007). This prohibits all discrimination including discrimination on the grounds of race, colour, ethnic or social origin, genetic features and membership of a national minority. Section 2 contains a reference to the stipulation in Article 18 TFEU on the basis of which, within the sphere of operation of the EC Treaty and the EU Treaty, and 'without prejudice to special provisions of those Treaties', all discrimination on grounds of nationality is prohibited.

The information systems discussed will not only be consulted at external borders, but also by law-enforcement authorities within EU territory. Such controls and the use of biometrics in visas and residence documents could contravene the stipulations mentioned above if these are applied selectively, based on nationality, without objective legitimate grounds for doing so. Although EU subjects will also be increasingly subjected to these kinds of controls, including the biometric passport, for example, the systems discussed above such as the SIS, VIS and Eurodac will primarily affect non-EU subjects. Although in the case of *Moustaquim* v. *Belgium* the ECtHR accepted that the preferential treatment of EU citizens in national law is objectively and reasonably justified as a means of discriminating within the framework of granting specific rights, it does not justify every difference in treatment within the framework of EU measures (*Moustaquim* v. *Belgium*, 18 February 1991, 12313/86). The protected position of EU citizens (or the non-EU family members of EU subjects) does not mean that within the framework of data storage and the recording of biometric characteristics all discrimination between EU subjects and those from third countries or between different groups of third-country citizens is also legitimate. In various judgments issued by the ECtHR it has established that differentiated treatment in relevant comparable cases without an objective and reasonable legal justification also results in prohibited discrimination in accordance with Article 14 of the ECHR (*Mamatkulov and Abdurasulovic* v. *Turkey* (I), 6 February 2003, 46827/99; *Gaygusuz* v. *Austria*, 17 September 1996, 17371/90).

### Non-discriminatory application of data protection law

As well as the general application of non-discrimination clauses, another area frequently ignored is the non-discriminatory nature of the right to privacy and data protection. Article 8 of the ECHR (the right to a private life) and Articles 7 (private life) and 8 (protection of personal data) of the EU Human Rights Charter explicitly apply to anyone, without distinction in terms of nationality or origin, religion or status. However, in the light of the measures outlined above, the question remains as to whether the non-discriminatory application of data protection law is in fact guaranteed. The developments detailed above suggest that certain standards, such as the purpose limitation principle, the storage terms and transparency are not protected for third-country nationals in the same way as they are for national subjects or EU subjects. In certain circumstances, the storage or making available of biometric data or information about religion or ethnicity, for example, will violate the protection of special or sensitive data provided for in Article 8 of EC Directive 95/46.

In this context an interesting judgment has been issued by the Court of Justice in the case *Heinz Huber* v. *Germany* (C-524/06, 16 December 2008). The case involves the registration of EU subjects in the German central aliens records system *Ausländerzentralregister* or AZR. Questions have been posed to the EU Court of Justice about the legitimacy of this registration by the Supreme Administrative Court (*Oberverwaltungsgericht*) in North-Rhine Westphalia. The case itself involved the registration of an Austrian citizen, Mr Huber, in the AZR. The questions related on the one hand to whether the registration of EU subjects in the central AZR did not violate the prohibition on discrimination on the grounds of nationality, and on the other hand whether such a registration system was not in contravention of the principles of EC Directive 95/46 on the protection of personal data. In his opinion issued on this case on 3 April 2008, the Advocate General (AG) Maduro already concluded that there may be violation of the prohibition of discrimination based on nationality in so far as the registration contains more data about EU subjects than the data as specified in Article 8 (3) of Directive 2004/38/EC dealing with administrative formalities for Union citizens. The AG explicitly highlighted the danger of stigmatization of EU citizens. According to Maduro, the fact that EU citizens are registered separately means that the German government is monitoring EU nationals 'much more strictly and systematically' than it is German nationals (see para. 15). This argument could also be applied to non-EU subjects. In its final judgment, the EU Court of Justice, partially on the same grounds as the AG, found that the German central registration of EU citizens violated their right to non-discrimination. This conclusion was based on a strict application of the condition of necessity as laid down in Article 7 (e) of the EC Directive 95/46. Amongst others, the German legislator had failed to justify the necessity of the centralized nature of the database, the storage of individualized personal data in the AZR for statistical purposes, and the possible use of the personal data on EU citizens for law-enforcement purposes. The Court of Justice's judgment on this case could prove significant within the context of more general developments in data processing. Despite the fact that this case only concerned the central data processing of EU citizens, it is not inconceivable that similar arguments may feature in a future case concerning the registration of migrants in the SIS, VIS or Eurodac.

In this context, there has been a highly disappointing ruling issued by the Dutch Supreme Administrative Court (ABRvS) concerning the Reference Index on Antilleans (*Verwijsindex Antillianen* – VIA) (ABRvS 3 September 2008, LJN BE9698). This case, brought by the Dutch Caribbean Consultative Body (*Stichting Overlegorgaan Caribische Nederlanders*, OCaN), concerns the question of whether the Dutch Data Protection Authority was justified in granting a discretionary permit for this reference index to the established. According to the OCaN, the VIA constitutes illegitimate (because it was unnecessary) registration based on ethnicity and is therefore in contravention of the non-discrimination principle of Article 14 of the ECHR since it only includes data about young Antilleans considered to represent a risk. In its judgment, which may also be criticized on several other grounds, the Supreme Administrative Court ruled that the registration in question did however serve a legitimate purpose (managing a specific group of young people considered to constitute a risk) and was also an appropriate means of achieving that purpose. Although the VIA has meanwhile been replaced by a general index of 'youngsters at risk', this proposal was an important example of a more general development whereby it is increasingly considered acceptable to collect personal records only about specific groups of people, based on their nationality or ethnic background.

## Data profiling and non-discrimination

In the process known as data profiling, different databases are compared on the basis of specific criteria fitting a general personal profile in order to ascertain whether a particular individual is included in different databases. This is part of an effort to reach an ever-smaller list of 'suspect persons'. In the report *A Surveillance Society?* published by the British Parliament in May 2008, profiling is defined as follows: 'Databases may be searched automatically or "mined" using a formula or algorithm – which may itself have been created automatically by a computer program – in order to identify and classify individuals into categories or groups on the basis of their recorded preferences or activities' (House of Commons, Home Affairs Committee 2008: 17). Profiling is used in both the private and public sectors generally as a means of working more effectively and can prove advantageous for both clients and citizens (Goldschmidt and Rodrigues 2006: 42). Governments who use this method take the conscious decision to also include innocent citizens in closer investigation methods by means of this profiling, assuming that those who are innocent will automatically be filtered out at a later stage. In view of this filtering method, it is also known as *Rasterfahndung* in Germany.

This data collection and exchange by the police based on ethnic or religious profiles is however at odds with the non-discrimination principle especially since these methods mean that certain population groups will be subjected to more controls than others. This was also established by the German *Bundesverfassungsgericht* in a judgment issued in April 2006 on the application of *Rasterfahndung* or data profiling by the German police in the wake of the attacks of 11 September 2001 in the United States (Judgment of the Bundesverfassungsgericht, 4 April 2006, 1 BvR 518/02 published on 23 May 2006). The German police had deployed this technique to detect suspect young Arab Muslims. The judgment concerned a complaint made by a Moroccan student about whom information had been collected from various databases. The *Bundesverfassungsgericht* concluded that this data profiling was illegitimate because it constituted a disproportionate breach of his right to protection of his personal life. In justifying its conclusions, the *Bundesverfassungsgericht* referred to the extensive scope of the data collection, the use of different databases and the increased risk for the persons involved of becoming the target of criminal prosecution. It is important to note that the *Bundesverfassungsgericht* also explicitly referred to the likelihood of a group of people becoming stigmatized in public life, especially since in this case the practice of data profiling focused on a group of people of a specific nationality who are also Muslims (para. 110–12 of this judgment).

## Conclusions and recommendations

### The need for boundaries

Within the framework of migration policy, terrorism prevention or crime detection, border control is a legitimate duty of government. However, the measures and proposals currently being introduced focus primarily on the enhanced monitoring of the movements of travellers in and out of the territories of EU member states (Data Protection

Authorities 2008). The trends described involving the centralization of data storage, multifunctional use, automated decision-making and profiling are at odds with important legal standards intended to protect individual rights and freedoms.

It is clear that the application of the proposed entry-exit system, linked to the use of the VIS, will lead to the monitoring of the movements of non-EU subjects and especially those migrants who require a visa. But also those who do not require a visa will increasingly find themselves confronted with controls designed to determine their identity and/or the legitimacy of their residence based on biometrics and a comparison of data in databases. If no account is taken of the legal boundaries when developing such systems, the government measures based on these systems will increasingly often be declared to be illegitimate by the courts and by data protection authorities. Ideally, these legal boundaries should already be taken into account by the system designers. As stated by one of the spokesmen of the IT industry during a hearing in the British House of Commons on digital surveillance: 'In general, the technical developments which will come about will still basically be in a context in which the privacy issues remain the same and the principles for how one should address those privacy issues will also remain the same. The challenge would be ... when one is a system designer remembering to take account of those principles and not just getting captivated and dazzled by the potential of what the technology could do.'[14]

However, it is in the first place the responsibility of the legislator to safeguard fundamental rights and freedoms when adopting measures implying the use of (migration-) technology. As Prins pointed out, with reference to the proposed expansion of Eurodac discussed above: 'any politician who takes the issue of privacy seriously, must at least demand that his fellows engage in a fundamental discussion on the darker side of the plans to use Eurodac – the European databank for fingerprinting asylum seekers – for the purposes of crime detection. ... In this context, leadership means: raising questions about the move to create an implicit link between asylum seekers and criminality' (Prins 2006: 411).

This monitoring task of politicians also entails the need to assess in advance the necessity and effectiveness of any measures proposed. The fact that this task is not taken sufficiently seriously is illustrated by the inclusion of the fingerprints of minors in travel documents. In the face of repeated claims by experts that these fingerprints are not yet suitable for identification purposes, politicians have still opted to record and store biometric data from children from the age of six (Lodge 2007).

The proposal for an entry-exit system presented by the European Commission also offers no convincing evidence of the effectiveness or even the necessity of such a measure. The impact-assessment study published alongside this proposal did evaluate the advantages and disadvantages of different alternative methods of border control but it paid scant attention to the human rights consequences of the proposal. Furthermore, the report explicitly referred to the negative consequences for the detection of terrorists and criminals if the personal controls carried out by experienced and trained border-surveillance officers were to be replaced by so-called automatic portals on the external borders of EU countries. Despite this conclusion, in its ultimate proposal the Commission persisted in the application of automatic border controls or 'e-borders'.

The report *A Surveillance Society?*, issued by the British House of Commons Home Affairs Committee in 2008, emphasizes that the loss of privacy caused by excessive surveillance systems can undermine the confidence of individuals in the government and fundamentally change the relationship between citizen and state. As various experts pointed out during the hearing in the House of Commons, citizens who no longer have confidence in their government and the way in which it handles their data are no longer willing to cooperate with the government. As a result, surveillance measures and data profiling could ultimately prove counterproductive for governments. One of the central recommendations included in the report is that in the formation of policy and systems for data collection, the government should apply the 'principle of data minimization': the government must only collect what is essential and store it for only as long as it is necessary.

### 'Impact assessment' and 'data minimization'

Both the European Parliament and national parliaments play an important role in the developments described above: this applies both to the decision-making itself as well as to the scrutiny to which the implementations of these decisions are subjected. The people's national representatives must make sure that the necessity of the proposed measures has been sufficiently established by means of an impact assessment before any proposed legislation is submitted at national or European level. These impact-assessment studies will also need to be conducted by independent expert organizations. In the context of these developments, the lack of any prior reticence or scrutiny among politicians is undesirable for several reasons. One reason is that, as established by the

Dutch Chamber of Audit (*Algemene Rekenkamer*) in a study on large-scale computerization projects, ongoing projects are not easily halted even if they are no longer professionally justified. According to the Chamber of Audit: 'from a political perspective, decisions already taken are often difficult to reverse' (Algemene Rekenkamer 2007: 37).

Another reason for parliamentary scrutiny is the need to ensure effective governance. The expansion of existing systems and the increasing sharing of data also entail a risk to the reliability of the data. In the report mentioned above, the Dutch Chamber of Audit also highlighted this problem in relation to the unreliability of the data systems used by the government caused by the linking up of corrupted and antiquated data systems within government (see Algemene Rekenkamer 2007: 23). The rejection by the European Parliament of the EU–US SWIFT agreement on the transfer of bank account data of EU citizens to the USA is a good example of the active role parliaments may have when dealing with proposals affecting data protection and fundamental rights. In its resolution of 11 February 2010, adopted by a majority of 378 to 196 votes, the European Parliament found that the agreement violates the basic principles of data protection law on necessity and proportionality of data processing and lacks sufficient guarantees in order to protect the rights of citizens.

Whenever the choice is made for specific systems or the storage of data, the regulations that apply to them must contain adequate safeguards. There must also be a clear and unambiguous description of the powers of the relevant authorities, the categories of people who may be monitored and the situations in which data may be collected. The making available of data to third states or private organizations must be prohibited as far as possible, especially when it relates to data about asylum seekers. Finally, the government staff involved must be educated and trained in such a way to ensure that the systems are used appropriately and rights of data subjects sufficiently accounted for.

## Human rights assessment

When setting up new data systems or applying existing systems more widely and when using data profiling, legislators must carry out a more comprehensive human rights assessment as, for example, proposed by Goldschmidt and Rodrigues with reference to the use of ethnic profiling (Goldschmidt and Rodrigues 2006: 56–60). They propose that the effectiveness of profiling should be evaluated regularly. According to them, profiling must always be temporary and its use outlawed once the reason for its application no longer exists. In their 'human rights standard', they also emphasize the general precondition that the necessity of the measures for the democratic society to protect public order and safety must have been demonstrated and there must be a balance between the intended goal and the fundamental rights of the data subjects. It is important in this context, as I argued above, that decision-making is not based on an artificial opposition between privacy on the one side and security on the other, with the latter being cited as another basic right. There is no doubt that in carrying out its general duties, including security policy, there are specific situations in which the government may restrict individual human rights such as the right to a private life, but this interference must meet the conditions described in this chapter.

Although this chapter does not examine this aspect in further detail, it is clear that the protection of human rights also includes the protection of refugees. In accordance with international law, EU member states are obliged to handle with care the personal data provided by asylum seekers during the asylum process. The authorities in the asylum seekers' countries of origin must be prevented from gaining access to these persons' asylum dossiers. For this reason, the data stored about asylum seekers in Eurodac for purely administrative purposes must not be made available to law-enforcement authorities and security agencies. This would not only contravene their right to data protection, but also violate the protection they are entitled to in accordance with international refugee law. The fact that the likelihood of EU authorities passing on asylum data to the authorities in the countries from which the asylum seekers originate is not completely illusory is demonstrated by the report issued by the Spanish refugee organization in June 2008, in which it warned against the exchange of asylum data between the Spanish and Colombian authorities.[15]

### Controls by individuals and supervisory authorities

Quite aside from the parliamentary control mechanisms, the controls carried out by the citizen and by independent supervisory authorities also need to be enhanced. This is necessary firstly because of the expansion in the provision of information to the individuals themselves. They need to be informed in advance about the collection of personal data, or if such collection takes place as part of the protection of internal security, at least after the appropriate measures have been taken. The authorities also need to take measures to counteract the illegitimate distribution of personal data and to safeguard the quality and protection of sensitive data.

The data protection authorities must be given increased financial resources and powers. The latter includes the possibility to issue binding advice if the data protection authority judges that the proposed instrument is unconstitutional or contravenes international (human rights) treaties. It is also worth considering extending the data protection authorities' powers to block illegitimate data processing and making it compulsory for them to subject existing large-scale systems to more regular scrutiny.

Finally, the options for sanctions and damage compensation could also be expanded. An important step towards this has been made in Article 49 of the SIS II Regulation in accordance with which member states must subject any misuse of data or exchange of supplementary information that contravenes this Regulation to 'effective, proportionate and dissuasive penalties in accordance with national law'. It is regrettable in this context that the EU legislator did not see fit to formulate minimum sanctions. It is highly revealing that such minimum sanctions were imposed with regard to the obligation of airlines to provide passenger data to border-surveillance officers. In accordance with Directive 2004/82, airlines must be fined between €3000 and €5000 for failure to provide this information.

Current developments demand a critical and balanced approach on the part of the legislator. Both the European and the national legislators must ensure that they, along with their administrators and IT developers, do not allow themselves to be carried away by current events or the 'dazzling' potential of information technology. In the adoption of new measures relating to migration technology, government boundaries and the rights of citizens must be placed centre stage.

## Notes

1. The exact source of the judgments cited can be found in the case-law section at the end of this chapter. The details of these cases are described in Brouwer (2008b: 147–76).
2. See the comment on *Examining the Creation of a European Border Surveillance System (EUROSUR)* COM (2008) 68 and concerning *Preparing the Next Steps in Border Management in the European Union* COM (2008) 69, 13 February 2008.
3. See for example the advice issued by the Belgian Privacy Commission no. 17/2008 dated 9 April 2008 on the processing of biometric data for the authentification of individuals, www.privacycommission.be/nl/docs/ Commission/2008/advies_17_2008.pdf (p. 9).
4. Like information registers, statistical registers also have an information purpose. The difference is that if statistical information concerns the population or groups within it, the information stored is not about the separate individuals but is anonymized.

5. Council document 16892/06, 20 December 2006, not public, but published on: www.statewatch.org/news/2007/jan/05eurodac.htm and Council document 17102/06, 22 December 2006, published on: http://register.consilium.europa.eu. See also the critical comments in response to this proposal from the Standing Committee of experts on international immigration, refugees and criminal law (Meijers Committee) dated 18 September 2007 and 6 November 2007, www.commissie-meijers.nl. See also: *Dutch Government Gazette*, no. 226, 21 November 2007.
6. Response from State-Secretary Albayrak to questions from member of the Dutch Labour Party (PvdA) Spekman, 27 February 2007, Annex no. 875 in Handelingen (Official report) 2006–07.
7. See the judgment of UK Immigration and Asylum Tribunal YI (Previous claims – Fingerprint match – EURODAC) Eritrea [2007] UKAIT 00054, 24 May 2007, Senior Immigration Judge Batiste, included in *Nieuwsbrief Asiel en Vluchtelingenrecht* 2007, with a note by E.R. Brouwer.
8. See the press release dated 4 January 2008 and earlier, the press release of 20 April 2005, on the lack of funding to deal effectively with the increasing number of requests for information about police records, www.cnil.fr.
9. During a meeting of the European Parliament on 8 July 2008, see the report 'Border Management: Striking the Balance between Freedom and Security', www.europarl.europa.eu/news/.
10. Wijziging van de Wet op de inlichtingen en veiligheidsdiensten (Amendment to the Information and Security Services Act), Handelingen Eerste Kamer (Official report on proceedings in the Upper Chamber of the Dutch Parliament) 2007–08, no. 30 553, C: 1–16. For the advice issued on this legislation by the CBP, see the press release dated 20 December 2007, www.cbpweb.nl.
11. For a detailed discussion of this subject, see Brouwer (2008a).
12. CETS no. 177, this protocol was enacted on 1 April 2005.
13. Regulation 562/2006 establishing a Community Code on the rules governing the movement of persons across borders, 15 March 2006, *OJ EC* L/105, 13 April 2006. See Article 6 Section 1 and Article 4 (2).
14. Pete Bramhal, Manager of Privacy and Identity Research at Hewlett-Packard Laboratories 12 June 2007 (House of Commons, Home Affairs Committee 2008: 42).
15. See the report *Spain/Colombia: Information Exchange Puts Colombian Asylum Seekers at Risk*, www.statewatch.org/news/2008/jul/01spain-columbia-cear.htm.

# Bibliography

Algemene Rekenkamer (2007) *Lessen uit ICT-projecten bij de overheid*, Rapport deel A, 29 November.
Beuving, J., J. Heuver and W. van Helden (2006) 'Etniciteit, profilering en het gelijkheidsbeginsel', *Nederlands Juristenblad*, 34: 1492.
Boeles, P. (2005) 'Europese burgers en derdelanders: wat betekent het verbod van discriminatie naar nationaliteit sinds Amsterdam', *SEW*, 12: 500–13.

Brouwer, E. (2007) 'Van de Schengengrenscode, via Frontex, naar SIS II en VIS. Nieuwe ontwikkelingen in het EU buitengrenzenbeleid', *Migrantenrecht*, 6: 232–9.

Brouwer, E. (2008a) 'Derdelanders en de "e-grenzen" van de Europese Unie. Differentiatie of discriminatie?', in A. Böcker, T. Havinga, P. Minderhoud, H. van de Put *et al.* (eds) *Migratierecht en Rechtssociologie, gebundeld in Kees' studies. Migration Law and Sociology of Law, or Collected Essays in Honour of Kees Groenendijk* (Nijmegen: Wolf Legal Publishers).

Brouwer, E. (2008b) *Digital Borders and Real Right: Effective Remedies for Third-Country Nationals in the Schengen Information System* (Leiden and Boston: Martinus Nijhoff Publishers).

Brouwer, E. (2008c) *The Other Side of Moon: The Schengen Information System and Human Rights: A Task for National Courts*, CEPS Working Document, no. 288, April (Brussels: CEPS).

Brouwer, E. (2009) *The EU PNR System and Human Rights: Transferring Passenger Data or Passenger Freedom?*, CEPS Working Document, no. 320, September (Brussels: CEPS).

Brouwer, E., P. De Hert and R. Saelens (2007) 'Ontwerp kaderbesluit derde pijler holt bescherming persoonsgegevens uit', *Privacy & Informatie*, 1: 9–13.

CNIL (2004) *L'expérimentation de visas biometrique: la position de CNIL*. www.cnil.fr.

CNIL (2007) *Occupation des locaux de la CNIL à Paris*. www.neteco.com.

Data Protection Authorities (2008) Declaration at their Spring Conference, Rome 17–18 April.

Dutch Data Protection Authority (2007) Symposium report, 1 November (The Hague): 35.

Elgesem, D. (1999) 'The Structure of Rights in Directive 95/46 on the Protection of Individuals with Regard to the Processing of Personal Data and the Free Movement of Such Data', *Ethics and Information Technology*, 1: 283–93.

Enschedé, C. (1974) 'Het interimrapport-Koopmans: een discussiebijdrage', *Nederlands Juristenblad*, 32, 28 September: 1025 ff.

Future Group, The (2007) *New Ideas for a Free and Safe Europe: Report for the First Meeting of the Future Group* (Eltville, Germany), 20 and 21 May.

Goldschmidt, J. and Rodrigues, P. (2006) 'Het gebruik van etnische of religieuze profielen bij het voorkomen en opsporen van strafbare feiten die een bedreiging vormen voor de openbare orde en veiligheid', in J. van Donselaar and P. Rodrigues (eds) *Monitor Racisme & Extremisme. Zevende rapportage* (Amsterdam: Anne Frank Stichting).

Groenendijk, K. (2006a) 'Citizens and Third Country Nationals: Differential Treatment or Discrimination?', in J. Carlier and E. Guild, *The Future of Free Movement of Persons in the EU* (Brussels: Bruylant).

Groenendijk, K. (2006b) 'EG migratierecht en de grenzen bij bestrijding van terrorisme', *Migrantenrecht*, 6–7: 231–7.

Groenendijk, K. (2007) 'The Long-Term Residents Directive, Denizenship and Integration', in A. Baldaccini, E. Guild and H. Toner (eds) *Whose Freedom, Security and Justice? EU Immigration and Asylum Law and Policy* (Oxford: Hart Publishers).

Guild, E. (2005) 'The Legal Framework: Who is Entitled to Move?', in D. Bigo and E. Guild, *Controlling Frontiers: Free Movement into and within Europe* (Aldershot: Ashgate).

Hert, P. de, W. Schreurs and E. Brouwer (2007) 'Machine-Readable Identity Documents with Biometrical Data in the EU: Overview of the Legal Framework and Critical Observations (Parts II, II and IV)', *Keesing Journal of Documents & Identity*, 22, 23, 24.

Hirsch Ballin, E. (2007) Speech at the symposium of the Dutch Data Protection Authority, 1 November. www.cbpweb.nl/downloads_pb/pb_20071101_speechHirschBallin.pdf.

House of Commons, Home Affairs Committee (2008) *A Surveillance Society? Fifth Report of Session 2007–08*, vol. II (London: The Stationery Office).

Legomsky, S. (2005) 'The Ethnic and Religious Profiling of Noncitizens: National Security and International Human Rights', *Boston College Third World Law Journal*, 25: 161–96.

Lodge, J. (ed.) (2007) *Are You Who You Say You Are? The EU and Biometric Borders* (Nijmegen: Wolf Legal Publishers).

Muller, E., H. Kummeling and R. Bron (2007) *Veiligheid en privacy. Een zoektocht naar een nieuwe balans* (The Hague: Boom Juridische uitgevers).

Prins, C. (2006) 'Etno-selectie', *Nederlands Juristenblad*, 8: 411.

Schmid-Drüner, M. (2007) *Der Begriff der öffentlichen Sicherheit und Ordnung im Einwanderungsrecht ausgewählter EU-Mitgliedstaaten: Status quo und Reformbedarf auf europäischer Ebene* (Baden-Baden: Nomos Verlag).

Scholten, S. (2008) 'Verantwoordelijkheden van vervoerders in grenscontrole. Nut en noodzaak van doorgifte van passagiersgegevens', *Privacy & Informatie*, 4: 179–83.

## Case law

*Al-Nashif* v. *Bulgaria*, 20 June 2002, no. 50963/99, JV 2002/239.
*Amann* v. *Switzerland* 16 February 2000, no. 27798/95 ECHR 2000-II.
*The Association for European Integration and Human Rights and Ekimdzhiev* v. *Bulgaria* 28 June 2007, no. 62540/00.
*C.G. and others* v. *Bulgaria* 24 April 2008, no. 1365/07 ECtHR 2008/79 with note by A. Woltjer.
*Christine Goodwin* v. *United Kingdom*, 11 July 2002, no. 28957/95 (unpublished).
*Friedl* v. *Austria*, 31 January 1995 (decision of the Court to strike the case from the list, amicable settlement), no. 15225/89, Series A 305B.
*Gaskin* v. *United Kingdom*, 7 July 1989, Series A no. 160.
*Gaygusuz* v. *Austria*, 17 September 1996, no. 17371/90.
*İletmiş* v. *Turkey*, 6 December 2005, no. 29871/96 (unpublished).
*Klass* v. *Germany*, 6 September 1978, no. 5029/71.
*Kruslin and Huvig* v. *France*, 24 April 1990 (combined cases) nos. 11801/95 and 11105/84, Series A 176 A and B.
*Leander* v. *Sweden*, 26 March 1987, no. 9248/81, Series A no. 116.
*Lupker and others* v. *the Netherlands*, Commission decision of 7 December 1992, no. 18395/91, unreported.
*Lupsa* v. *Romania*, 8 June 2006, no. 10337/04 JV 2006/311.
*Malone* v. *United Kingdom*, 2 August 1984, no. 8691/79, Series A 82.
*Mamatkulov and Abdurasulovic* v. *Turkey (I)*, 6 February 2003, no. 46827/99 (unreported).

*Moustaquim* v. *Belgium*, 18 February 1991, no. 12313/86.

*Peck* v. *United Kingdom*, 28 January 2003, no. 44647/98 *ECHR* 2003-I.

*Perry* v. *United Kingdom*, 17 July 2003, no. 63737/00 *ECHR* 2003-IX.

*P.G. and J.H.* v. *the United Kingdom*, 25 September 2001, no. 44787/98 *ECHR* 2001-IX.

*Rotaru* v. *Romania*, 4 May 2000, no. 28341/95 *ECHR* 2000-V.

*Segerstedt-Wiberg and others* v. *Sweden*, 6 June 2006, no. 62332/00 *ECHR* 2006, 89.

*Smirnova* v. *Russia*, 24 July 2003, nos. 46133/99 and 48183/99 *ECHR* 2003-IX.

*Z.* v. *Finland*, 25 February 1997, no. 22009/93, *Reports* 1997-I.

# 7
# Reclaiming Control over Europe's Technological Borders

*Huub Dijstelbloem, Albert Meijer and Frans Brom*

## Surveillance by government and citizens

Migration policy and border control in Europe and its member states increasingly take place in a surveillance regime that is focused on control. The surveillance regime consists of the intertwining of migration, integration and security policies on the one hand with a technological apparatus for the control of the movements of people on the other (Haggerty and Ericson 2000; Lyon 2009). Surveillance of citizens, migrants and illegal aliens is not only executed by the state but also by private companies and medical professionals working for the state. Next to that, the surveillance regime is not only regulated externally but travellers internalize security in voluntary behaviour. As a consequence, surveillance is not only exercised by control 'from above' (Big Brother) but also 'from aside' (Little Sister) and 'from within' (Voice Inside).

In this concluding chapter, we will describe how surveillance and control affect the citizen: regular inhabitants of the several member states, travellers, migrants and illegal aliens. Moreover, we will sketch the need for a thorough rethinking of the position and the rights of these citizens because of the consequences technological borders have, for instance, on their privacy, bodily integrity, mobility, quality of data, information storage and exchange, and opportunities for correction. We want to reclaim the role of citizens as *subjects* who are actively involved in controlling and shaping Europe's technological borders.

To elaborate on this perspective, it is useful to remember that originally the term surveillance was introduced as a means not for the government, but for the people. By the time of the French Revolution it referred to a form of public oversight that was celebrated as the main remedy for dysfunctional institutions (Rosanvallon 2008: 13). These powers of oversight could function beside the parliament to strengthen public control, for instance by the execution of watchdog functions and civic vigilance. Surveillance is not the privilege of the state apparatus, but a means of control that can be executed by citizens and independent authorities such as supervisors and audit committees as well. Conceptually and historically, the term thus offers some space to broaden the surveillance regime with forms of counter-control by citizens 'from below'. Such counter-control is needed all the more because we cannot expect the several technological systems to work without problems.

A political imperative to reconsider the position of citizens in the oversight of the technologies that are deployed in migration policy and border control is given by the recent changes in the constitution of the European Union since the Treaty of Lisbon (Chapter 2 by Balch and Geddes in this book). These changes include, amongst others, a strengthening of the position of the European Parliament as the representative of citizens. More programmatically, attention for the position of citizens in the area of freedom, security and justice has been asked for in the Stockholm programme of the European Council (Council of the European Union 2009). It highlights migration as a priority area and includes integration, illegal migration, migration and development, labour migration, asylum seekers and rights of third-country nationals (people from outside the European Union) amongst its action points (Collett 2010). Although the Council considers that technology can play a key role in improving and reinforcing the system of external border control, and encourages the EU agency Frontex to continue its work on automated border control, the programme pleads for a greater opportunity for citizens and representative associations to debate and publicly exchange views on these topics. Moreover, the rights of non-EU citizens ('default citizens' – Aas 2009: 319) are also specifically considered.

The role of citizens is not only of importance for the European Parliament, but also for the national parliaments. Although migration policy and border control are increasingly integrated and harmonized at a European level, member states and other states involved in the Schengen area still have sovereignty on many tasks and instruments. Moreover, in some respects there is a discrepancy between national and European initiatives. With regard to biometrics, for instance, European systems such as the SIS, Eurodac and VIS focus mainly on the use of fingerprints while many national governments (e.g. the United Kingdom and the Netherlands) experiment with systems using iris scans. Interoperability between systems is a strong incentive at the European level, but it remains unclear if and how national systems will fit in a common European system in the near future, especially because cooperation on migration issues demands much more than 'technical solutions'. As the UK's House of Lords has stated in its report *Surveillance: Citizens and the State* (2009: 79): 'technological solutions, if not pursued within a wider design framework, may help to limit surveillance and protect privacy, but they should not be seen as a standalone solution. This is because the specific rules, norms and values – for example, data minimisation, access controls, and the means of anonymity – that may be built into technological systems must come from outside those systems themselves.'

The complex relations between national and European responsibilities, and between national and European technological systems for migration policy and border control, make it all the more important to analyse the problems arising for citizens and to explore the opportunities to strengthen their position.

## Technology out of control

The sum of the systems that are used in Europe in migration policy and border control that create a surveillance regime has been labelled in this volume as a 'machine'. This machine is a cross-border policy apparatus for limiting the movement of aliens and for making choices about the migrants (desirable/undesirable) who report to the borders. It consists of laws, policy measures and implementation officers, and not forgetting a considerable amount of technology. It comprises everything from age testing by means of bone scans on underage asylum seekers to the body scans at European airports, and everything from passport control to enormous European databases. As a result, checking the movements of persons to the EU or even their movements worldwide (Redpath 2007) is increasingly becoming a technological issue.

The technology is needed to carry out the complex tasks that European governments are faced with in implementing migration policies and in checking the migrant flows. The dynamics of migration, the employment market and criminal networks have increased enormously, thus demanding important adjustments in migration policy implementations. In order to deal with all the complex processes, increasingly complex forms of control methods are needed (Beniger 1989).

Still, it remains unclear to what extent the 'growth' of the machine can be regulated. In general, issues that have been framed as technological issues tend to remain within the technological domain. Many scientists and artists have warned us of the dangers of 'technics-out-of-control' or 'autonomous technology' (see the influential and still surprisingly relevant work of Winner (1977) for an overview). In a way the migration machine has already developed its own dynamic, with technical system questions dominating the decision-making around policies and their implementation. The logic of a machine that is trying to perfect itself plays an important role here.

From within the technological frame, deficiencies – such as the impossibility of establishing with any certainty someone's identity from documents – are considered as problems that can be solved technically. Information systems are linked up to each other to an increasing degree, thereby giving added value. Technology is 'greedy' and the danger is that it will come to dictate political decision-making.

Technological developments allow questions from the 'real world' to be translated into system requirements. Technology, however, never allows a one-to-one translation. Some social meaning is lost in translation, and the political environment in which the technology is developed can also cause distortions. In the SIS, the complex behaviour shown by migrants is simply translated into the presence or absence of an observation (hit/no hit). But behaviour is in general more complex than the yes/no dichotomy allows. If one fails to recognize the political character of the techno-social simplifications involved, the machine may run out of control. This leads to machines that develop their own dynamic and that take away room for political choice.

Can we make adjustments to the migration machine in order to keep it under control? Before we are able to develop adjustment strategies, we need to have a clearer view of the risks, issues and unintended problems that arise from insufficient reflection on the deployment of migration technology. This final chapter therefore focuses mainly on the negative side of using migration technology. We sketch risks, issues and unintended problems with the help of four questions on the functioning and management of the migration machine:

- Does the migration machine deliver?
- Is the migration machine just?
- Can the migration machine be managed?
- Is the migration machine subjected to public control?

The objective of these four questions is to assess whether – and maybe more precisely: to what extent – a 'machine' has been created that functions properly within its political, legal, humanitarian, administrative and technological parameters. To what extent are we still in control of technology?

## Does the migration machine deliver?

In an ideal textbook scenario, the migration machine achieves its goal – the implementation of migration policy – effectively and efficiently. In addition, it does function in a reliable manner and makes a limited number of mistakes. The means the migration machine uses to achieve this goal are proportional in relation to the infringements it makes on people's lives. In short: the ideal machine strengthens policy implementation. In practice, however, things look different.

A fundamental question regarding the deployment of migration technology is whether or not the required target is being achieved. The effectiveness of migration technology is often difficult to measure. In many cases there are no data or they are not publicly available. Very often, evaluative reports fail to be written when existing systems are replaced or are succeeded by new systems such as the SIS. We cannot assess whether Europe's electronic borders actually enhance the effectiveness of immigration policies.

In addition, it is often not clear how narrowly or how broadly the effectiveness should be interpreted and whether the effectiveness ultimately achieved corresponds with what had been envisaged. The purpose limitation principle demands that information about migrants, collected for a particular reason, is not without a proper reason applicable for another requirement. The principle restricts the use of information for other goals than it was originally gathered for. If this principle is not adhered to and, for example, a databank is set up to achieve a certain aim but is then used for other reasons, one may speak of function creep. The association between migration and security in particular is significant here, with the risk that contributions to security policy also form part of the evaluation of the effectiveness of migration technology, especially since after the attacks of 9/11 the fight against terrorism gained a much stronger position worldwide (Bigo and Tsoukala 2008).

Related to effectiveness is efficiency. Large government ICT projects are often overloaded with political ambitions that can lead them to collapse under their own weight. It is difficult to predict the gains of large technological systems because thorough analyses of costs and returns are generally lacking. Technology is often presented as the only way forward without systematically analysing the costs and benefits of technological options.

Next to effectiveness and efficiency, proportionality is important. The collection and storage of personal details (especially sensitive information) can have a serious effect on one's personal life. The question should then be asked: is such an infringement commensurate with the aim? There is no general standard for proportionality. In practice, the government, organizations (that implement measures) and judges often interpret proportionality in their own individual way and this leads to discussions about deploying technology such as bone scans and databases intended for security purposes. In that sense, border control in the European Union is not merely enforcing legal norms created by the European Union. Instead, legal norms are modified by local actors who adapt international, European and national law and assert their own claims at their conveniences (Klepp 2010: 20).

Reliability is another of the basic criteria for testing the machine. Technology is often thought to eliminate the arbitrary nature of human decisions and ensures that equal cases are always treated equally. When systems are implemented, the reliability of the technology is often taken for granted. In many cases, technology is indeed a reliable partner. The accuracy of DNA tests used in family reunification cases is almost 100 per cent. However, no biometric system is infallible, as every form of identification is fundamentally unstable (Chapter 4 by Van der Ploeg and Sprenkels).

The reliability of the large databases (mainly European) should also be queried. Error detection is playing too limited a role, at any rate in the national information systems. In the present SIS, personal data are not always deleted within the period of time or according to the conditions legally established (Chapter 6 by Brouwer). The various technologies are enormously complex and involve considerable organization so it is very difficult to guarantee reliability of data.

In sum, it is hard to tell whether the machine actually delivers. Lack of evaluations, shifting goals and an unbalanced proportionality trouble a clear judgment on this point.

## Is the migration machine just?

From a legal perspective, the ideal migration machine should function in accordance with the legal demands that have been formulated through democratic and legal processes. Equal treatment of equal cases is a key principle and a well-functioning machine should respect it. Other requirements are respect for the human body and people's privacy. The ideal machine respects the general requirements that have been formulated for government. However, in this case too the practice of migration policy raises many questions.

The protection of migrants who are subjected to the migration machine can be conceptualized in terms of guaranteeing (or violating) the protection of migrants' privacy, their equality before the law and their integrity (Chapter 6 by Brouwer). This integrity has to do with preventing data being misused by governments, civil servants or third parties. 'Everyone has a right to the protection of his personal data' (Art. 8 EU Charter for Fundamental Rights). Therefore, protecting information and creating clear rules for the lawful access to data is of crucial importance (Chapter 4 by Van der Ploeg and Sprenkels). After all, migrants are required to supply data about themselves, so it is very important they can rely on there being no misuse.

At the same time, the extent to which the machine can still do justice to migrants' individual situations can be questioned (Chapter 6 by Brouwer). A properly functioning migration machine can increase equality before the law as migrants are not then at the mercy of one individual civil servant's decision. However, there is also a risk of increasing inequality. Some migrants are offered a DNA test; others are not. This leads to differences in potential ways of collecting evidence. Also, age testing is carried out in different ways in different EU countries, thus causing possible inequality before the law. The practice of data profiling seems at odds with the principle of non-discrimination (Chapter 6 by Brouwer). The migration machine makes use of a way of social sorting (Bowker and Starr 1999; Lyon 2003) and can be characterized as a sorting machine that provides some people with privileges whilst excluding others (Chapter 3 by Broeders). After all, selection is, after restriction, the main aim of the policy (Chapter 1 by Dijstelbloem *et al.*).

Migrant protection is also expressed where a technique uses the body as point of intervention: as information storage device or even as way to verify a migrant's story. A possible side effect is an infringement of the integrity of a migrant's body. According to Alterman in an article with the telling title 'A Piece of Yourself', collecting biometric data acquires a fundamental privacy interest because it has an impact on one's right to control the use and disposition of one's body. Moreover, according to him we should be concerned about having biometric images created, reproduced or circulated (Alterman 2003: 145–6). So, in general, technologies making use of information the human body provides are far from innocent. As European Data Protection Supervisor Peter Hustinx stated in 2007: 'Biometrics are not just another information technology. They change irrevocably the relation between body and identity, in that they make the characteristics of the human body "machine-readable" and subject to further use. Even if the biometric characteristics are not readable by the human eye, they can be read and used by appropriate tools, forever, wherever the person goes' (in Ludford 2007: 3).

Other risks are that the human body is actually put in danger or at the risk of being damaged. An example of possible infringement of the bodily integrity is exposure of minors to X-rays in order to establish that they really *are* minors. This exposure to X-rays is not justified by a valid medical reason, because those seeking asylum are, after all, not ill and have not reported to a medical authority; they simply wish to be considered for a residence permit. The investigation being carried out is also not a medical but an anthropological one. It is far from clear whether the aim justifies the infringement of the human body.

Another potential side effect is stigmatization of migrants. The EU guidelines regarding migration should be applied without reference to race, skin colour, ethnic or social background or religion, but databases and biometrics make it increasingly easy to distinguish between people on the basis of these features. This means that certain forms of 'categorical surveillance' can arise, and also discrimination against migrants (Chapter 4 by Van der Ploeg and Sprenkels). The migration machine can sort on ethnicity and origin by referring to body material and this seems to be developing into data profiling. Some people may be stigmatized and this could be seen as an attack on their personal life. The risk of stigmatization increases when databases are also used for security policy. The idea behind this appears to be that every migrant is a potential criminal if data analysis shows that they belong to a high-risk group.

A third potential side effect is the establishment of a class of 'migration-machine operators'. The migration machine is adequately characterized by the idea of vulnerable individuals who are being steamrollered by a large governmental machine. It is more realistic to analyse the roles of individuals from the perspective of who benefits from the 'sorting machine' function and who does not. The official narrative is that a functioning machine separates the migrants who satisfy all the migration requirements imposed by government from the migrants who ask to migrate for dishonest reasons. A side effect, however, is the establishment of bureaucratically competent middlemen who assist migrants in playing the migration machine successfully. This makes bureaucratically less competent migrants dependent on people smugglers – the people who can support them sufficiently in playing this game.

And, finally, Europe's electronic borders do not only distinguish between the 'good ones' and the 'bad ones' but also between ethnic groups (Chapter 3 by Broeders). For certain ethnic groups, there is a problem with fingerprints, hand shapes and facial characteristics (Chapter 4 by Van der Ploeg and Sprenkels). Thus, although the migration machine may have succeeded in reducing the bias showed by individual civil servants, this individual bias may well have been replaced by a system bias.

In sum, the functioning of the migration machine should not be analysed purely in terms of decreasing or increasing migrant flows; the advantages and disadvantages (and which groups experience one or the other) also need to be analysed. In this respect, the importance of impact assessment and a human rights test should be emphasized, to which a periodic evaluation could be added, as it is extremely important to guarantee that the migration machine is not adversely affecting the wrong groups (Chapter 6 by Brouwer).

## Can the migration machine be managed?

Europe's electronic borders are managed by bureaucratic authorities in the various member states. In theory, the migration machine is controlled by bureaucrats and does not infringe upon the principles of bureaucratic organization. These principles are important to ensure the government policies are implemented according to the demands of bureaucracies' political masters and with respect for the law. The migration machine needs to be comprehensible and controllable to the various layers of bureaucratic organization (Chapter 5 by Meijer). Again, in practice many questions arise.

The relationship of the civil servants making the decisions to the automated processes deserves some special attention (Lyon 2003). Strictly speaking, technology and automation apply to all processes in which information is registered in documents or databases and to all processes that are automated or supported by the use of information databases to such an extent that the character of the administrative processes is strongly affected. Such systems do not replace civil servants, neither do they confirm that civil servants are an extension of technology. However, they do structure situations because, for practical reasons, it is rather difficult to diverge significantly from the route traced out by information technology. That makes it difficult to guarantee a civil servant's discretion and to separate automated decision-making from structured decision-making.

The quantity of data on individuals that the migration machine collects, processes, enhances and combines is formidable. Examples would be the use of the SIS and VIS: by 2005, 30,000 terminals in the Schengen territory already had access to the SIS and more than 260,000 records had been entered. The estimate is that 20 million visa requests are processed annually in VIS. However, it is often unclear precisely which data are collected and used. Individuals are not normally aware of what information is collected by which government and in which situation.

A relevant question is to what extent migrants can have insight into the migration machine. For example, in order to make a tax law effective taxpayers should not be aware of precisely which criteria the Tax Administration uses when carrying out checks. In general, surveillance to discover unlawful practices demands a degree of non-transparency. Non-transparency, however, needs checks and balances, for instance forms of checking, monitoring and appeals. Non-transparency should, thus, be limited and be subject to countervailing powers. Statutory rules therefore grant asylum seekers a right to sufficient information to be able to check the claims against them. The practice of informing migrants, however, deserves serious consideration and monitoring (Chapter 6 by Brouwer).

An important concept here is *Einzelfallgerechtigkeit*; in other words, the necessity to take account of the circumstances specific to the case (Chapter 5 by Meijer). If the migration machine applies the rules of implementation strictly, it may have the effect of not doing justice to the circumstances specific to that case. Open standards are a manner of creating the possibility of doing justice to these individual cases. If the open standards are limited to only one interpretation because of technological systems, individuals risk being crushed in the cogs of the machine. The development of the migration machine, however, leaves fewer and fewer opportunities for 'street- level bureaucrats' to judge individual cases on their merits (Chapter 3 by Broeders; Chapter 5 by Meijer). '[T]he migrant becomes what the computer says he or she is' (Chapter 3 by Broeders). But at the same time there should be no doubt here that this computer dominance also brings many advantages. It is no longer possible to make judgments that are coloured by preconceived ideas about certain groups of people because computers render the judgment objective. However, the autonomy of 'street-level bureaucrats' offers the possibility of looking at individual situations.

In sum, the migration machine does not like exceptions at all: these need to be categorized so the machine can process them using agreed rules. This means that management becomes complicated in the sense that exceptional cases cannot be dealt with in a correct manner. Discussions on the further development of the machine should contain the question as to which possibilities still exist for doing justice to exceptional cases. That raises the question of how much room is left for practical judgment 'in the spirit of the law'.

## Is the migration machine subjected to public control?

Europe's technological borders may be managed perfectly, but without any oversight by politicians these borders are not subjected to popular control. In theory, the migration machine is controlled by the public: that is, directly or indirectly by politicians who are accountable to Parliament and citizens (Winner 1980). In addition, independent authorities play a supplementary role in ensuring that the migration machine does not get 'out of control'.

Arrangements for carrying out inspections are required to ensure that those implementing the rules also keep to them. However, the question is if internal and external monitoring authorities have sufficient insight into the functioning and effects of technology. If sufficient data are not publicly available, the technology being deployed cannot be evaluated in public and political discussion. The information density of the present policy is such that increasing amounts of data concerning migrants are stored and used by more and more organizations. In addition to the fact that it is no longer possible to monitor which information is used by whom, it has also become impossible for a migrant (or the person representing his or her interests) to request the data in order to check for accuracy, let alone correct them if necessary.

Monitoring authorities such as the EDPS (European Data Protection Supervisor) or national data protection authorities are not authorized to give binding advice and their non-binding advice is often pushed to one side. Moreover, there is often a problem in the relationship between staffing and the powers that are wielded, so in fact there are insufficient authorized staff to monitor the situation. In 2007, the Data Protection Authority was unable to deal with every individual request for advice because of lack of resources (Chapter 6 by Brouwer).

As made clear above, monitoring is especially important when it concerns non-transparent surveillance measures because, in such cases, individuals have little or no chance to monitor what governments are doing. The European Court of Human Rights is very critical of national governments that have created too few opportunities for monitoring the way in which surveillance takes place. Not only monitoring the implementation is important, though; in the course of further developing and extending the migration machine there should also be guarantees in place that the machine develops within the human rights frame. An *ex ante* evaluation is one way of guaranteeing this. Making a human rights test part of such an *ex ante* evaluation helps to guarantee that the functioning of the migration machine does not lead to a violation of human rights.

The final question concerns public control over the migration machine and the opportunity for exercising democratic control over the use of migration technology. This can take place by means of political discussion in both national and European parliaments (depending on the technology) and through public discussion, but often both together.

For Europe there is the complicated question of the relationship between the national and European parliaments. Since there is no real public European political discussion the possibilities for exercising political control over migration technology at both national and European levels are insufficiently clear. Their individual roles are not always totally clear for citizens when it comes to making decisions about technology that is implemented at a European level (and that at the same time has an effect on national policy of individual member states).

In sum, to reach political legitimacy, both the functioning and the regulation of the machine are crucial. However, due to opaque European decision-making the actual control seems to be lost to system developers and to a European level. When for instance large-scale databases (some of them European) are used, political commitment and supervision in the use of this technology is, by contrast, limited. The 'front end' of the migration machine is discussed whereas the 'back end' and the coupling between these two remain outside the public debate.

## Controlling the migration machine

Our fourfold assessment has resulted in a list of risks, issues and unintended problems of the migration machine. There are reasons to think that the migration machine does not deliver what it promises and that it infringes upon legal requirements. Bureaucrats work with the migration machine but are not able to control it, and complexity hampers public control.

The migration machine is not 'ready'; it is still very much in development. This development, however, takes a specific direction. Firstly, instead of being based primarily on accurate procedures, the machine relies increasingly on the use of new technologies. It moves away from procedures in which meticulousness is all important and where time and attention are valued more than speed and quantity ('slow-tech'), towards a use of the most up-to-date features of biometrics and database technology ('high-tech'). Secondly, facilitation of travellers and migrants in the bordering process is being replaced by broad screening of citizens. The machine is less focused on processing requests of individual migrants quickly and accurately ('service'), but emphasizes the broad screening function of the migration machine to rationalize policy and safeguard security ('screening').

In this twofold respect, the migration machine is out of balance. But even a balanced machine still needs to be controlled to prevent the dystopic vision of technics-out-of-control. If specific measures are not carefully considered with due regard to necessity, privacy and proportionality, we might, according to Baroness Sarah Ludford, Member of the European Parliament and rapporteur on the Visa Information System, risk instead of creating a safer society to be midwife to a surveillance society (Ludford 2007: 6).

In our modern, large-scale democracies, the issue of control is a layered and complex one that leads us to questions about bureaucratic subservience, (parliamentary) democracy and the rule of law. The crucial point here is that a migration machine in this modern age needs to be controlled from various angles. The rise of the surveillance state in migration policy demands new countervailing powers, because 'the developments in European Union migration politics are neither following a fixed scheme, nor are they always driven by democratically legitimate or obvious actors. They should be closely observed because they constitute an arena in which the parameters of the future of the EU and its core values are under threat' (Klepp 2010: 21).

The migration machine is a typically 'modern' machine, not only because a great deal of information technology relevant for this machine is 'new' and 'present day', but mainly because the expectations aroused by this machine and the way in which it has been developed and is being managed is entirely within the spirit of modernism. It relies on a rationalization of working processes by efficiency, a division of labour, functional specialization, refined administrational procedures, and it is goal-oriented. In short, these are the ingredients which typify a policy model rooted in command and control.

Often, the rise of the surveillance society is illustrated with the metaphor of the 'Panopticon' or 'Big Brother' (Fernandez 2009: 199), but the 'modernist' spirit spoken of here is represented perhaps best of all in the film *Modern Times* (1936). Charlie Chaplin played a factory worker who struggled with the machines and production work at the conveyor belts. The fact that this was a comedy does not hide that the film was just as tragic as it was hilarious. In this film, the main character comes to grief. It is amazing to see how Chaplin's machine generates the same questions as those presented in this volume: how can we prevent the machine becoming an uncontrollable and unmanageable monster that takes on more and more functions but also becomes increasingly anonymous in the way it implements things, thereby in line with Mumford's (1970) famous but worrying analysis of the machine transforming the people it deals with into cogs in the mechanism?

However, there are possibilities of winning back ground from this machine. The machine should be stopped every now and again when there is danger of overloading it or of its grinding to a halt. Interim evaluation, more openness about the effectiveness and efficiency of the policy, a deliberation on proportionality, political and public discussions on justice, and validated research into the reliability of technology can all help to create such periods of rest. The machine can also be programmed in another way. Technological and administrative determinism should leave room now and again for political and public voluntarism. Taylorism and the factory conveyor belt have, after all, been replaced in many cases by less hierarchical and more intelligent and flexible technological and professional processes. With the correct use of technical aids, these can do justice to the specific expertise that professionals are required to have. Migration policy should not be carried out according to the administrative paradigms of the factory where Chaplin was working a century ago.

We therefore propose to subject the migration machine to a way of scrutiny, in line with Rosanvallon's (2008) opening-up of the concept of surveillance at the beginning of this chapter, as not only a form of control from above, but also a form of public oversight. Control by citizens is an important but understudied form of counter-surveillance that can contribute to the political, administrative and legal control of the migration machine, especially now the emphasis of the machine is on the use of high-tech and its main goal has shifted towards the screening of citizens and aliens.

In the introductory chapter of this volume it was already obvious that technology is deployed in decision procedures, the outcomes of which have enormous consequences. After all, someone can be prevented from entering the country or from being allowed to settle here. It also became obvious that migrants, in a political sense, have a weaker position, because they, for instance, have limited possibilities for fighting decisions in the courts. Within the migrant population, underage migrants are even more vulnerable. In general, migrants who are non-EU subjects without residence status are often unable to represent themselves properly and only have the right to speak indirectly – via refugee organizations, asylum lawyers or the sporadic media attention. They risk being handled not as citizens but as aliens.

Citizens are generally regarded as the objects that are processed by the migration machine: they need to be 'packaged' and 'framed' so that the machine can process them. The migration machine by its nature tends to dehumanize the people it needs to process. Human histories and characteristics need to be translated into measurable indicators which can be stored in databases. These transformations will distort the information and, therefore, they can lead to unjust treatment of citizens. Forms of public control can create the opportunity for bringing back the subject (Monahan 2006). Citizens will need to know what information is stored in the system so that they can challenge this information or even neutralize it, although actions to prevent this should not be underestimated (Marx 2003, 2009). The position, however, of these citizens is often problematic since they are not nationals and do not have the same legal position as the inhabitants of a country. Their condition as 'aliens' should not result in a denial of fundamental rights for citizen control since, in the end, these forms of control are needed to prevent the construction of an inhumane migration machine.

Instead, migrants should not automatically be regarded as objects of policy or even as input for the migration machine. It is crucial that migrants are seen as subjects who can interact with governments because of their own life story. It is therefore crucial that migrants, migrant organizations and their representatives are involved in debates on judging this machine and the choices of design. The design of technological borders is a democratic, legal and humanitarian issue which deserves more attention and which needs the inclusion of the experiences and opinions of citizens and migrants as well.

## Bibliography

Aas, K.F. (2009) 'Surveillance: Citizens and the State', *Surveillance and Society*, 6(3): 317–21.

Alterman A. (2003) 'A Piece of Yourself': Ethical Issues in Biometric Identification', *Ethics and Information Technology*, 5: 139–50.

Baldaccini, A. (2008) 'Counter-Terrorism and the EU Strategy for Border Security: Framing Suspects with Biometric Documents and Databases', *European Journal of Migration and Law*, 10: 31–49.

Beniger, J.R. (1986) *The Control Revolution: Technological and Economic Origins of the Information Society* (Cambridge, MA: Harvard University Press).

Bigo, D. and A. Tsoukala (2008) *Terror, Insecurity and Liberty: Illiberal Practices of Liberal Regimes after 9/11* (New York: Routledge).

Bowker, G. and S. Leigh Starr (1999) *Sorting Things Out: Classification and its Consequences* (Cambridge, MA: MIT Press).

Collett, E. (2010) 'The European Union's Stockholm Program: Less Ambition on Immigration and Asylum, But More Detailed Plans', *Migration Information Source*, www.migrationinformation.org/Feature/display.cfm?ID=768 (16 June 2010).

Council of the European Union (2009) *The Stockholm Programme – An Open and Secure Europe Serving and Protecting the Citizens*. Doc. 17024/09. Brussels, December.

Fernandez, L.A. (2009) 'Is Resistance Futile? Thoughts on Resisting Surveillance', *Surveillance and Society*, 6(3): 198–202.

Haggerty, K.D. and R.V. Ericsson (2000) 'The Surveillant Assemblage', *British Journal of Sociology*, 51(4): 605–22.

House of Lords (2009) *Surveillance: Citizens and the State* (London: The Stationery Office).

Klepp, S. (2010) 'A Contested Asylum System: The European Union between Refugee Protection and Border Control in the Mediterranean Sea', *European Journal of Migration and Law*, 12: 1–21.

Ludford, S. (2007) 'The Implications of Using Biometrics in the VIS', speech delivered 2 October 2007 for the *European Biometrics Forum*.

Lyon, D. (2003) *Surveillance after September 11* (Cambridge: Polity Press).

Lyon, D. (2009) *Identifying Citizens* (Cambridge: Polity Press).

Marx, G. (2003) 'A Tack in the Shoe: Neutralizing and Resisting the New Surveillance', *Journal of Social Issues*, 59(2): 369–90.

Marx, G. (2009) 'A Tack in the Shoe and Taking off the Shoe', *Surveillance and Society*, 6(3): 294–306.

Monahan, T. (ed.) (2006) *Surveillance and Security: Technological Politics and Power in Everyday Life* (New York: Routledge).

Mumford, L. (1970) *The Myth of the Machine: The Pentagon of Power* (New York: Harcourt Brace Jonavich).

Redpath, J. (2007) 'Biometrics and International Migration', *Ann Ist Super Sanità*, 43(1): 27–35.

Rosanvallon, P. (2008) *Counter-Democracy: Politics in an Age of Distrust* (Cambridge University Press).

Walters, W. (2006) 'Border/Control', *European Journal of Social Theory*, 9(2): 187–203.

Winner, L. (1977) *Autonomous Technology: Technics-out-of-Control as a Theme in Political Thought* (Cambridge, MA: MIT Press).

Winner, L. (1980) 'Do Artifacts Have Politics?', *Daedalus*, 109(1).

# Index